EPHESIANS

A Bible Commentary in the Wesleyan Tradition

MARK A. HOLMES

General Publisher: Nathan Birky
General Editor: Ray E. Barnwell
Senior Editor: David Higle
Managing Editor: Russell Gunsalus
Editor: Kelly Trennepohl

CONTENTS

EDITOR'S PREFACE

This book is part of a series of commentaries seeking to interpret the books of the Bible from a Wesleyan perspective. It is designed primarily for laypeople, especially teachers of Sunday school and leaders of Bible studies. Pastors will also find this series very helpful. In addition, this series is for people who want to read and study on their own for spiritual edification.

Each book of the Bible will be explained paragraph by paragraph. This "wide-angle lens" approach helps the reader to follow the primary flow of thought in each passage. This, in turn, will help the reader to avoid "missing the forest because of the trees," a problem many people encounter when reading commentaries.

At the same time, the authors slow down often to examine particular details and concepts that are important for understanding the bigger picture. Where there are alternative understandings of key passages, the authors acknowledge these so the reader will experience a broader knowledge of the various theological traditions and how the Wesleyan perspective relates to them.

These commentaries follow the New International Version and are intended to be read with your Bible open. With this in mind, the biblical text is not reproduced in full, but appears in bold type throughout the discussion of each passage. Greater insight will be gained by reading along in your Bible as you read the commentaries.

These volumes do not replace the valuable technical commentaries that offer in-depth grammatical and textual analysis. What they do offer is an interpretation of the Bible that we hope will lead to a greater understanding of what the Bible says, its significance for our lives today, and further transformation into the image of Christ.

David A. Higle
Senior Editor

AUTHOR'S PREFACE

One of great joys of life is the occasional unexpected surprise which makes a radical impact on one's life. Such was the case when I answered the phone to hear Dave Higle ask if I would be interested in writing a commentary. My acceptance of this opportunity has both challenged and blessed me.

A commentary is a compilation of comments made regarding a certain subject. This book is a gathering of comments made in consideration of Paul's letter to the Ephesians. I am a minister, and make no claims of scholarship. This book is not presented as a definitive work, but rather as the product of a pastor wrestling with the Word of God. As such, I invite the reader to join with me in grappling with God's truths, that together we might gain insight, and benefit from the experience. I have attempted to write as a shepherd to his flock, maintaining simplicity, yet hopefully revealing the meat of the text. It has been a challenge to keep this balance. If I have erred too strongly in one direction or the other, I ask readers their patience in my occasional indulgence.

Frederick S. Dellenbaugh once wrote, "A completed book is a mirror of the writer's shortcomings." As this is true, I fear I have created a rather large mirror by which my errors will be reflected. A written record of thoughts leaves one vulnerable to one's peers. I pray that mine will be understanding and gracious.

As with any book, the time and effort needed for its creation was considerable. To accomplish the task, I am indebted to a number of people: my wife, Jenny, who accepted the many evenings alone while I was busy in the office; my children, Amos and Rachel, who were understanding even when Dad's time on the computer took away opportunities of their own; the people of Hillview and Darrow Road Wesleyan Churches who graciously allowed me the time to work on this project; numerous friends who shared words of encouragement which came at the right moments; and most especially God, for ever extending to me the grace by which I have come to know Him, and for His Word which He has allowed me the privilege to study over the years. It is my prayer that the reflections contained within this book will be used to glorify Him and further the kingdom of God on this earth.

Mark A. Holmes
Superior, Wisconsin
September 1997

INTRODUCTION

B y his own admission, the Apostle Paul had a message that was unheard of—Gentiles becoming heirs to the promises of Israel, coming together with Jews to form a new body called the church (see Ephesians 3:4-6). But here is Paul, the "Apostle to the Gentiles" (see Romans 11:13), proclaiming what he understands to be the "mystery" of God's plan of salvation to humankind. Paul's letter to the Christians living in Ephesus would have been received as radical in the first century. Its claims are bold, its depiction of God's church unique, and its commands sweeping regarding Gentile behavior. By reading its message, one can easily understand how the controversy between Paul and the Jewish community developed, resulting in his imprisoned predicament during the writing of this epistle.

THE OCCASION OF THE LETTER

The book of Ephesians is known as one of Paul's prison letters because it is believed he wrote it while incarcerated. He refers to himself as "the prisoner of Christ Jesus" (Eph. 3:1); "a prisoner for the LORD" (4:1); and "an ambassador in chains" (6:20). The fact that Paul is a prisoner at the time of his writing is obvious. What is not so obvious is where he was imprisoned.

Tradition maintains that Paul was in Rome under house arrest when he wrote the epistle around A.D. 61 or 63. This imprisonment was the result of his having been arrested in Jerusalem after he returned from his third missionary journey (see Acts 21:27-36). Accused of defiling the Temple by bringing Gentiles into the inner court, an angry mob closed in, but he was rescued by a commander of the local Roman troop and placed under arrest. Being warned of an assassination plot, he was transferred to Caesarea where he was tried by Felix, then governor of the region. Desiring to fill his pockets with money from Paul, Felix left him imprisoned at Caesarea for two years, at which time Felix was replaced by Porcius Festus.

Festus, having just arrived at his new position, was confronted by the Jewish leaders, who sought to have Paul transferred back to Jerusalem so that they might kill him. Festus ordered Paul to appear before him in order to hear Paul for himself. It was during this confrontation that Paul exercised one of his fundamental rights as a Roman citizen—he appealed to Caesar in Rome. Because of that appeal, Paul was sent to Rome, where we know he continued under house arrest for approximately two years. It is during this two-year imprisonment that tradition holds he wrote his epistle to the Ephesians.

However, not everyone is convinced that Rome was the location of Paul's writing. Some have suggested a possible imprisonment in Ephesus itself, which is not recorded in Scripture. There are three specific imprisonments of Paul mentioned in Scripture: Philippi, where he and Silas converted the jailer and his family as a result of an earthquake (see Acts 16:16-34); and the Caesarea and Rome experiences described above. However, several places in Scripture imply that we do not have a complete record of Paul's imprisonment history. In 2 Corinthians 11:23, Paul attests to having been imprisoned a number of times because of his faith. If our dating of Paul's letters is accurate, the two letters to the Corinthians were written after Paul's Philippian experience and prior to his Caesarean/Roman incarcerations. Since he testifies to having been jailed on a number of occasions, we can only assume that these experiences happened but were never listed by Luke in the book of Acts.

In 1 Corinthians 15:32, Paul recounts that he fought wild beasts while in Ephesus. Though some believe he is speaking figuratively of opposition to his message, others feel that this is a mention of an imprisonment that caused him to fight against animals as a prisoner. To add to this concept, he mentions in 2 Corinthians 1:8-11 hardships suffered in Asia (the area around Ephesus), expressing even the possibility of a death sentence. Later, in his letter to the Romans (see Romans 16:3-4), Paul mentions a rescue made on his behalf by his traveling companions, Priscilla and Aquila, who had accompanied him during his ministry in Ephesus.

Additional arguments that favor an Ephesian imprisonment are made in consideration of Paul's experience with the runaway slave Onesimus, and Paul's subsequent letter to Onesimus's owner, Philemon, written at the same time as the epistle to the Ephesians. Paul requested that Philemon prepare a room for him, because he hoped to be released from prison as a result of Philemon's prayers. In Paul's Roman letter, which was written during his third missionary journey, Paul mentions a travel itinerary that would allow him not only to visit Rome, but to travel on to Spain, farther to the west, because "there is no more place for me to work in these regions" (Rom. 15:23). If Paul's intent was to leave the areas he had already ministered to for new parts farther west, why would he instruct Philemon to prepare a room for him at Philemon's residence which—if Paul was imprisoned in Rome—would have been a thousand miles east of Paul's location? Reason would suggest that Paul, upon release from his house arrest in Rome, would have set off westward as he intended in the first place.

Actually, Paul's Philemon letter and experience with Onesimus support a third possibility for the location of Paul's writing—Caesarea. Paul was held in prison there for two years before being sent to Rome. His letters could have been written between A.D. 59 and 61 from a cell in this coastal town. A runaway slave—Onesimus—may have been more likely to travel by land than sea, and the distance between Colosse and Caesarea is greater than that between Colosse and Ephesus. An additional influence to our thinking on Caesarea is a statement written by Paul to the church at Philippi (see Philippians 2:24) expressing plans to go to them once he was released. Some view these plans as a change from Paul's original intent to go straight to Rome and eventually Spain. Through a less-than-direct route, Paul could have intended to fulfill his earlier Roman trip, but by making his way through the churches he had established in Asia, much as he did during his second journey (see Acts 15:36). Thus, once being released from Caesarea, he could make his way west, visiting Colosse where Philemon lived, Philippi where the church was preparing for his visit, and then Rome and Spain.

One final argument for an Ephesian imprisonment is aroused by Paul's behavior while traveling back from his third missionary journey. Luke records that instead of landing at Ephesus, Paul sailed past the city and went ashore at Miletus, a town located to the south. From there he sent for the leaders of the church at Ephesus, who went to fellowship with him (see Acts 20:16-38). Luke states that Paul did this to avoid spending time in Asia because he was in a hurry to get back to Jerusalem by the day of Pentecost.[1] The unanswered question is, what was it that Paul feared would hinder his travel plans—the popularity of a man who had ministered in the area for a number of years, or the potential repeat of his earlier experience in the local jail? Had Paul been banished from Ephesus?

Whether it was written from Caesarea, Rome, or Ephesus, this letter is the result of Paul's pastoral concern for Christ's church. Paul was an apostle, called of Christ to serve in building and forming the church, especially among the Gentiles. During various incarcerations, he directed a number of his letters to churches or individuals, instructing them on some aspect of the faith, as well as sharing insight and encouragement with his readers. Those held to be letters written from prison include the books of Ephesians, Colossians, Philippians, 2 Timothy, and Philemon. Of these, Ephesians, Colossians, and Philemon were probably written at about the same time and delivered by a man named Tychicus (see Ephesians 6:21-22) who was accompanied on his journey by Onesimus (see Colossians 4:7-9). It is obvious from the close similarity found between Colossians and Ephesians that not only were they written at about the same time, but they were also motivated by the same concerns and interests. Some of their passages compare almost word for word. An additional aspect that makes Colossians and Ephesians unique is the fact that by Paul's acknowledgment (see Colossians 1:7-9) and implication (see Ephesians 3:2-13; 4:21) he had not personally met the recipients of these letters, but had come to know of them through word of mouth.

THE RECIPIENTS OF THE LETTER

Two observations have been made about the Ephesian epistle that require consideration. If the letter was written to the church at Ephesus, as its modern title claims, then it is doubtful that Paul wrote it. If it was indeed written by Paul, as Ephesians 1:1 claims, then it is doubtful that it was written to the church at Ephesus. Several pieces of evidence support these observations.

First, it is obvious from reading the letter that the writer and recipients have no firsthand knowledge of each other. In Ephesians 3:2-13, Paul feels it necessary to explain who he is by means of his ministerial duties and calling. His uncertainty of their knowledge is expressed by the statement, "Surely you have heard. . . ." This same statement is repeated in 4:21 in regard to what they had been taught in relation to their life in Christ. Such a statement would seem out of place to a group to whom Paul had personally ministered.

Second, there is a distinct lack of personal references made by the writer regarding common experiences or acquaintances. Luke records in the book of Acts that Paul had spent a long and fruitful ministry of up to two years in and around Ephesus (see Acts 19:10). His influence was such that all the Jews and Gentiles in the region of Asia had heard the word of the Lord. It seems peculiar, then, that there is no mention in the letter of any specific activity that had taken place during this ministry, such as that found in 1 Corinthians 1:14-16 and 2 Corinthians 13:1-3, nor are there the customary greetings or specific mention of individuals as Paul makes in his other letters (see Romans 16:3-15; 1 Corinthians 1:11, 14; Philippians 4:2-3). Apparently, there was not a close relationship between the readers and the writer. The challenge that remains is whether Paul was the author or Ephesus the destination.

Three schools of thought have been developed regarding the authorship of Ephesians: (1) the letter was indeed written by Paul; (2) the letter was written by a secretary on behalf of Paul, yet under Paul's direction; or (3) the letter was written by another individual after Paul's death, as a tribute to the man.

Some have argued against the authorship of Paul because the letter contains a high number of words used only once in all of the Scriptures. Did Paul choose these words, or are they evidence of another writer? Some of these words have been found only in literature that was written in later centuries. There is also a number of places where the style of writing and phrases used are not in keeping with Paul's normal style. Others argue that, because of the close similarity between Colossians and Ephesians, the latter is merely a copy of the other epistle presented in the name of Paul. As well, there is the recognition that some of the teachings found in Ephesians reflect a distinct difference from teachings Paul presents in other letters. Because of Paul's use of terms like "mystery," some see a connection with a heretical group known as the Gnostics that developed late in the first century (for further discussion of the Gnostics, see comments on the theme of the letter).

A theory of authorship growing in popularity has been described by William Barclay in his commentary on Ephesians.[2] This position holds that the letter was written as a memorial to Paul after his death. One individual suggested as the memorial writer is Onesimus, the returned slave who accompanied Tychicus, the deliverer of the letter. Barclay relates the interesting story of Ignatius, one of the early church fathers, as he was being led to Rome under arrest and to eventual martyrdom. Along the way, he wrote letters, of which some copies are still in existence, to the various churches. From the town of Smyrna, he wrote a letter to the church at Ephesus, encouraging the people to be obedient to their bishop, whose name happened to be Onesimus. Those who propose the memorial theory of authorship believe this bishop is the same slave Paul returned to his owner. Because of the obvious influence Paul had on this man's life, it is not difficult to believe that the potential of a memorial could exist. However, there is no evidence that the bishop and the slave are one and the same. The remainder of the theory is argued from silence, as there is no further mention in history of the letter as being a memorial to Paul.

An explanation for the presence of unusual words and phrases found in the work can be made by considering the possibility that Paul used an amanuensis (secretary) to write the epistle. This was not an unusual practice in Paul's day, and support for this explanation can be found in Romans 16:22. There, Paul's secretary, Tertius, greets the recipients of the letter and acknowledges that he is the actual writer of the Roman epistle. In Galatians 6:11, Paul draws special attention to his own penmanship as evidence that he wrote the letter, as he also does in reference to the greeting in 1 Corinthians 16:21. The need for this remark becomes obvious if there were other letters circulating for which Paul had used a secretary. The difference in handwriting might have aroused suspicion as to authenticity. The similarities between Ephesians and Colossians are probably due to the fact that they were written at the same time and to the same region of people. A final evidence in favor of Paul's authorship is the fact that it is mentioned twice in the letter (see Ephesians 1:1; 3:1), with the earliest manuscripts we have in existence containing both of these references.

If Paul was the author of the letter, it is doubtful that the recipients were Ephesian residents—unless we accept, as some have suggested, that it was written to a very specific group in Ephesus whom Paul had not met. New Testament scholar Marcus Barth suggests this group was made up of Gentiles converted to Christianity *after* Paul's last visit, or of Gentile Christians who lived in cities in and around Ephesus that Paul never visited.[3] The weakness of this argument is found in the lack of any specific address by Paul to this group, and the lack of any specific or personal message to others in the church, specifically the Jewish Christians.

In addition to the lack of firsthand knowledge experienced between the writer and the recipients, some of the earliest and most reliable manuscripts lack the phrase "in Ephesus" found in 1:1. (For a discussion of variations in scriptural texts, see the appendix.) These manuscripts, which were copies of Paul's letter, do not include the words we have in our present translations. Instead, they simply read, "To the saints who are." The fact that this was the accepted form of the letter at the time is proven by a study written on this verse by Origen, an early church father. The study was an attempt to explain what Paul meant by "the saints who are." This implies that Origen and the people of his time were unaware of an address to Ephesus. The words "in Ephesus" do not begin to appear in the manuscripts until around the second century A.D.

The reason for this lack of address can easily be explained by viewing the letter as a general epistle drafted for the encouragement of the Gentile

14

Christians found throughout the region of Asia. It was not uncommon for letters of this nature to be written and circulated. Evidence that Paul encouraged the exchange of his letters can be found in Colossians 4:16, where he instructs his readers to share that letter with the people in Laodicea, and to read the letter he had sent to the Laodicean people as well.

This instruction by Paul may shed some light as to the actual identity of the Ephesian letter. As stated above, Ephesians, Colossians, and Philemon were written at the same time and delivered by the same person, Tychicus. We have no existing manuscript of a "letter to the Laodiceans." Yet, Paul testifies to its having been written, presumably at the same time as the Colossian letter. The potential is high that what we regard today as being the Ephesian letter is really the Laodicean letter mentioned by Paul, and, because it was written without a specific recipient addressed, it was circulated throughout the area of Asia and subsequently found its home at Ephesus. In time, the letter would have become associated with the church that retained it, thereby being referred to as the "Ephesian letter." Being general in purpose, this would explain the absence of any specific mention of people and experiences.

From its contents, it is obvious that the book of Ephesians is written to Gentiles about their understanding and expression of the faith. The emphasis is found most markedly in 1:11-14; 2:1-10; 3:1-13; and 4:17-32. Some, however, have sought to make a distinction between Paul's mention of the "saints" and the "faithful" (1:1) as Jews and Gentiles, respectively. That Paul makes a distinction in the letter between Jew and Gentile is obvious, but not in the sense that he is addressing both groups. Rather, he enlightens the Gentiles regarding their faith experience by comparing it to the experience of the Jews. The letter is unmistakably written to Gentiles. Any reference made to the Jews is for the Gentiles to understand their place within the body of Christ.

THE PURPOSE OF THE LETTER

The purpose of Ephesians is best understood by considering its structure. The letter can be divided in half, with the first three chapters containing mostly theological discussion, and the last three chapters expounding more on the practical expression of the faith in daily living. Paul is exercising his responsibility as an apostle to direct the church, forming its theology and practice so as to accurately reflect the image of Christ.

The theology Paul presents to the Gentile readers is an explanation of God's design of salvation, planned for their benefit from before Creation.

Paul describes the inner workings of the church as a unified result of diverse activities and expressions. His message to these people, who formerly were considered outside the grace of God, is that they have been included in God's plan as recipients of God's grace and participants in His kingdom. They are now fellow heirs with the Jews. They have been saved by grace through faith. The distance between them and God has been closed. The hope of eternity has been made possible. The witness of God's presence is now a fulfilled promise.

However, this inclusion within God's salvation plan does not come without responsibility. Much will need to be changed in their lives as a result. Their lifestyle and understanding of God will need to come under the direction of God. This will require some radically new expressions in life and worship. Relationships with the world and society must change. Goals, dreams, worship practices, and even the means by which one follows the will of God will require a different approach. Paul elaborately expounds on all these issues throughout the letter.

THE THEME OF THE LETTER

The main theme of the Ephesian letter is God's great plan of salvation revealed, experienced, and lived out among the Gentiles. Paul understands that the plan of God to save the world includes *all,* which includes the Gentiles, and although presently incarcerated because of his connections with the Gentiles, Paul writes to expound the faith and encourage them in it.

A main expression of this salvation theme is Paul's assurance that it did not come to God as an afterthought. This plan was made even before the beginning of the world. Though its revelation took some time in coming, and was in fact kept hidden from those who were the first to believe (the Jews), it was now being made manifest to the world through the ministry of the prophets and apostles of Christ, of whom Paul was one.

This predetermined salvation plan of God was fulfilled through the obedient sacrifice of Jesus Christ, God's Son and our Lord. Everything about humankind's experience of salvation can be traced to this action of Christ which brought to fulfillment the Father's eternal plan. It was the Father who exerted the power of resurrection in Christ's experience, and Paul assures his readers that this same power would be experienced in everyone who believed by faith in Christ and His sacrifice. Lives, conditions, and relationships would radically change. It is Jesus that makes it all possible, and Jesus that brings us all together. Paul relates the Christian experience by the oft-repeated phrase "in Christ." This becomes the relational state in which all believers, Jew and Gentile, now find themselves. They were once in the world, or in sin, but now they are in Christ. Thus, the obedient sacrifice of Jesus enabled God the Father to relate to humankind by grace, and enabled humankind to relate to and experience the Father. Christ is the means of relationship with God.

Paul explains this salvation experience as a mystery revealed to humankind in the present age. Although the Father may have determined how He would rescue humankind from their sin—even before the plan was necessary—He did not choose to reveal this plan until after Christ's sacrifice on the cross. The specifics of this plan were kept hidden from the world prior to this time. But now it was the message of Paul and the other enlightened people that God had commissioned to serve as apostles and prophets.

Paul's use of the term "mystery" has raised a certain amount of suspicion by some, who endeavor to associate his thought with a late first-century heresy known as Gnosticism. Gnosticism was a mixture of Greek philosophy, Eastern religion, and Christianity. Among its many beliefs, it held that one's salvation resulted from knowledge received from certain secret rites and messages referred to as "mysteries." Gnosticism held that one was delivered from the fleshly, physical state into a pure spiritual state through this special type of knowledge. But the similarities between Paul and the Gnostic use of "mystery" end with the use of this term. Paul never implies that this is a secret rite of passage. With Paul, "mystery" was a public expression of hope to all who would hear and believe. It was a mystery because God chose to withhold its understanding until after the provision of salvation had been fulfilled by Christ. Once this was done, the mystery became a common message of the church to all who would hear it. Also, the mystery which Paul speaks of does not cause the salvation of humankind. Salvation does not come by knowledge, but by faith and trust in the grace of God. It was not what the readers of the letter would *know* that would save them, but whether they were in Christ as a result of their *faith in His sacrifice* on their behalf.

Unmistakably, the Ephesian letter was written specifically to Gentiles. Its theme develops their experience in God from sinful state to glorified existence. Its message is that those outside the Jewish faith can now be included in a personal relationship with their God as a fellow heir to the Kingdom and a brother to the Israelite. This does not require the customary circumcision and other activities that make one Jewish, but rather blends both Jew and Gentile together into a unique hybrid which Paul calls the church. So radical is the concept Paul expounds that it no doubt was received with both elation and reserve, enlightenment and, at times, confusion. The Apostle to the Gentiles eloquently presents this message from God.

The latter half of the letter (chapters 4–6) becomes a lesson in daily living. Paul repeatedly challenges his readers to live (walk) in a number of specific ways as a result of their new life in Christ. Their lives are to be worthy of the calling they received in Christ. They are to live no longer as Gentiles, but to be changed from within so that their practice reveals the person of Christ to the world. Their lives are to be lived in love, just as Christ also loved them. Wisdom will replace folly among them in both faith and expression. Their lives will be marked by humility and submission in their common daily relationships. Husbands and wives will relate through submission and self-sacrifice. Children will obey as fathers carefully instruct. Slaves will obey their masters and live honestly with them. Masters in turn will treat their slaves as Christian brothers.

One final major theme is Paul's call to arms. He makes no false claims or easy promises. The Christian life is one of challenge— challenge resulting from social influences, supernatural opposition, and one's own sinful temptations. The follower of Christ must be a realist and must willingly take up his or her place in the cause of Christ to wage war against these attacks, overcoming our Enemy by God's provision. The call to the Christian is a call to arms. The warfare is daily. The Enemy relentless. The opposing forces awesome in power. Yet, none of these realizations allows for excuse or ease, as God has also provided a variety of means by which we can fulfill our militant duties on behalf of self and Kingdom.

If ever there were an owner's manual for the Christian, the Ephesian letter would be it. It comes complete with background, so as to assure proper understanding of the experience. It also comes with specific instructions as to the daily operation and function of each follower. Written to a group of unfamiliar Gentiles, Paul succeeds in revealing the heart of God, the obedience of the Son, the sustaining power of the Holy Spirit, and the heart of a faithful apostle called to share God's good news with the Gentile people.

ENDNOTES

[1]In the New Testament, Pentecost primarily refers to the event when the Holy Spirit was given to the church; this occurred on the day of Pentecost. The Greek

term which *Pentecost* comes from means "fiftieth" or "the fiftieth day" and is literally the fiftieth day after the end of the Passover. It is also known as the Jewish Feast of Weeks, a day that is part of the Jewish observances, and was the beginning of the offering of first fruits.

[2]William Barclay, *The Letters to the Galatians and Ephesians,* The Daily Study Bible Series, rev. ed. (Philadelphia: The Westminster Press, 1976), p. 275.

[3]Marcus Barth, *Ephesians 1–3,* The Anchor Bible, vol. 34 (Garden City, New York: Doubleday and Company, Inc., 1982), p. 11.

EPHESIANS OUTLINE

I. OUR BLESSINGS IN CHRIST (1:1–3:21)
  A. **Paul's Greeting (1:1-2)**
    1. 1:1a   Paul Identifies Himself
    2. 1:1b   Paul Identifies His Readers
    3. 1:2   Paul Gives a Twofold Blessing
  B. **Paul's Litany of Praise (1:3-14)**
    1. 1:3-10   The Blessings of God
    2. 1:11-14   The Benefits of Believing
  C. **Paul's Thankful Prayer (1:15-23)**
    1. 1:15-16   Paul's Unending Thankfulness
    2. 1:17-19a   Paul's Continual Petitions
    3. 1:19b-23   God's Resurrection Power
  D. **Relationships Reconciled in Christ (2:1-22)**
    1. 2:1-10   Reconciliation Between Humankind and God
    2. 2:11-22   Reconciliation with One Another
      a. 2:11-13   Between Jews and Gentiles
      b. 2:14-22   Jesus Our Peace
  E. **Paul's Prayer for Power and Love (3:1-21)**
    1. 3:1-13   Paul's Ministry and Message
      a. 3:1   Paul the Prisoner
      b. 3:2-6   Paul the Administrator
      c. 3:7-13   Paul the Servant
    2. 3:14-21   Paul's Second Prayer

II. LIVING THE FAITH (4:1–6:24)
  A. **Living Worthy of Your Calling (4:1-16)**
    1. 4:1   An Ironic Command
    2. 4:2-6   Celebrate Your Unity
    3. 4:7-13   Exercise Your Diversity
    4. 4:14-16   Anticipate Your Maturity
  B. **Living No Longer As Gentiles (4:17-32)**
    1. 4:17-19   The Gentile Life Described
    2. 4:20-24   The Christian Life Contrasted
    3. 4:25-32   The Specific Commands Given
  C. **Living a Life of Love (5:1-7)**
    1. 5:1-2   Being Imitators of God

Part One

OUR BLESSINGS
IN CHRIST

Ephesians 1:1–3:21

D iamond cutters are intriguing. These artisans take a rough-shaped stone and study it for a period of time, becoming familiar with its unique shape and properties. Then, having determined its structure, they carefully place a cutting tool at the precise point and, striking it with a hammer, cleave the stone into two brilliant gems. Paul's letter is like this, as it too can be divided into two lustrous parts. The first three chapters deal with doctrine, while the remaining three expound on practice. Like diamonds in a matched set, each section can be studied for what it has to reveal, but they must never be separated, or else both will lose their value. So it is with the Christian faith. Doctrine and practice are dependent upon each other for their fulfillment. Those who *know* the faith, and yet fail to *live* it, are cold and lifeless. Others who *live* their faith without *knowing* its content become shallow and confused. Obviously, Paul was aware of this truth when he wrote this letter, and he masterfully balances these two necessities for his readers' benefit.

We all enjoy receiving letters that begin with a phrase like, "Congratulations! It is my pleasure to inform you. . . ." We anticipate that something good is being offered for our benefit. Such is the case with the first section of this letter. If we were to describe its contents, it would be with the word *blessing*.

As Paul plumbs the depths of some of his most profound theology, he keeps the information immersed within the context of the personal benefits these truths hold for his readers. He expounds on themes of salvation and holiness, adoption and regeneration, while all the time reminding the reader that these blessings are God's gift to humankind. He writes of estrangement—separation between humankind and God, as well as between Jew and Gentile—only to reveal that these divisions have been restored, the chasms have been bridged. He uses words such as *heir* and *adoption* to inform the world that we are not just forgiven, but are united with God and our fellow believers in ways never before experienced. He shares God's revealed *mystery* with its good news of reconciliation to all.

This section is not a cold and boring treatise on theology. It is a vibrant message of benefit to all who will accept its claims by faith. "Congratulations," Paul writes. "It is my pleasure to inform you that although you were sinners separated from God, He has both planned and fulfilled what is necessary for you to be forgiven and at one with Him forever."

1

PAUL'S GREETING

Ephesians 1:1-2

A
s would be expected with any letter, Paul begins his message with a greeting in keeping with the style of his day. This section gives us insight into the recipient, the writer, and the writer's feelings toward the people he is addressing. Although we often overlook these introductory passages, close consideration should be given to these two verses because their content is deeper than what appears at first glance.

In an age and culture where Bibles are readily available to anyone desiring them, it is difficult to appreciate the excitement which the epistle we refer to as Ephesians would have stirred among its original recipients. Christianity was still in its fledgling state, struggling with its foundational beliefs and expressions. Churches were in their infancy, inhabited by first-generation Christians who themselves were young in the faith. Confusion, conflict, and controversy often sprang up within this environment. Letters from the apostles were extremely helpful for the people to gain insight into their faith and its expression.

Somewhat different from our own, a particular style of writing was used by the people of Paul's day when it came to letters. They normally began with a greeting which contained the identification of both the writer and the recipient, as well as a brief blessing. These sections are often glossed over quickly in our reading, viewed as simple expressions of formality. However, the Ephesian letter does not allow that privilege. There is uncertainty in these opening verses regarding the author and the readers. (For a fuller discussion regarding these issues, see "The Occasion for the Letter" in the introduction.)

1. PAUL IDENTIFIES HIMSELF 1:1a

Paul begins his letter by using his name and official title in relationship to the church and Christ. Paul was no stranger. His name and influence were well known among the churches, many of which he started by visiting the towns and cities throughout the Mediterranean area. Even those churches at Colosse and Laodicea, who had never seen Paul, recognized his position and calling in Christ's church. The words they would hear would be sound words of faith and wisdom. Words they could trust with their eternal existence.

The writer introduces himself as **Paul, an apostle of Christ Jesus,** though this was not the only way he had been known to the church. His Jewish name was Saul. He was the offspring of Jewish parents who, as residents of Tarsus, were Roman citizens. He was a well-educated Pharisee (see Philippians 3:5) who received his instruction as a boy in Jerusalem under the tutelage of Gamaliel, one of the leading teachers of his day (see Acts 21:39–22:3). Paul was also a Roman citizen, which afforded him a number of civil rights not enjoyed by the other apostles. This made it possible for him to move in and out of both worlds. He could address crowds at each town's synagogue, while at the same time argue his rights before Roman authorities (see Acts 14:1; 16:37-40). He was knowledgeable in the faith and practices of the Jews, as well as the mythologies of the pagan world. This bicultural existence would prove to be quite effective in the task of propagating the gospel.

The church's first experience with Paul was far from positive. Luke introduces him in the book of Acts as Saul, a witness to the stoning of Stephen, the first Christian martyr (see Acts 7:58; 8:1). The event opened the door for Jewish persecution of the Christians, to which Saul was a willing participant. On his way to Damascus in a zealous attack upon the church, Saul was confronted by the risen Lord. As a result of this encounter, Saul, who became Paul, was not only convinced of Jesus' true identity and the validity of the Christian faith, but he was also assured of his own call by Christ into the ministry of the church. His office would that of an apostle. His ministry would be to the Gentile people (see Acts 22:6-21).

His claim of apostleship afforded Paul certain privileges within the Christian faith. The office of **Apostle** was a unique position that required three specific experiences: (1) he had to have seen Jesus; (2) he had to have been an eyewitness of Jesus' resurrection; and (3) he had to have been personally called by Christ.[1] Each of these requirements was met by Paul's encounter at Damascus. His vision was not only of Jesus, but Jesus in His resurrected state. His commission came from the lips of the Lord himself, to which Paul testifies in his letter to the Corinthian church (see 1 Corinthians 15:8-9). As a result of this encounter, Paul not only saw himself as an apostle, but as the least and an unworthy recipient of the title because of his earlier persecution of the church.

Just as the office of an apostle had its unique requirements, it also had its distinct privileges. The office was a gift given to the church by Christ to fulfill a number of needs: (1) an apostle was to proclaim the gospel of Jesus Christ; (2) his words would in time become the message of the church as they determined, defined, and expressed the faith among its people; (3) his words would carry a unique authority as they spoke for Christ, and would be received as inspired by God (see 1 Corinthians 7:10-12); (4) the authority of an apostle's words would demand obedience and adherence among the brethren as they determined policy across the known world; and (5) the apostle would not be the product of the church as much as the church would be a product of his faithful ministry (see Ephesians 2:20). The office would not continue beyond Paul, as he would be the last one privileged to be called into and to exercise it. Thus, his introduction, **Paul, an apostle of Christ Jesus by the will of God,** went beyond identification to authentication. The letter was not being received from anyone other than an apostle, specifically and uniquely called of God.

Because the office of apostle was closed with Paul, in no way does it negate the activity of apostleship in the church today. We may not be apostles in the formal sense of the office, but we can still exercise the gift of apostleship (see 4:11). The Greek word for "apostle" is *apostolos* and simply means "to be a messenger." Every person who has experienced the saving grace of Jesus Christ comes under His commission to go and share this good news with others (see Matthew 28:19-20). We are all messengers of Jesus Christ; we are just not given the same level of authority as the original men we know as the apostles. We are a product of the church. Our words, though often eloquent and profound, are merely a reflection or elaboration of the words these men proclaimed and wrote for Christ. Where we enjoy cooperation, we do not hold the same authority within the church as these men. We are apostles in the sense of being messengers; we are just not apostles as those Christ appeared to and called.

2. PAUL IDENTIFIES HIS READERS 1:1b

The second half of Ephesians 1:1 shares information regarding the recipients of the letter. Traditionally, the letter has been associated with the church at Ephesus, as Paul's written introduction seems to imply. However, the certainty of this statement is not as solid as one might believe. (For a further discussion on the identity of the recipients of the letter, refer to the introduction.)

Paul's greeting to the recipients is an expression of his view regarding people's experience once they have received God's saving grace. Salvation results in a twofold experience that is both active and passive in nature. Salvation is active in that it prompts people to be **faithful** in their relationship to God. It is passive in that it expresses the result of God's action toward people, making them **saints.**

Paul's reference to the recipients as **saints** introduces a major theme in the Christian faith. The Greek word used here is *hagios* and means literally "the holy." This concept carries two specific meanings which speak of both a condition and a position. The condition relates to the actual purifying work God does in the lives of people who repent: the cleansing of sin. The positional understanding expresses something that happens in people's relation to God: they are separated or set aside to serve God. Holiness (or "saintliness") refers to those individuals who have been touched by God in purification from sin, and consecrated ("set aside") by God to a distinct life of service. Paul is expressing his understanding of the experience in the lives of people who have received this touch of God. Those who are recipients of God's grace are those who live a life of purity and identity remarkably like God's.

A second term Paul uses to define the recipients' experience in Christ is **faithful.** If being "saints" is the passive experience from God to humankind, being "faithful" is the active counterpart from humankind back to God. Being faithful holds an understanding of commitment. Our entire relationship with God is based upon our faith in Him (see 2:8). The faithful are those who have heard the claims of the gospel and embrace them as true (see 1:13). The righteous shall live by faith (see Habakkuk 2:4; Romans 1:17). **Faithful** (Eph. 1:1) also carries the understanding of being consistent and reliable. Here is our response back to the Father each moment of our lives. As God leads, rebukes, corrects, challenges, and changes us, we remain committed to Him and His call. Therefore, the mark that identifies believers in Christ is the purified and separate condition in which they live, coupled by the consistent and obedient expressions they faithfully extend back to the Father.

The glue which holds this description together is the phrase **in Christ.** This is a phrase well used by Paul, referring to one's relationship with God. By Jesus' own confession, "No one comes to the Father except through [Him]" (John 14:6). Our salvation and the subsequent benefits are a direct result of our association with Jesus

Christ and His sacrificial death. The hallowedness and faithfulness of these recipients would be possible by no other means. It is only as they became related **in Christ** (Eph. 1:1) that they experienced God's life-changing ministry and separation. Nothing we ever do makes us fit for heaven. It is only because of what Christ has done for us by way of His sacrifice, and what God does for us by way of His acceptance through grace, that we truly become both saints and faithful.

3. PAUL GIVES A TWOFOLD BLESSING 1:2

To bless someone is to invoke a divine favor upon the person. This was a common practice included in letters of Paul's day. Paul's blessing in Ephesians 1:2 calls for two experiences—**grace and peace.** The source of each is found in both the Father and Jesus Christ.

Grace, within the Christian context, has always been understood as the expression of unmerited favor bestowed upon the believer by God. Usually we refer to this within the action of salvation: "It is by grace you have been saved" (2:5b, 8a). But we must be careful not to limit the experience of grace to just the experience of salvation. If properly understood that grace is the unwarranted expression of favor to humankind by God, then any and every consideration given or expressed by God toward humankind is an exercise of grace. There is nothing about humankind that merits God's consideration. His actions toward us are based solely upon His sovereign love. For God to even think about us, let alone extend himself toward us, is a benevolent act of His wonderful grace. Where the experience of salvation is the most obvious and significant expression of God's unmerited favor, it is well for us to remember that the totality of our relationship and interaction with God is possible only through His marvelous grace. Paul's blessing then, is for the people to be the recipients of God's divine attention, to experience the benevolence of God's audience.

John Wesley emphasized this concept of God's continual expression of unmerited favor upon the world, referring to it as "prevenient grace." "This is God's grace extended and expressed to humankind long before we ever realized that He existed. It is that grace that rescues infants and the mentally disabled of our society from the curse of hell. It is that grace that beckons and reveals to humankind the existence of God and His provision of salvation. It is that extension of God to the world, that prevents it from sinking into a completely depraved and hellish existence. . . . God breathes into us every good desire, and brings every good desire to good effect."[2]

All that is good in this world is the direct benefit of God's prevenient grace. All that is wrong is the fruit of our rejecting this grace.

Peace is the product of grace. The recipient of God's unmerited favor discovers that life has taken on a new meaning and experience. Jesus referred to this in John 14:27 when He promised the disciples a peace that comes as a gift from God incomparable with the world's peace. The peace of the world is elusive and short lived. It merely exists as that brief pause experienced between trials and troubles. It is the one thing we cry for most in this world, yet fail the greatest to achieve when attempting to find it.

The 1960s and 1970s were turbulent times for American society. The civil rights movement and the Vietnam War resulted in a number of protests and activities to promote more civility within the nation and world. The rallying slogan quite popular with young people at the time was one word—"Peace." It was expressed in symbols, and saluted to one another by means of hand signs. The expression, "Peace, man," replaced traditional words of greeting and parting. Yet, as prominent as this desire became, it resulted in few lasting, beneficial results. The basis for obtaining peace was based on the utopian desire for everyone to come to an understanding and acceptance of one another. In this way, conflict would disappear. However, universal understanding and acceptance never developed.

Peace sought by the world requires the absence of turmoil and strife. The peace of God is quite different, as it is often found in the very midst of turmoil and strife. It comes not so much from harmony within humankind, as from harmony of the soul with God. It is the assurance, resulting from God's grace extended to us, that although the rest of the world falls away, God's favor and benevolence will continue to be extended. Peace in this way is still relational—not between humankind and our fickle expressions and desires, but rather with God and His consistent, unchanging love expressed through grace. Even though all the world crumbles around us, we can be at peace. Paul's blessing for believers is not only that they would experience God's unmerited consideration, but that they would also benefit from the resulting peace of this experience.

In the Hebrew language, a common phrase equivalent to our phrase "How are you?" literally inquires, "What is your peace?" This is a timely question for all to answer. In the ongoing experiences of this world, what is your peace? Is it the result of the occasional respite enjoyed from life's ongoing struggle? Or is it the certainty that above and beyond all else in life, there is a loving Heavenly Father extending His unmerited favor toward us, resulting in an unworldly relationship of peace? What is your peace?

ENDNOTES

[1]Herman Ridderbos, *Paul: An Outline of His Theology,* John Richard DeWitt, trans. (Grand Rapids, Michigan: William B. Eerdmans Publishing Company, 1975), p. 449.

[2]*The Works of John Wesley*, vol. 6, 3rd. ed. (Grand Rapids, Michigan: Baker Book House, 1986), p. 508.

2

PAUL'S LITANY OF PRAISE

Ephesians 1:3-14

I t has been said that John 3:16 is "the gospel in a nutshell." If this is true, our present section is the tree from which this gospel nut fell. Having concluded his greeting, Paul jumps headlong into one of the most profound discussions regarding God's salvation plan for humankind found in the Bible. He explains its origins from before Creation, illustrates the parts fulfilled by each expression of the Trinity, and concludes by outlining how humankind experiences the benefits of this gracious plan. It is a complex section that challenges all of us with its depth of insight and breadth of vision. We are stretched to think the complex thoughts of God, while confronted with the need to embrace these claims by faith. These topics, difficult by nature, have long been controversial within the history of the church. However, we can embrace these truths with the realization that our salvation is not determined by our *understanding* of how they are possible, but rather by the faith that believes they are possible.

A fifth-grade Sunday school teacher once arranged a tour of a local farm. The children from his class had never been to a farm, so the trip would afford them an opportunity to experience a number of new things. The farmer proved to be an excellent tour guide, sharing many interesting facets of farm life with the children. The tour progressed to where they entered the barn itself. There they beheld a large variety of farm animals. As they walked past the various pens of livestock, the farmer expounded on their characteristics and use. The teacher was certain his students were benefiting from this man's insight, as well as their firsthand experience at seeing these animals. He turned to observe the responses on their faces, only to discover that he and the farmer were standing alone at one end of the barn. The children were at the other end, gathered in a group around something that had caught their interest.

Wondering what exotic creature they had discovered, the teacher went back to the children and peered over their shoulders to see the subject of their concealed interest. There in the middle of the group, on a hay bale, sat a common, ordinary, house cat. The teacher stood shaking his head in disbelief. He had brought them out to see animals they had never seen before, and what had caught their interest was a creature that they could see every day.

This same potential remains with our study of this section. We can easily fixate on the terms and topics to which we have become accustomed, at the expense of the special items we should be discovering. Often it is the controversial topics that catch our attention, though they are rather minor in regard to the text. One example is the issue of predestination and divine election mentioned by Paul. We see these terms and fixate upon them, ignoring the greater message that surrounds them. While we must consider what Paul meant by these truths, the blessing from God that Paul is excited about deals with God's salvation plan: holiness, adoption, redemption, and God's revealed mystery.

Controversial themes are found within this section, but one must be careful not to spend time stroking a house cat when there are far more pertinent matters at hand. What was primarily written as an expression of praise to God, has become recognized as a theological treatise filled with deep and controversial topics. The challenge to anyone desiring to unpack the truths of this section is to keep a broad perspective of the whole and not allow oneself to become narrowed to its subtopics at the expense of its major themes.

1. THE BLESSINGS OF GOD 1:3-10

Having concluded the formalities of greeting and blessing, Paul moves into the body of his letter by giving praise to God for all that He has done in providing salvation to humankind. This passage is an expression or litany of praise and blessing. The Greek word for "blessing" that Paul uses in Ephesians 1:3 is based on the word *eulogetos,* which means "to bless." It is the word from which we derive our English term *eulogy.* We are more accustomed to hearing the word *eulogy* in the context of a funeral, when a person shares with those present the positive characteristics of the deceased. But Paul is referring to the wonderful plan God made for our salvation.

Simply stated, the reason for Paul's exuberance before God is the salvation plan God has made and fulfilled on our behalf. It is a provision preplanned by the Father, made possible by the Son, and bestowed upon and sealed for the believer by the Holy Spirit. Paul blesses *God* for blessing *us* with all spiritual blessings in **the heavenly realms.** In one long, twelve-verse sentence, Paul folds back the spiritual curtain that normally obscures our view of God's behind-the-scenes provision, to reveal each segment of our experience provided for in God's salvation plan. Each expression of the divine godhead is portrayed by their individual roles. **God** the Father is presented as the originator of the plan, extending its possibilities to humankind. It is He who blesses us with all spiritual blessings; who chose us to be holy and blameless before the creation of the world; who predestined us to be adopted as children of God; and who lavishes us with grace and reveals the mystery of His will (see 1:3-5; 8-9).

Our Lord Jesus Christ (1:3), God's Son, is revealed as the one who makes the entire plan possible. Two oft-repeated phrases are **in Christ** and **in him,** when relating to Jesus. They are phrases of instrument, pointing to *the means* by which this plan was made possible for humankind. Being **in Christ** refers to the unexpressed sacrificial death of Jesus and to the relationship and intervention made by Christ daily on behalf of His redeemed.

The plan was determined by the Father before the creation of the world (see 1:4), and yet its fulfillment came through the death and resurrection of Jesus Christ. His cry from the cross, "It is finished!" (John 19:30), was a statement revealing the completion of the events necessary to satisfy God's great provision. Now what had been determined before time could be extended to humankind by way of God's grace and blessing, but only as it was made possible through Jesus Christ. There is no salvation except through His death and resurrection. Thus, the Father blesses us with all spiritual blessings **in Christ** (Eph. 1:3). His choice of us is made possible **in him** (1:4). Our adoption is made possible **through Jesus Christ** (1:5). God's grace is given to us **in the One He loves** (1:6). Our redemption is **in him . . . through his blood** (1:7). God's will (salvation plan) was put into effect **in Christ** (1:9), which will result in all things being brought together under one leader, **even Christ** (1:10). Paul's distinctive description of himself and others is the "first to hope **in Christ**" (1:12), while he reassures his readers that they were also included **in Christ** when they believed in the gospel, for they were marked **in him** (1:13).

The **Holy Spirit** (1:13), the third expression of the Trinity, enjoys a much shorter mention, mainly as a "seal" giving evidence that God's saving grace has been extended to the individual: having believed in the gospel, they have been marked with a seal, **the promised Holy Spirit.** Paul describes the Spirit's particular task as a deposit, guaranteeing our inheritance with God until the day His salvation plan is fulfilled in all believers by their resurrection to heaven. This is an echo of Christ's earlier promise given to the disciples before His crucifixion (see John 14:16, 25-26; 16:5-15). The presence of the Spirit working in the believer has always been an evidence of God's salvation existing with the believer, as we read in the book of Romans, "The Spirit himself testifies with our spirit that we are God's children" (Rom. 8:16).

Paul's description of God's salvation plan extends beyond people to include a time frame. Paul writes that this plan was not a secondary thought with God, but was developed even **before the creation of the world** (Eph. 1:4). A problem, however, is understanding who or what was predetermined or **predestined** in the first place. Historically, two options have been considered: (1) God chose the *individuals* whom He would save; or (2) God chose the *plan* by which individuals would be saved. Paul presents the topic by referring to God's choosing (see 1:4, 11) and predestining (see 1:5, 11). Both imply a prior decision by God resulting in a present experience.

Central to this topic is the question, to what extent does God's prior knowledge of these matters (called God's "foreknowledge") influence their outcome? Also, how exacting is God's foreknowledge? Does it include the specific people who will benefit or just the general plan of salvation? This idea of God's foreknowledge has long been a controversial topic within the church.

Those who prefer to interpret God's foreknowledge as a specific choice of persons stress heavily His ultimate wisdom, power, and sovereignty—He chooses whom and what He desires based on His perfect will. We are the creation; He is the Creator and, as such, holds unquestionable control over us. This is called determinism. In its extreme version, this says that it is God's individual choice of those He will save and those He will condemn. Those who support this idea believe the recipients of this divine decision are to be thankful for God's plan on their behalf, whether this includes salvation or damnation. This may be hard for mere mortals to comprehend, but proponents of this view hold that this is what happens when God is God among His people: "His ways are above our ways." Although it may be confusing to us, we are to accept it by faith and trust that God will do only what is ultimately right.

A drawback to this interpretation is that it takes the emphasis away from God's love. Determinism appears to be inconsistent with what we understand about God being perfect love. To say God has predetermined those who will be saved is also to say God has predetermined those He will condemn, causing some to be hopelessly lost no matter what their personal desires toward God might be. A rewriting of John 3:16 would seem necessary: "God so loved the *predestined* [not "the world"], that He gave His only begotten Son."

Another drawback to this position is its consideration of justice. Is it fair to preselect people for damnation before they are even born? Even before they have committed an act of sin? Is it just to condemn people on the grounds that no atonement was made for them, while at the same time redeeming others because of a divine choice? To condemn someone implies responsibility for one's actions. One of the understood responsibilities of each person would be to accept God's salvation. But if there are no true choices available, how can one be blamed for taking the only possible course in life? It would be like prosecuting a person based on gender. True, we are all guilty before God because of willful and inbred sin. But, in this narrow understanding of predestination, God cannot truly hold us responsible for our sin. This lack of choice denies us responsibility and, therefore, frees us from prosecution. This kind of determinism would condemn people merely because they had the bad fortune of not being elected by God.

A third drawback to determinism is that it contradicts what we understand from Scripture regarding God's will for humankind. This limitation was expressed by John Wesley: "If you ask, 'Why then are not all men saved?' the whole law and the testimony answer, First, not because of any decree of God; not because it is His pleasure they should die; for, 'As I live, saith the Lord God,' 'I have no pleasure in the death of him that dieth.' ([Ezekiel] 18:3, 32 [KJV]). Whatever be the cause of their perishing, it cannot be His will if the oracles of God are true; for they declare, 'He is not willing that any should perish, but that all should come to repentance;' (2 [Peter] 3:9;) 'He willeth that all men should be saved.'"[1]

Another interpretation of God's predetermination emphasizes the *plan* of salvation, and not the individual. In this sense, God's plan is understood by Paul as being "predetermined" or designed prior to its being carried out in history. The specifics of the determination would be the events of the plan, and not its participants. God's choice in Ephesians 1:4, **He chose us in him before the creation of the world to be holy and blameless in his sight,** would refer to the opportunity to become holy and blameless before Him. His predestination would be the adoption made possible to all who would desire it (see 1:5). God's plan would provide the means of redemption and the bringing of all things back together under the Headship of Christ (see 1:10). God's sovereignty is expressed through the plan in its development and execution, allowing His love to be held high. His love is expressed by extending to all people the opportunity to embrace His salvation. This love is also expressed in that God, knowing full well that humankind would turn from Him, created us anyway, even though to do so would cost the life of His Son, Jesus Christ. This is the beauty of Paul's litany of praise before God—not just that God would provide this heavenly blessing, but that it was determined even before the fall of humankind (see Genesis 3), which would make it necessary.

A criticism cited against the predetermination of the plan is its limitation of God's sovereignty and the empowering of humankind's authority. This is referred to as "free will"—the ability of all people to accept or reject God's salvation. Here again we see the theme of love come to the foreground. God chose to limit His supreme authority so that He could relate His love to us. In doing so, He took the risk that, even though He loves us and lavishes His grace upon us, we can and may reject Him. However, this risk also allows those who do choose to respond to His love to develop a personal relationship not possible through determinism. God becomes both lover and beloved, as does humankind.

Another criticism of a predestined plan is that free will makes us all responsible for our own salvation, making our rescue a type of "works righteousness." This argument assumes that our ability to choose is much broader than God has allowed. Christianity has always understood the primary dependence of humankind upon Christ for salvation (a fact well explained by Paul in this section). The only human factor involved in our salvation is the acceptance of God's grace by faith; everything else, both before this time and after, is the result of God's grace working in our lives (see 2:8).

I have mentioned in chapter 1 the reality of prevenient grace, which God extends to all of creation to prevent it from hellish decay. Within the actions of this grace is God's revelation of himself to all people by His existence, love, and salvation. It is through this grace that we come to know Him and understand our need of Him (see John 6:44). Even the very faith that we need to extend for our salvation is provided by God, through Jesus Christ (see Hebrews 12:2). Our freedom—our free will—to embrace or reject the gracious provisions of our salvation is a God-given ability. Our justification, adoption, redemption, and holiness are all the result of being in Christ. We are totally dependent upon God as He works His great salvation in and through us; but we are allowed to accept or reject this grace.

Having discussed the various themes that relate to God's great plan, consideration should be given to the actual parts which make up this great blessing. Paul speaks of four aspects: holiness, adoption, redemption, and mystery.

The fact that God planned for humankind to be holy is expressed in Ephesians 1:4. We were chosen **to be holy and blameless.** Herein is one of the great themes of salvation that deals with the extent of God's restoration of humankind. Two things become evident regarding our relationship to God, and both are a result of the Fall: (1) all humankind is guilty of sin (see Romans 3:23); and (2) we all have a desire to commit sin against God (see Romans 1). Paul's first point explains the extent to which God's plan addresses our restoration from sin. Two words describe the full extent of God's restoration: **holy** and **blameless** (Eph. 1:4).

First, **holy** is taken from the Greek word *hagios,* which refers to both the position and condition of our relationship with God (see chapter 1 of the commentary). The *position* of holiness is the setting aside of something for a special purpose. The offering plates and communion-ware of our churches serve as a good illustration. These items have been established by the church for one purpose: to receive God's tithe and dispense the elements of His Eucharist.[2] If these utensils are used for any other reason, they are made common or blasphemed. In the same way, God's salvation for humankind is such that we are separated unto God. Holiness is a separation by God from sin and a consecration to himself. It is the position in which God's redeemed are to exist within this world. The church has always understood this separation toward God. It is inherent in the Greek term used for the church—*ecclesia*—which literally means the "called out ones." Jesus prays that this provision would become a reality in the life of His disciples (see John 17:15-19). In this, God's plan for His redeemed is not one of a split allegiance, but of a separation and consecration of His people to himself. God's plan is realized in our lives as we are moved away from the world and drawn unto Him.

Second, **blameless** (*amomous* in the Greek; Eph. 1:4) literally means "without blemish or spot." In using this word, Paul refers not to our position, but to our *condition* before God. This is the moral result of

God's grace. It was not enough for God to simply restore our relationship to Him by the blood of Christ, which allows for our forgiveness. God's plan also includes complete restoration. It was not enough for His people to be forgiven; they also would be given victory over sin so as not to have to live under its daily controlling influence. Holiness, in this light, speaks not of separation, but of cleansing. This is not an act performed by us through our ability and obedience. It is an extension of God's grace, provided by the person of Jesus Christ and driven in us by the Holy Spirit. This very idea was written earlier by Paul to the Thessalonian church: "From the beginning God chose you to be saved through the sanctifying work of the Spirit and through belief in the truth. He called you to this through our gospel, that you might share in the glory of our Lord Jesus Christ" (2 Thess. 2:13b-14).

Paul gives a description of this purification as he writes in Ephesians 5:25-33 of Christ's ministry. The end result of this ministry is the making holy of Christ's church—"cleansing her by the washing with water through the word"—so that we might be presented to Him as a radiant church "without stain or wrinkle or any other blemish, but *holy and blameless*" (5:26-27, my emphasis). Some would argue that this is a condition credited to us by Christ who, being holy, infuses His holiness within us so that we benefit from a passive righteousness, a righteousness not necessarily our own. While this is true, it does not limit holiness to this one experience. Christ's holiness may be credited to us, but it is also accomplished within us. Christ is not our substitute for holiness, but rather our source.[3]

The first great blessing Paul lists for humankind regarding our salvation is its *complete work of restoration.* God did not plan to just forgive us of sin, but to separate and cleanse us from sin.

The second of God's blessings regarding our salvation is found in a *restored relationship through adoption.* Sin's tragic effect upon humankind was to sever the original relationship with God once enjoyed by the first couple, Adam and Eve. Because of sin, we no longer are children of God by virtue of our creation; now we must rely upon God's adoption for the relationship to be restored.

Adoption is found as an Old Testament theme relating to the redemption of humankind through God's choice of Israel. This reclamation was defined as a father-son relationship. To King David, God promised to become a father to David's son, Solomon (see 2 Samuel 7:14). God's fatherly benevolence and power over Israel is related in the Psalms: "You are my son; today I have become your Father"

(Ps. 2:7). Jeremiah speaks to the elders of Israel for God regarding God's relational desires: "How gladly would I treat you like sons. . . . I thought you would call me 'Father'" (Jer. 3:19). John develops this concept of adoption in his introduction of Jesus (see John 1:12), stating that those who would accept Jesus would be given the right to become the children of God.[4] Later in this Gospel, we find Jesus in a hot debate with the Jewish leaders regarding their lack of adoption. The leaders claimed relationship with God because they were children of Abraham. Jesus countered the claim by saying they were not children of God, or they would have recognized Jesus' true identity (see John 8:31-42).

But it is Paul who develops our most comprehensive understanding of adoption. In reaching out to Gentile believers, he needs to develop a Christian expression that includes them, a group previously excluded by Judaism (generally speaking).[5] In his letter to the Romans, Paul recognized the role played by God's covenant with Abraham in establishing relationship with God: "Theirs is the adoption as sons" (Rom. 9:4a). But with the coming of Jesus Christ into the world, a new covenant was established, one that came through the shed blood and broken body of the Son of God. Adoption no longer was achieved through the covenant of Abraham, but by faith in the Son of God, as we read in the book of Galatians: "You are all sons of God through faith in Christ Jesus" (Gal. 3:26). This would be a spiritual adoption conceived by faith and germinated by grace. Paul referred to this spiritual adoption by teaching that "those who are led by the Spirit of God are sons of God" (Rom. 8:14; see also 8:12-13).

This adoption by God carries with it a number of benefits (see Romans 8:15-17): (1) it frees us from fear; (2) it allows us an intimate relationship, even to cry out "Abba"[6]; (3) it provides an inner certainty of relationship as God's Spirit testifies with our own; and (4) it promises an inheritance equal to that of Christ's—we become coheirs with Him. This second part of God's great plan assures our reinstatement back into an ongoing, vibrant, and endearing relationship with God. With regard to salvation, God would not settle for a secondary relationship. We would be not only forgiven, but adopted and made fellow heirs with His Son, Jesus Christ.

The third part of God's salvation plan is experienced through *redemption.* The late James Herriot, English veterinarian and author, wrote of an old English farmer whose milk cow had long passed its prime. He sold the cow to the local slaughterhouse, but, after some time of reflection, realized his strong attachment to the animal. Leaving the farm, he sought out the buyer and purchased the animal back, allowing her to live out her days at the farm instead of suffering her fate at the slaughterhouse. In order for God to deliver us from our death because of sin (see Romans 3:23), our debt was paid as well. Paul calls this purchase by God our redemption. He uses the Greek word *lutro,* which literally means "to buy back." Originally it referred to the setting free of captives and slaves. This is the experience of Christians described by Paul in his first letter to the Corinthians: "You are not your own, you were bought at a price" (1 Cor. 6:19b-20a).

The price that was expended on our behalf was not of perishable items such as silver or gold, but rather the life blood of Jesus Christ, the Lamb of God (see 1 Peter 1:18-21). This is the one whom John the Baptist introduced to the public at the Jordan River by proclaiming, "Look, the Lamb of God, who takes away the sin of the world!" (John 1:29). This is the one who Paul explained took away the curse of the law[7] (death) by allowing himself to be made a curse (be put to death) for us (see Galatians 3:13). Because of this act, Jesus is the only one found worthy in all of heaven and earth to open the great seals described in the book of Revelation. The entire celestial audience cries out His worthiness, proclaiming, ". . . You purchased men for God . . ." (Rev. 5:9).

God's great plan of redemption recognized that, because of humankind's sin, a price would have to be paid to redeem us back from death: "Without the shedding of blood, there is no forgiveness" (Heb. 9:22b). The price would be the life blood of His Son so that those dead in sin may be set free. As we were slaves to sin, Christ died for us, so that the blood necessary for our purchase could be supplied (see Romans 5:8).

Paul recognizes the great part grace plays in this event. It is not simply given; it is **lavished** upon us (Eph. 1:8). One can picture here an Old Testament vision of anointing with oil as done by Samuel to Saul and later David. We understand that such an act was not performed by a mere drop or two, but by the pouring of oil so that it ran down the sides of the head and face, through the beard of the man, until it flowed on the ground. Our redemption, our purchase by God, is the result of great anointing. We are covered by the sacrificial blood of Jesus Christ, the Lamb of God, revealing the cost by which we have been purchased. Our souls drip from the lavish amount of grace God has poured upon us, revealing the love that makes it possible.

The last item in Paul's description of God's salvation plan refers to its revelation to humankind. As wonderful as its provisions are, they would be meaningless if we were unaware of them. Where this may seem an act of common sense, God's revealing His salvation is another great expression of grace, and is thereby a blessing to us. Paul's choice of words to describe this revelation has stirred up a certain amount of controversy. He refers to the entire plan as a *mystery*.

Mystery carries with it a number of understandings. It can refer to an event wrapped in secrecy and kept so obscure that it conjures up a sense of magic. This is the idea we find in what are referred to as mystery religions, quite prominent in Paul's day (see comments on "mystery" in the introduction). Because of their popularity, there are some who argue that Paul's use of the term implies his own participation in the mystery religions.

One of the more popular of these groups contemporary with Paul was known as Gnosticism. It was a hybrid religion developed by crossing Eastern and Greek thought with Christianity. Generally, Gnostics believed that flesh was evil and spirit was good. Each person is challenged in this life because they are encased within evil flesh and, therefore, are the victims of its desires and actions. The goal (salvation) was to free themselves from the flesh and obtain a pure spiritual existence that would return back to God. The means of finding their freedom from the flesh came by way of "mysteries"—secretive, ritualistic concepts which, once utilized, would result in deliverance. It was a way of having the "inside track" on spiritual issues. Those who would like to define Paul as a Gnostic cite these passages, claiming his understanding of the Christian faith to be influenced by these early cults. Some of our modern-day cults rely on this age-old idea that secret wisdom, once known, can deliver. This is not the **mystery** (1:9) expressed by Paul, for several reasons.

First, Christianity does not see our task as the separation of spirit from flesh. While we do recognize that the flesh has certain desires that must be controlled, it is not understood to be evil in itself. Sin, even that which is acted out through the flesh, begins as a spiritual issue long before it becomes physical (see Matthew 5:21-22, 27-30). By Paul's own description, the person returning to God after death does so not in spirit, but in a bodily resurrection (see 1 Corinthians 15:42-43).

Second, our salvation is not the result of exercising mysterious rites, but embracing a truth revealed to all people by God's prevenient grace. Paul develops this thought in his benediction at the end of his Roman epistle (see Romans 16:25-27). His claim is that God is able to establish the Romans (and us) by the gospel and the proclamation of Jesus Christ in accordance with the revelation of the mystery. This mystery is described as having been withheld from humankind for ages, but as being now revealed and made known by way of the prophetic writings. The reason for this revelation is so that "all nations might believe and obey

Him" (Rom. 16:26). It is God's desire that everyone understand this withheld revelation so that they all come to salvation.

Third, we are saved by the blood of Christ, and not by what we know. Knowing the mystery would result in education, but experiencing the Savior results in salvation.

Mystery can also mean an act that is incomprehensible, or unexplainable. This is a good description of God's salvation plan. As much as we might discuss, define, and develop our understanding of it, we realize that it extends far beyond our wildest thoughts and deepest discernments. How do we begin to fathom the depths of God's love and mercy (see Ephesians 3:18)? How do we comprehend the unique intricacies of those legal aspects necessary for our justification? Can we ever understand fully the love which motivated our Lord to go to the cross? In light of these and so many other considerations, God's revelation will always come to us as that which is both knowable and yet never completely known, at least on this side of heaven. John Wesley agreed, defining mystery as ". . . the gracious scheme of salvation by faith, which depends on His own sovereign will alone. This was but darkly discovered under the law; is now totally hid from unbelievers; and has heights and depths which surpass all the knowledge even of true believers."[8]

Mystery can also mean something that is known only through faith, and not human reason. Here is the central aspect of Paul's meaning. The depths and workings of God's great plan are not only beyond our ability to understand, but contradict our rational thought. There are a number of items contained within God's salvation plan that go beyond reasonable explanation, contradicting human logic. These items are often referred to as "antinomies," which means that which is against reason or logic. For example, how can Jesus Christ be 100% man, while at the same time 100% God? How could Jesus die, being God and, therefore, eternal in existence? How can God be sovereign and all knowing, yet at the same time allow us the freedom of choice? These and many other examples are aspects of God's salvation that go beyond explanation, and because of this they must be accepted by faith. To each of these unknowable conflicts comes the Christian's faithful response, as we read in Mark's gospel: "With man this is impossible, but not with God; all things are possible with God" (Mark 10:27).

In his description in Ephesians 3:6, Paul specifically states that the mystery enables Gentiles to become fellow heirs with Israel in the Kingdom—they are to be members of the same body and sharers of the same promise. To some in Paul's day, it was unexplainable how God could make available to the Gentiles what they had determined was exclusively for the Jews. This was often a point of contention between Paul and the Jewish leaders of his day. More than once, Paul was accosted on this very topic, driven from town, imprisoned, and even stoned and left for dead. In fact, the original charge against Paul, which resulted in the present arrest during which he wrote his epistle to the Ephesians, was that he dared to take Gentiles into the inner court of the Temple in Jerusalem (see Acts 21:28). Paul's description of the mystery in Ephesians 3:6 is actually a testimony of his calling (see Ephesians 1:7-10) to explain and reveal this mystery to all, including Gentiles.

It is an unexplainable experience when we see God working the seemingly impossible in this world. Surely there were Jews of Paul's day who firmly believed in the total lostness of the Gentile race; after all, they were outside the covenant and were "sinners." Even today there are people we may have difficulty seeing as fellow heirs—members of the Body and sharers of Christ's promise. This, too, is a mystery. How can God work His grace, resulting in new life, among those who seem hopelessly lost? How does God turn sinner to saint? How does He melt a hardened heart? How does He draw to himself a person whose interests and understandings appear as complete contradictions? It is a mystery that goes beyond our understanding and requires us to accept and anticipate by faith. Paul shares several specifics about God's intentions regarding the **mystery** (1:9).

First, its existence was intended by God's own **good pleasure** (1:9). The Greek word used describing this desire is *eudokian,* which can mean "pleasure, good will, favor, or delight." God chose to reveal the mystery to humankind, not out of some solemn, regretful necessity, but out of a desire to share His pleasure with us. God's news of salvation is good news, from the vantage point of both the one sharing and the one receiving.

Second, the mystery was **purposed in Christ** (1:9). In other words, it was made possible through Jesus Christ. Again, we find Paul using his understanding of the instrument of Christ in God's redemption. Whatever else can be said of the mystery, it must always find its central expression in the life, death, and resurrection of Jesus Christ on our behalf.

Third, the mystery was **put into effect when times reached their fulfillment**—that is, when the time was right (see 1:10a). To understand the timing of God, we must remember that this plan was established before the foundations of the earth were established (see 1:4). Humankind and creation awaited the arrival of God's perfect time so that this plan could be both enacted and revealed (see Romans 8:19-25). The fulfillment of this awaited time has been understood to be the coming of

Christ into the world: "You see, at just the right time, when we were still powerless, Christ died for the ungodly" (Rom. 5:6). John the Baptist introduced Jesus to the world by stating, "The time has come . . ." (Mark 1:15). Paul, when writing to the church at Galatia, stated, "When the time *[chronos]* had fully come, God sent his Son . . ." (Gal. 4:4).

God's timing itself is a mystery to humankind, as we will never fully understand why He does certain things at certain times. Apparently it is determined by criteria quite different from our own. If, after all, God's plan was to save humankind, why did He wait several thousand years into the creation experience before sending His Son to bring about its fruition?

The Greeks had two words for time with different meanings. *Chronos* referred to quantity of time, as regulated and measured by our watches. It is where we get our modern word *chronometer. Kairos* expresses quality of time, referring to the nature of an experience, such as, "A good time was had by all." In this verse, Paul uses *kairos.* Apparently, he believed that God is not so much moved by the quantity of time (considering He is eternal) as He is with its quality. We might say that when God felt the time was just right, he revealed the mystery. He did not set a predetermined date and time for the event, but rather chose it by a given condition and situation which only He knew.

In relation to this idea, we presently await the return of our Lord which has been determined to happen at a certain time. Many attempt to set this occasion by using *chronos* time (dates and years) in place of *kairos* time (situations and conditions). Jesus' teaching to His disciples tells us that no one knows the day or the hour of the event *(chronos),* except the Father. Perhaps this is because God's timing is determined by *kairos.*

When the situation is right, God acts. This is not always a comfort to us as we sometimes find ourselves waiting on God to answer a prayer and provide a need. We realize from our perspective that He is passing up a number of great opportunities to act on our behalf. However, when the time comes and He acts, we realize it could not have been done at a better time. This is Paul's statement about the fulfillment of God's plan: it could not have come at a better time. It has been said that God answers our prayers in one of three ways: "Yes," "No," or "Wait." Although the first two might be preferred because of the immediacy of the response, we can accept God's call to wait, because we know that while His time is not our time, His time is right.

Last, the mystery's final result was **to bring all things in heaven and on earth together under one head . . . Jesus Christ** (Eph. 1:10). Essentially, this would reverse the effects of sin and the fall of humankind.

The consequence of humankind's disobedience toward God has resulted in a number of separations that continue to influence us even today.

There is the separation of humankind from God. This separation is evident in the account of God looking for Adam and Eve after they had sinned. Aware of their sin, they were hiding from God in fear (see Genesis 3:10). Sin severs us from God because He is holy and cannot look on sin without the need for judgment.

There is a separation of humankind from paradise. Adam and Eve were expelled from the Garden to prevent their eating from the Tree of Life (see Genesis 3:23). Since then, humankind has desired to regain what it has lost, to hear the words of our Lord: "Today you will be with me in paradise" (Luke 23:43b).

There is a separation between humankind and the rest of creation, as God cursed the ground on humankind's behalf so that it would not easily produce its crop. There is a separation between man and woman, with a marked distinction placed upon roles and responsibilities that continue to be debated even today (see Genesis 3:16-17). There is a separation within families, as sin would influence us to turn against one another for any number of reasons (see Genesis 4:8). There is a separation within humankind itself, begun at Babel, as we distinguish one another into hierarchies determined by sex, age, race, color, social status, or nationality (see Genesis 11:5-8). There is also the division made evident in this letter between Jew and Gentile, which Paul sees closed by the person of Jesus Christ (see Ephesians 2:14-22).

The list of these divisions could continue, as the effects of sin within our world have relentlessly divided us further into isolation from God, humankind, and our world. God's plan through Jesus was to redeem the world, restoring severed relationships, and to reverse the process of sin in the individual as well as in the whole world. Sin brings chaos from order. God's grace brings order from chaos. All things in heaven and on earth would be affected by being reunited under the lordship of Jesus Christ, the instrument of God's plan.

In summary of the mystery, Paul has listed the major areas of concern. The "what" of God's plan deals with the salvation of humankind to a complete restoration of holiness and blamelessness. The "why" is discerned by the motives described—His pleasure and will. The "how" is revealed by the experiences in humankind's transformation, wrought by the death and resurrection of our Lord Jesus Christ—namely holiness, adoption, and redemption. The "who" must be understood as referring to all people, and not just a prechosen few. The "when" was the right moment, determined by the quality of time, and not its quantity. The "where" is that juncture where heaven and earth meet in the unity and person of Jesus Christ (see Ephesians 1:10). This is the ultimate fulfillment, when that which has been divided and torn by sin can once again be brought to unity through grace—grace determined and extended by the Father, made possible through the Son, and executed by the Holy Spirit. We can all join with Paul in his litany of praise to God: **Praise be to the God and Father of our Lord Jesus Christ, who has blessed us in the heavenly realms with every spiritual blessing in Christ** (1:3).

2. THE BENEFITS OF BELIEVING 1:11-14

As much as we recognize Paul's ministry to the Gentiles, and read his letters both defending and defining their incorporation into the Christian faith, he still makes a distinction between the Jews and Gentiles. Paul's distinction in this section of Ephesians is subtle. Throughout the first ten verses, Paul has used common first-person pronouns when referring to the recipients of God's favor: "we," "us." They are used in an inclusive sense, referring to humankind in general. However, beginning with verse 11, this expression changes, with a greater distinction made between "we," in verses 11 and 12, and "you," in verse 13. What distinguishes the identity of the "we" from the "you" is the order in which they received the gospel message. The "we" group is defined as **the first to hope in Christ** (Eph. 1:12)—those who had been chosen and predestined by God to bring about praise. The "you" group (1:13) was incorporated into Christ, not by predestination, but by their belief in the gospel when it was first shared with them. The result of their belief has made them the beneficiaries of God's Holy Spirit, who marks them with a seal.

This distinction may actually find its beginning in 1:9, as it relates the reception of the mystery to a specific group: "He made known to *us* the mystery of His will" (my emphasis). Paul's later mention of this reception in 3:2-3 implies that it was part of his original call, made known to him, of which he had already written briefly (3:3). This mention obviously points to his reference in 1:9.

There is a noted distinction made by Paul in this letter between Jewish Christians and Gentile Christians. But an issue that remains is whether Paul is referring to Jewish Christians as a whole, or to a group of predestined individuals selected from this broader category.

An argument can be made for a generalized reference to Christian Jews, as they are those chosen by God through the covenant of Abraham to reveal God's glory to all the world (see Isaiah 49:6). Their acceptance of Jesus Christ as Savior would usher them into the new covenant already endowed by God's earlier commission. The Jews were originally chosen by God, via the covenant, and selected to be God's voice to the nations. In this passage, Paul is referring to Christian Jews in general, seeing their unique position in God's plan of salvation as the link between the old and new covenant. They are the ones, by virtue of their race, who had an initial claim to God. Now, in addition to this, they are among the "first to believe" (early Christians) and, as such, are part of the new covenant. They are not the people, like the recipients of this letter, who were uncircumcised, separated from Christ, lacking citizenship, foreign to the covenant and promises, living "without hope and without God" (Eph. 2:11-12). Thus, Paul's exclusive reference could be to the continued responsibility placed upon Christian Jews to finish what God had originally covenanted with them to do through Abraham. In this way, the Christ event is a necessary step for God's original call to be fulfilled through the Jewish nation (see Ephesians 2:12-13).

Another suggestion is found in 3:5 where Paul states that the mystery was revealed by the Holy Spirit to "God's holy apostles and prophets." To this group, Paul connects himself by testifying to having become a "servant of this gospel" (3:7). This distinction could be narrowed even more to the immediate context of Paul's writing and those Jewish Christians who were present with him in Rome: Tychicus, Aristarchus, Mark, Barnabas, and Jesus called Justus (see Colossians 4:10-11).

As Paul reassures the Gentile readers of their incorporation in Christ, he shares a number of *necessities* that are part of our salvation.

There is *the necessity of hearing*—they believed when they **heard the word of truth** (Eph. 1:13). This may appear a mere observation of the obvious, but it is a reality we must be reminded of continually. Paul asks the timely question in his epistle to the Romans: "How, then, can they call on the one they have not believed in? And how can they believe in the one of whom they have not heard? And how can they hear without someone preaching to them?" (Rom. 10:14). We must never forget that our primary duty as believers is to share God's words of truth regarding how each person may be saved.

There is the *necessity of the gospel*. Paul emphasizes the content of the necessary message: **the word of truth, the gospel of your salvation.** The importance of a message is found in its contents. It is not enough for us to be aware of the need to proclaim God's truth. It is equally important to be aware of the message God wants us to proclaim. Purity of the Word is always a concern for the conscientious Christian. It is far too easy for personal bias or ignorance to taint our message with an errant slant. There is a temptation to speak for Scripture, rather than allowing Scripture to speak for itself. Our theology and doctrine all clamor for attention and, if allowed, would distort the pure message of God with our human confusion.

The gospel presents a number of influences upon people. To one person, it may be a hard message which contradicts a misguided behavior or attitude. To another, it may be words of healing to a deep inner need. To still another it can be a word of hope to an otherwise desperate life. It can be an intellectual answer to a great thinker, or it can be a simple claim of truth to a child. The important part is for us to remain true to its message and guard against the temptation to adapt it as we would see fit. The world, like entertainment, tends to give people what they want. The gospel, in its truth, gives people what they need.

There is the *necessity of believing the gospel.* The Greek word used in this phrase **having believed** means "to express faith in" or "embrace with faith." But there is the danger of mental assent here. To agree with a statement is to exercise a certain amount of faith in its claim. Sometimes this comes as a result of previous experience. I believe the lights in my office will come on when I flip the switch on the wall. I do not doubt this, as it has always happened. But belief in the gospel requires a different exercise of faith. It cannot be that which results from experience, but a faith that accepts its claims with a response of trust.

In 1860, Blondine, a famous tightrope walker, strung a 1,000-foot cable 160 feet above the roaring waters of Niagara Falls. Large crowds gathered on both sides of the falls to watch while he performed his fearless acts of daring. Having made a number of trips back and forth over the wire, he came down to his audience and asked them, "Do you believe I can walk across the wire one more time?" A resounding cheer of affirmations erupted from the crowd. Again, the daredevil queried the people: "Do you believe I could cross the wire while carrying a man on my back?" Again, the crowd roared their conviction. To this, the performer asked, "Which one of you will be first?" The air went silent as everyone looked at the ground, avoiding his inquiring gaze. It is easy for us to believe in something that demands little from us. The faith required to accept the gospel is one which embraces our Lord with the wholehearted trust that Christ can do what He claims.

Paul now moves from discussing what the people know as their experience to the less obvious workings of God in their salvation. Their part had been to hear and accept the gospel in faith; God's part would be to extend to them the benefits of His salvation plan.

They were **included in Christ** (1:13). We have looked at the meaning of Paul's term "in Christ" and have understood it to mean the inclusion or incorporation into the gracious relationship with God, made possible through Jesus Christ. Specifically, though, this inclusion in Christ refers to the incorporation of the Gentile believers into the kingdom of God, giving them equal status with those who were "the first to hope in Christ." Because of their birth, they were Gentiles and, therefore, uncircumcised and separated from Christ (2:11-12). But now, in Jesus Christ, this has all changed, and they enjoy the same full relationship with God that the Jewish Christians enjoy.

They **were marked in Him with a seal, the promised Holy Spirit** (1:13). The purpose of this **seal** is to assure the believer that all God has promised regarding salvation will be done. The **Holy Spirit** is **promised** to God's children in a number of places within Scripture. In John 14:16-31, Jesus comforted His disciples just prior to His crucifixion with the promise that once He was gone, He would pray to the Father to send in His place the Holy Spirit. The purpose of this Spirit would be mainly benevolent, in that He would take the place of Jesus' presence in leading, instructing, and ministering to the disciples. In Luke 24:49, Jesus reassured the disciples, just before His ascension, that He would send what His Father had promised. The disciples were to wait in the city until that promise was fulfilled. This account is repeated in Acts 1:4. This is also part of Peter's message to the witnesses of Pentecost, that the phenomena before the people was the result of Jesus' faithfulness in pouring out the Holy Spirit upon them.[9]

The presence of the Spirit is also a testimony to the believer that the grace of God has been applied to his or her life (see Romans 8:16). This infilling marks us with a holy presence signifying to whom we belong. It is a mark of identity God places upon us which says to the world, "Property redeemed by God." There has been a long debate as to how this **seal** (1:13) is expressed within the believer.

The first evidence or expression is the mystical revelation by God to believers, assuring them of His grace, such as described in Romans 8:15-17. This experience is as varied as the people experiencing it, but its results are the same. The believer knows that he or she has been redeemed by God and has been adopted into the family of God as an heir with Christ.

A second evidence of the Holy Spirit's presence is understood by some to be the Spirit's influence on a person's life. This influence is usually stressed by differing groups as proof of God's mark upon the person. There is the influence of wisdom, which enlightens the Christian in the ways of God. First Corinthians 2:6-16 relates Paul's discussion of this influence on his life and the lives of other believers. The Spirit enables the Christian to understand what God has freely given. This wisdom is taught to us by the Spirit, using spiritual thoughts and words. It is the "unspiritual" (those lacking the Holy Spirit) who are unable to receive or understand these truths. In short, they lack spiritual discernment. Spiritual persons, on the other hand, have the discernment necessary to make judgments of all things.

A third evidence of the Holy Spirit has been understood as the gifts of the Spirit. These special abilities given by God enable Christians to minister for God in special ways. Though often controversial, these gifts are the empowering graces necessary within the church for it to perform the work of God. Paul lists these gifts in several places within Scripture (see Ephesians 4:11; Romans 12:6-8; 1 Corinthians 12–14). The danger of abuse of these gifts is seen when we understand the gifts as evidence of the Spirit's presence, and as easily mimicked by people who may not have them. It requires the spiritual ability of discernment to determine the genuineness of some expressions.

A fourth evidence recognizing the Holy Spirit's presence is the fruits of the Spirit. Listed in Galatians 5:22-26, they reveal the changed nature of the inner person. Because of this, the "fruits" are less easy to mimic and tend to be a more accurate reflection of God's work within the person.

In addition to different understandings of the expression of the Spirit's **seal** in our lives (Eph. 1:13), a controversy also exists over what exactly Paul meant by the seal of the Holy Spirit. The conflict usually revolves around two possible interpretations.

First, the seal mentioned prohibits any tampering of the item until its rightful owner receives it. An illustration of this view can be seen in the use of sealing wax on a document. Once marked with a signet, the wax would fasten the paper and mark the document so that anyone handling it would recognize the owner and leave it alone. Those who embrace this understanding believe that God has sealed the believer so that his decision for salvation will never be lost. Once God has redeemed a person, he or she never can be taken away from God. Paul eludes to this provision in 2 Corinthians 1:21-22, where he states that it is God who enables us to stand firm in Christ. Because of this, He anointed us, set His seal of ownership upon us, and put His Spirit in our hearts as a deposit of guarantee.

Second, and that held by John Wesley, is the view that the Holy Spirit is present within the person, but more as a witness, and not as a lifelong seal. In Wesley's book, *Plain Account of Christian Perfection,* he answers a question directed specifically to this issue.

> Q. Does St. Paul mean any more by being "sealed with the Spirit," than being "renewed in love?"
> A. Perhaps in one place, (2 Cor. 1:22), he does not mean so much; but in another, (Eph. 1:13), he seems to include both the fruit and the witness; and that in a higher degree than we experience even when we are first "renewed in love;" God "sealeth us with the Spirit of promise," by giving us "the full assurance of hope;" such a confidence of receiving all the promises of God, as excludes the possibility of doubting; with that Holy Spirit, by universal holiness, stamping the whole image of God on our hearts.[10]

Apparently Wesley saw the seal of the Holy Spirit as a sign that one has been saved by Christ ("renewed in love"). However, regarding this passage in Ephesians, Wesley sees a combination of both the seal and its effect on the believer's life in a stage of maturity beyond initial salvation. He sees the seal and its accompanying witness of full assurance as that which helps block the potential of doubt; faith stays strong. Thus, the Holy Spirit, being applied to the person in this context by way of "universal holiness," stamps the entire image of God on the heart of the believer.

But does this mean that a person, once sealed with the Spirit of God, will be unable to fall from grace? In response to this possibility, Wesley lists six ways expressed by Paul by which a person so marked with the Spirit can break its seal: (1) by "unprofitable" conversation that lacks a ministry of grace to people; (2) by developing a bitter attitude; (3) by allowing anger to control the person, developing a less-than-tender-hearted attitude; (4) by failing to forgive one another; (5) by vulgar speech; or (6) by gossip and backbiting which centers around the faults and shortcomings of another. Obviously Wesley believed that the seal of the Spirit did not guarantee our continued salvation.

What a blessing is ours as a result of God's salvation plan! In one long, rambling sentence, Paul has chained together the most profound, life-changing truths known to humankind. He begins his letter with this message as a stepping-stone to the results of faith worked out in our lives. Truly we have been blessed by all the spiritual blessings God has provided for us through Christ Jesus.

ENDNOTES

[1]John Wesley, *The Works of John Wesley*, vol. 7, 3rd. ed. (Grand Rapids, Michigan: Baker Book House, 1986), p. 381.

[2]Eucharist commonly refers to the Lord's Supper or Communion. The Greek word it comes from means "thanksgiving." There is no direct link in the Scriptures between thanksgiving and the Lord's Supper, except possibly in 1 Corinthians 14:16, which may refer to giving thanks over the elements taken in the Lord's Supper. A form of the word is also used in the accounts of the Last Supper (see Matthew 26:27; Mark 14:23; Luke 22:17, 19; 1 Corinthians 11:24).

[3]W. T. Purkiser, Richard S. Taylor, and Willard H. Taylor, *God, Man, and Salvation: A Biblical Theology* (Kansas City, Missouri: Beacon Hill Press of Kansas City, 1977), p. 467.

[4]The Gospels include the New Testament books of Matthew, Mark, Luke, and John.

[5]Judaism is the life and belief system of the Jewish people and involves a covenant relationship with God. Though there are various branches of Judaism, the underlying theme among them has been monotheism and a recognition of the Law, or the Torah. The Hebrew word from which *Torah* comes is translated *law* and refers to divine instruction and guidance. The Torah is comprised of the instructions and directions given to Israel by God. Torah is another name for the Pentateuch (the first five books of the Old Testament: Genesis, Exodus, Leviticus, Numbers, and Deuteronomy), also known as the Law of Moses. It is considered the most important division in the Jewish Scriptures, with highest authority, since it was traditionally thought to have been written by Moses, the only biblical hero to have spoken with God face-to-face.

[6]*Abba* is an Aramaic word of endearment that can be loosely translated as "Daddy."

[7]Law here refers to the Levitical Code (all God's rules and regulations).

[8]John Wesley, *Explanatory Notes,* vol. IV (Salem, Massachusetts: Schmul Publishers, 1975), p. 489.

[9]In the New Testament, Pentecost primarily refers to the event when the Holy Spirit was given to the church; this occurred on the day of Pentecost. The Greek term which *Pentecost* comes from means "fiftieth" or "the fiftieth day" and is literally the fiftieth day after the end of the Passover. It is also known as the Jewish Feast of Weeks, a day that is part of the Jewish observances, and was the beginning of the offering of first fruits.

[10]Wesley, *The Works of John Wesley,* vol. 11, pp. 423–24.

3

PAUL'S THANKFUL PRAYER

Ephesians 1:15-23

aving concluded his mind- and faith-stretching passage on God's redemptive plan in Ephesians 1:3-14, Paul allows both his excitement for the message and his loving concern for his readers to carry him into an expressed prayer on their behalf. It is a prayer that is motivated by what Paul knows of his readers (their faith and love) and what he desires for them to receive from God (a spirit of wisdom and an enlightenment). In a sense, he concludes all of the wonderful news shared in the last section by celebrating in prayer that which his readers have already enjoyed and from what they might still benefit.

One day a letter came from the local Salvation Army. I opened it curiously, having not anticipated a correspondence from this group. Inside was a printed piece of paper titled a "Prayergram" with a note written below telling me I had been prayed for on the date listed by the people who had signed their names at the bottom. I had been facing some particularly hard issues at the time, and the note could not have arrived at a more appropriate juncture in my ministry. I was immediately encouraged by the thought that I was not alone in my plight, but that others, unknown to me, were making mention of my needs to God. No doubt, this same feeling was experienced by the readers of the Ephesian letter as they read Paul's claim of faithful intercession for them. Ever since he had heard of their faith in Jesus Christ, he had made it a practice to pray for them. What a wonderful gift God has given to us through prayer! What a wonderful thing to know that one like Paul was praying on your behalf.

As we move into this prayer section of Paul's letter, it is interesting to note that he is just beginning his third sentence in the original Greek. As in the last 12 verses, Paul continues by using a long, complex sentence which extends through verse 23. It presents a prayer of thankful petition on behalf of the readers. But Paul arranges it in a manner different from his other letters. It is not that he expresses thanksgiving for the people (this he does in his other letters) or prays on their behalf (which he does in all of his letters, except 1 and 2 Corinthians). What is unusual is that his thanksgiving immediately follows the praise section of verses 3 through 14. Ephesians is the only New Testament epistle that has this construction. The motivation of Paul's thanksgiving and praise flows out of the context of the letter itself. We have already observed, in chapter 2, Paul's litany of praise to God for His great salvation plan by which He blesses all believers in Christ. His thankful prayer is directed to a more specific group, namely the recipients of the letter.

1. PAUL'S UNENDING THANKFULNESS 1:15-16

The **reason** (Eph. 1:15) for the prayer is based upon the information previously expressed in Paul's litany. Because God has predetermined this salvation plan for all humankind, and because the recipients of the letter have embraced it, resulting in their receiving God's Holy Spirit as a mark of their salvation, Paul shares his joy in knowing that God's good grace has become fruitful among them. The motivations for this prayer are closely paralleled with Paul's prayer on behalf of the Colossians (see Colossians 1:9-12). Paul gives two reasons for his faithful prayers on behalf of the Ephesians.

First, they are the beneficiaries of God's salvation, and the results of God's salvation are manifest in their lives. Paul has apparently received word regarding the practice of these people, which was expressed through their **faith in the Lord Jesus** and their **love for the all the saints** who also were in Christ (Eph. 1:15). The source of this information is not divulged, and yet Paul's delight in the news is obvious. Paul was an apostle who remained aware of the activities and conditions of the churches of his day. This was no small task, considering that letters and messages could take months to be delivered. Most of his letters make mention of his awareness of the church, revealing his personal interest and concern on their behalf. To the Roman church, Paul expressed thankfulness because their "faith is being reported all over the world" (Rom. 1:8). To the Corinthian church he was thankful for God's grace finding its enrichment in them (see 1 Corinthians 1:4-5). To the Philippian church he was thankful for their "partnership in the gospel" (Phil. 1:5). The Thessalonian church was recognized for their work produced by faith, their labor prompted by love, and their endurance inspired by hope, and because their faith and love were both growing (see 1 Thessalonians 1:3; 2 Thessalonians 1:3).

It is no secret that the integrity of the faith of any one person or church is evident in the living out of their beliefs. Sadly, it is far too common for a group of believers to become known for the wrong reasons. Churches that have become confused over time begin to manifest attributes that no longer reflect the Christian life. They no longer are known for attributes such as faith, love, hope, work, and endurance, but rather strife, discord, politics, legalism, rejection, hypocrisy, and coldness. It is sad, but one of the necessities often required today is to dissolve a church that has so lost its direction by God that it no longer has any vestiges of Christianity. Their people cannot get along. The damage is so great that in the secular community the name of the church becomes synonymous with hypocrisy and conflict. The negatives for which these churches are known far outweigh any ability to express God's grace. To rescue the work, the church is dissolved, the building sold, and the work relocated to another area under a new name, with the hope that the appropriate expression of God's church can once again be made.

Some ancient Greek manuscripts contain a different wording for the phrase that appears in the New International Version as "love for all the saints." Paul's word for "love" *(agapen)* is not found in many of the older manuscripts. Because of this, it is debated whether the word should be included in this verse. However, two views argue strongly that it should be.

First, without the word **love** (Eph. 1:15), it would imply that Paul is thankful for the faith the people have in Christ *and in all the saints.* While it is no great wrong to have faith in one's fellow believers, the phrase seems out of character for Paul when compared to his other letters (see especially Colossians 1:4). Paul uses the Greek noun for "love" *(agape)* more often in this letter than in any other of his correspondences, except 1 Corinthians, which is a much longer work. The Greek verb for "to love" is used more times in Ephesians than in any other letter by Paul.[1]

Second, the error can be easily explained by considering the Greek manuscript. There were no copying machines in the first several centuries A.D. Copies of a manuscript were made by hand, which made them prone to human error, errors that we easily commit even today. In the case of Paul's use of *agapen,* the word is both preceded and followed by the same Greek word, *ten.* Quite possibly, the scribe who was copying the manuscript read up to the first *ten,* and then wrote the words on his paper.

Looking back to the text, he returned to the word *ten* to begin the next portion. However, instead of going back to the preceding *ten,* the scribe began with the *ten* that *followed* the word "love" *(agapen),* which would have left the word "love" out of his copy. Such an error is known by scholars as a haplography. Because this manuscript would in turn be copied by other scribes who were unaware of the missing word, the error would have been included by them without realizing the problem. It was also customary for illiterate slaves to be used for the copying process, since all that was needed was an ability to write the letters, not understand them. Thus, words could be left out without any realization of the awkward structure that would result. (For further discussion of this issue, see the appendix.)

In light of these two views, it is probably more accurate to retain the word "love" than to exclude it.

It is significant to note that Paul's thankfulness is an ongoing action expressed to God through prayer. It would have been interesting to join Paul in one of his prayer sessions, to eavesdrop on this man of God as he poured out his heart on behalf of his work and the church. His thankfulness was not something that he kept to himself, nor was it expressed sparingly.

Thankfulness can become an endangered experience in our lives unless we are careful to guard it. When we fail to tell God we are thankful, our prayers and worship become little more than a list of wants and needs. When we fail to express it to those for whom we are thankful, our fellowship dies for want of edification. The Christian faith is a thankful faith. It recognizes the blessings that are ours because of God's grace, and because of faithful, loving brethren.

No doubt, the word of this church's spiritual activity was uplifting to Paul during his incarceration. It is quite possible Paul was experiencing discouragement as he realized that his life was coming to an end and that he might not be free to continue in his ministry much longer. Word that the church was alive and well could only serve to encourage him. Thus, Paul was thankful not only for what God had done in the lives of the people, but for the encouragement which such news brought to his life.

Paul continues his Trinitarian theme throughout this section. The office and activity of each expression of the Trinity is described. Paul's prayer is to God the Father. More specifically, the God who is the Father of our Lord Jesus Christ and who is "glorious," an expression used nowhere else by Paul. The prayer is that the people might receive the benefit of the Holy Spirit's ministry so that in the end, they might be endued with power similar to that performed by the resurrection and ascension of Jesus Christ the Son.

2. PAUL'S CONTINUAL PETITIONS 1:17-19a

Paul's prayer on behalf of his readers is for their enlightenment, which raises a question: How does one experience enlightenment? Enlightenment in the Christian sense refers to spiritual insight given to people by God through the ministry of the Holy Spirit. Paul's request is that God would give them a **Spirit of wisdom and revelation** (Eph. 1:17) so that they might know God better.

Verse 17 leaves us wondering as to the exact identity of the **Spirit** through which this enlightenment was to occur. "Holy" (as in "the Holy Spirit") is not mentioned, nor is there any definiteness associated with the word that would express a specific spirit—*"the* Spirit" as opposed to *"a* spirit." The question is important to answer. It determines whether **wisdom and revelation** are the benefits of the Spirit (the Holy Spirit), or if **the Spirit** is an expression of revelation and wisdom (in other words, the spirit *of* wisdom and revelation). The distinction is between entity or essence.

If, by **the Spirit,** Paul means the Holy Spirit, then we are dealing with a living being, and the experiences of wisdom and revelation are the results of His ministry to us. This would be in keeping with Jesus' original introduction and explanation of the Holy Spirit's responsibilities in John 14. There, in addition to being a comforter, the Holy Spirit was to be an enlightener and leader for the believer. It would seem that Paul's prayer is merely requesting that the ministry of the Holy Spirit, as described by Jesus, might be fulfilled in the lives of these believers. However, Paul may be referring to an abstract idea, expressing it in an easily understood fashion. The writer of Proverbs, for example, personifies wisdom as a woman who calls out warnings in the street to undiscerning people in the height of their passions (see Proverbs 1:20). Like a spirit, this woman is not encountered physically, but as an inward influence upon the person. Therefore, Paul is either praying for *the* Holy Spirit to come upon them, or for an *inner awareness of God's enlightenment* to be made known. Since Paul implies that the Holy Spirit has already been given to the readers of the letter as a result of their belief in the gospel (see Ephesians 1:13), it would seem Paul's request is for the people to become aware or retain an inner sense of God's wisdom and revelation. This would be made known through the Holy Spirit.

The reason for the prayer is found in Paul's statement, **that you may know Him better** (1:17). The pronoun **you** refers to the recipients of the letter, while the pronoun **Him** refers to the one to whom Paul is praying, namely the Father. Paul's overall desire is for his readers to have a better knowledge of God. This is not a desire that they strike off on a fact-finding mission. The Greek word for **know** here *(epignosei)* has a special type of construction that lends a special emphasis.[2] Usually, *epignosei* can mean anything from recognizing to understanding, but when used in this specific way, the meaning intensifies to express knowing something exactly and completely.[3] New Testament scholar Leon Morris explains that this construction is only used in the New Testament to describe religious or moral knowledge, and as such is used only in relationship to God.[4]

Paul's prayer speaks to the heart of a Christian's need. Most people desire a better understanding of God. When asked why we read our Bibles and attend church services, we often reply, "To learn more about God." But knowledge is not the same as knowing. What we often seek is breadth rather than depth. We errantly assume that the more facts we know, the closer we grow. But Paul's prayer is for depth, not breadth. His concern is not that the people know *of* God, but to *actually know* God. **Wisdom and revelation** from God (1:17) speaks of intimacy of relationship between the Father and the believer, the lover and the beloved. As with Paul's readers, so should it be today—that we, through the ministry of the Holy Spirit, might gain a sense of God's wisdom and revelation so we may search the depths of who He is. Paul prays for this more specifically in Ephesians 3.

To allow for the full effect of this knowledge of God, resulting from His revealed wisdom, Paul continues to pray poetically on behalf of his readers that **the eyes of your heart may be enlightened** (1:18). This descriptive phrase speaks not of the physical, but the spiritual and emotional aspects of humankind. In keeping with the meaning of *epignosei,* Paul desires that this in-depth enlightenment with God would have its effect upon the inner person. This is not a request for superficial religion, but the kind that cuts to the core of an individual and creates a change. Biologically, we understand that all thinking, reasoning, and emotion is a result of certain brain functions responding to various stimuli. Poetically, though, the source of emotion—the depth of the soul—is not found in the head, but in the heart. Paul does not want our experience of God's revelation to speak to our minds only, but to our souls, affecting the very fiber of our being.

There is a need for enlightenment among humankind. Sin originally displaced the light, allowing only darkness in its absence. It was against this spiritual darkness that Jesus came into the world, so that people might have light (see Isaiah 9:2; John 1:4). Darkness is simply the absence of light. Once light comes, however, darkness is dispelled.

The Christian is in constant need of God's shining His light of revelation into our lives; otherwise, it is naturally replaced by the darkness so prevalent in the world. God is the source of light. At the very beginning, God commanded, "Let there be light." Our need and dependence upon God for light was summed up by Paul when writing to the Corinthian church: "For God, who said, 'Let light shine out of darkness,' made his light shine in our hearts to give us the light of the knowledge of the glory of God in the face of Christ" (2 Cor. 4:6). This enlightenment by God, for which Paul prayed, would give his readers understanding of three things: the **hope** of their calling; the **riches** of His inheritance; and His incomparable **power** for the believer (Eph. 1:18-19).

Hope, in the Christian context (as understood in the New Testament), is somewhat different than that of the world. Hope often conjures up an image of a little girl before the glowing candles of her birthday cake. She has secretly made her wish, and now, with her fingers crossed and eyes closed, she blows really hard to extinguish the candles, all the while desiring her wish to come true. Hope, in this sense, is an intense but uncertain desire that is at the mercy of fate.

To the Christian, hope is not an intense *desire,* but an intense *certainty.* It is not the result of fate, but the product of faith. Hope is the fulfillment of God's promises and claims. As God reveals to us His will, it gives us a source of anticipation by which we live our lives. The hope in which God has called us is the certainty of His saving grace in our lives. The assuredness that all which Paul listed earlier in this chapter, regarding the predestined plans of God on behalf of humankind, is true and will be fulfilled in our lives. Later in this letter, Paul will speak of the unity of the Christian faith, the one hope resulting from our call. That call moves us toward one purpose in life, namely obedience and service to God. It is a call which assures us of one result of God's grace—eternity with Him as fellow heirs with Christ.

The names Howard Hughes, J. Paul Getty, and Aristotle Onassis are all synonymous with vast wealth. It is hard to imagine the money that these individuals amassed in their lifetimes. Their worth was so high that it took professional accountants to keep track of not only how much they had, but where it was all located. To comprehend these fortunes is mind-boggling. If this is true with earthly wealth, how much more so with heavenly wealth. Paul prays that his readers might know **the riches of his glorious inheritance in the saints** (1:18). Paul has already revealed

61

that God's plan provides not only the forgiveness of our sins, but the adoption of each believer as His child (see 1:5). It is an adoption resulting in our becoming heirs. To think that His believers will receive an inheritance from the One who owns all things goes beyond comprehension. No wonder Paul prayed that such incredible information as the riches of their inheritance be revealed. They could obtain it by no other means.

But there is another reason Paul prays for them to know the riches of God's inheritance. Not just so they could come to an understanding of what was in store in the future, but that they might have encouragement in the present. The call of Christ is to store up treasures in heaven, and not on earth. It is a call to self-denial, of seeking the Kingdom first in all we do. Of selling what we have and giving to the poor. Of giving freely what we have received freely. Of giving without seeking repayment. The path of God seldom leads to huge amounts of earthly wealth. It is in times of want when we need to be reminded that what we presently are experiencing is trivial. That which we surrender or refuse is but a pittance in comparison to what our Father has in store for His children: **the riches of His glorious inheritance** (1:18). We are heirs of the Kingdom.

When I was a child, my brothers and I could not endure the seemingly endless night before Christmas. The clock never moved, and sleep never came while we lay anticipating the many gifts we would enjoy the next day. Sometimes the wait got the best of us, and when we thought that our parents were asleep, we would sneak out of our rooms and down the creaky, old steps to have a preview of what the next day would provide.

Likewise, our souls get restless for God and home. The clock of life ticks slowly, and anticipation becomes strong. To this time of desire, Paul prays that we might come to comprehend the riches that God's great inheritance has for us all. What are these riches?

First, they likely include the riches of eternal life. An eternity with God is a concept beyond our perception. Peter and Gordon were popular singers in the 1960s. They sang a song about eternity which described it in terms of a mountain that was one thousand miles square and high. To this mountain a little bird would fly, once every one million years. It would sharpen its beak, then fly away. When this little bird had finally succeeded in wearing down the mountain to nothing, by way of its infrequent visits, the equivalence of this time would be one day in eternity. Those who are in Christ inherit *eternal* life.

Second, these riches likely include the riches of life without pain or illness. Pain and illness are actually beneficial feelings given to humankind by God. They tell us when our well-being is imperiled. While we may not enjoy pain or illness, they do serve as a reminder that our world is harsh to its inhabitants and that we suffer those consequences. But our inheritance is not of this world, and there comes a time when we will live in an environment no longer hostile, but hospitable. Jesus promised His disciples that He was going to prepare a place for them (and us), a place designed with His people in mind, where bacteria and environment, age and error will not corrupt or destroy.

Third, the riches of God's great inheritance include the riches of life without sadness. Sadness is the emotional experience resulting from our suffering in this world. It is the yearning of the soul for what it knows is better. We lament our loss and suffering because we know it could be different. In the book of Revelation, John describes God's merciful ministry to His children as He welcomes them home—wiping from their eyes the evidential tears of a life once suffered—and gives to them the desires of their hearts.

Fourth, included in the riches of God's inheritance are the riches of life in the immediate, unlimited presence of God. Even our most lofty thoughts of God fall short of reality. Moses wanted to see Him, but was only allowed a glimpse of His back (see Exodus 33:18–34:8). Paul tells us that we see now as through a dark glass, but then we will see Him as He is (see 1 Corinthians 13:12). Jesus was sent to reveal God to us, and yet in Philippians Paul writes that Christ, the obedient Son of God, did not demand equality with the Father, but emptied himself, taking on the form of a man (see Philippians 2:6-11). In John's gospel, we read Jesus' words to the disciples: "Anyone who has seen me has seen the Father" (John 14:9). Yet, even this identity was limited. We can come to understand a great deal about God through Jesus Christ, but not everything. That is coming on the day when humankind no longer needs to worry that seeing Him will destroy them, because we will see Him as He is.

Fifth, these riches include the riches of the glorified state—no sin. Try to imagine a world without prohibitions. A place where the only response possible is "yes" because there are no potential wrongs. Try to imagine living without being tempted or confronted with sin. Where every thought is continually noble and pure. Every motivation perfect. Every action springing from integrity. Welcome to glory. Paul wrote in 1 Corinthians 15 that our old bodies were sown in corruption, but were raised incorruptible. This is glorification, or that state wherein it is impossible for us to sin. The struggle of the soul is gone. All is at complete, peaceful surrender. What greater wealth could a person have than to be at complete rest with God, one's neighbors, and oneself?

Sixth, the riches of God's glorious inheritance include the riches of God's rewards. In several passages of Scripture, Jesus refers to our reception by the Father as being a reward. Rewards are usually the result of faithful stewardship of that which God has entrusted to us. There is also Jesus' encouragement for us to make investments in heaven, to lay up treasures where we can be assured that no theft or corruption will take them away. How many people have been redeemed by God as a result of our faithful service? How many have gone on before us and even now enjoy the riches we now struggle to comprehend? How many will be there in testimony of God's grace having worked through our lives?

Paul's last request before the Father is that we might know **His incomparably great power** (Eph. 1:19). One of the known attributes of God is His omnipotence, or unlimited power. God is so great that there is nothing He cannot do. Imagine the act of Creation alone—how, just by God's simple command, all things came into being. To comprehend the limitless is beyond our ability. Our minds cannot handle it, even if God did reveal it to us. So Paul is asking for a comparative expression of power which we might begin to understand. But even this limited expression finds the need of a strong emphasis in description.

3. GOD'S RESURRECTION POWER 1:19b-23

At this point, Paul seemingly breaks off on a side issue, caught up in the heady thoughts of God's great power at work. He elaborates on this power, describing its ability and expression. This incomparably great *power* of God **is like the** *working* **of His** *mighty strength* (Eph. 1:19, my emphasis). Leon Morris sees four different expressions regarding God's power in this statement: (1) God's **power** means His natural inherent ability; (2) God's **working** is His exercised expression of operation; (3) that God is **mighty** reveals a relative manifestation of him; and (4) God's **strength** expresses His physical, endowed power.[5]

Paul continues in his definition of God's power by using comparison. It is the power **like** that God exercised on behalf of Jesus when **he raised him from the dead** (1:20). Paul wants us to know God's resurrection power, that ability of God to raise one out of death into life.

This power is realized *spiritually,* as we were once dead in our sins, but now have been raised to new life in Christ (see 2:4-5). We see it in

God's restoration of the believer from sinner to saint, reprobate to child of God. Paul saw baptism as an outward symbol of this inner working of God's power (see Colossians 2:12). The resurrection power of God is not something we must wait for at the end, but it can be ours now as God raises us out of sin and despair.

God's resurrection power is also known *physically* (see Ephesians 2:6). Just as we are all destined to die, those who are in Christ will be raised from the dead. Two important realizations of this resurrection are necessary. First, it is a bodily resurrection. We must be careful that we do not fall into an old Greek idea that the flesh is shed and only the spirit returns back to God. The Greeks believed that flesh was evil and the spirit was good. Such a view is not in keeping with the Christian faith. God's resurrection power is one that raises us in incorruptible flesh. Second, it is a resurrection where we will never die again. Many view the miracle Jesus performed with Lazarus when He raised him from the dead as a resurrection (see John 11:38-44). Technically, it was not. It was a resuscitation. Lazarus, though raised from the dead, died again at another time. His body was corruptible. Paul wants his readers to know that the power of God's resurrection with Jesus is the same power He extends to us as well—a power that raises us from sin and death and hell, giving us victory over their influence.

God's power is a *celestial power*. Having resurrected Jesus, God raised him to heaven, **where he seated him at his right hand in the heavenly realms** (Eph. 1:20). This is a power that bestows honor, which is seen by how and where Jesus is seated. Jesus once instructed His disciples to be careful, when entering into a feast, not to take the prominent chair, but rather to choose the lesser seat and wait to be called forward by the master of the feast (see Luke 14:8-10). Jesus exemplified such humility. Choosing the lesser seat of human flesh, willingly accepting the degradation of the cross, submissively enduring the ungodlike experience of death, Jesus was raised by God to His rightful place of honor—a seat with the Father in heaven, at His right hand (see Philippians 2:6-11).

The **right hand** (Eph. 1:20) has always been known as the hand of honor in the Middle East. The left hand was used for certain acts of personal hygiene and, as a result, was considered to be unclean. The name Benjamin, given in honor by Jacob to his beloved second son of Rachel, literally means "son of my right hand."

In addition to Jesus' proximity to the Father's right hand, there is also the location of this seat. Paul describes it as **in the heavenly realms** (1:20).

This phrase is used five times by Paul, exclusively in the Ephesian letter. It is a term that cannot be limited to a mere reference to heaven, as it appears to take in a much broader realm. It is the location from which God's blessings have come to us (see Ephesians 1:3). In our present verse (1:20), it describes the place where Jesus sits in His resurrected glory. In 2:6 it describes where His people sit with Him in their resurrected state (see comments on 2:6). The term describes where the recipients of God's revealed mystery reside while He unveils this mystery throughout the church (see 3:10). It is also the battleground wherein God's people war against the evil principalities and powers (see 6:12). In general, "the heavenlies" have been described as meaning "the unseen world of spiritual reality."[6]

As much as it is important for us to understand God's workings of salvation *within* creation through Jesus Christ, the Ephesian letter also reveals those activities that continue to take place *outside* of creation **in the heavenly realms** (1:20). Paul assures us that here, amid so many other realities, is the presence of our resurrected Lord, at the Father's right hand.

God's power is further an *ultimate power* (see 1:21), where Jesus is given control over **all rule and authority, power and dominion, and every title that can be given.** This description is total! It suggests that Jesus' authority is greater than the claims of all other leaders, earthly or otherwise (**rule and authority**). It proclaims that Jesus' power is greater than any force that would endeavor to dominate (**power and dominion**). It announces a name that exceeds any other definitive title expressed or implied. We hear the echo of Philippians 2:9-11, where Paul recites what appears to be an early creed or hymn of the church, claiming that God's exaltation of Jesus is to the highest place, entitling Jesus with a name that not only is above all names, but through which all beings in heaven, earth, and under the earth will recognize His authority. This exaltation is in effect a restoration of Jesus back to the original state that He enjoyed with His Father even before the creation of time.

Paul explains that Jesus' coming among us was an act of humility by which He emptied himself *(ekenosen)* of all His divine claims and privileges. But these divine privileges and claims were restored by God in His resurrection and ascension. This original state of power and authority is described in Colossians 1:15-20. There, Paul writes that Jesus is not only the image of God, but the very one by whom all things were created "in heaven and on earth, visible and invisible, whether thrones or powers or rulers or authorities; all things were created by Him and for Him." Thus this power that God worked in the raising of Jesus was restorative, placing Him once again above the creation of which He willingly became a part, the creation that owes its very existence to Him. Jesus' ultimate authority over all rulers, authorities, powers, and dominions can be explained best by saying that that which is created is not greater than its creator.

Linked closely with Jesus' ultimate power is His timeless rule. His authority over all is not limited by time or situation, but is eternal, and **not only in the present age but also in the one to come** (Eph. 1:21). There is nothing physical or chronological that can usurp His reign. The distinction between the present age and the one to come is an inclusive expression by which all possibilities of time are considered.

God's power is also a *conquering power.* **God placed all things under his feet** (1:22a). Placing your foot on something or someone is an expression of dominance. Perhaps it is best understood in a military sense. When the ruling party of a defeated land was brought before their new king, they would bow before the throne of the monarch to express their surrender and submission. This act expressed their position as being beneath their new ruler. In David's song of praise to God for having delivered him from his enemies, David credited God with having made David's adversaries bow at his feet (see 2 Samuel 22:40). Later, David's son, Solomon, when writing to Hiram, king of Tyre, stated that David was unable to build a temple for God until the Lord "put his [David's] enemies under his feet." This militant task that God chose to work through David is described in Psalm 110:1. Later, Jesus would refer to this passage when debating His identity before the Pharisees of His day (see Matthew 22:41-46).

This dominance theme is echoed by the psalmist in describing the uniqueness of humankind within God's creation (see Psalm 8). Here it is proclaimed that God made humankind ruler over His creation, having "put everything under his [humankind's] feet." The writer of the book of Hebrews develops this idea further by applying it to mean our reign over the world to come (see Hebrews 2:5-9). We ourselves do not see it all, but we do see Jesus who, like us, was made a little lower than the angels, but since then has been crowned with glory and honor. This glorified dominance is presented as an inheritance for believers in Christ, who is not ashamed to accept them as brothers.

The subjugation of all things is described as an ongoing task of Jesus by Paul in 1 Corinthians 15:20-28. The theme is the resurrection of humankind, of which Christ is the firstfruit. The ultimate task of Jesus is to bring all things into submission and, as a last act of submission, present them all to the Father, to whom Jesus himself will submit in the end.

Paul's desire that we might know this conquering power relates to the potential we have of being victors over powers that desire to conquer and enslave us. There is the *natural realm,* from which we are continually challenged for survival. God's power comes to us through reason and understanding on how to be better stewards of the creation He has given us. There is also the *human realm,* from which we are attacked for any number of reasons. God's power can be enacted to bring peace where once there was only hostility. And there is the *spiritual realm,* for which we are encouraged by Paul, in Ephesians 6, to prepare ourselves for battle with spiritual armor and weaponry provided by God, in order to go against the powers and principalities of darkness.

Finally, God's power is the church's *primary power.* God, in raising Jesus from the dead, **appointed him to be head over everything for the church,** the body of Christ (Eph. 1:22). This theme is developed in a number of places by Paul, usually in describing diversity of people and gifts among which unity is found in Christ. Some have argued that the description of Christ as **head over everything** should not be considered as control oriented, but rather as leadership or being first. During the time of Christ, the seat of reason and thinking was associated with the abdomen and heart, not the head. There was no notion of control by the head over the rest of the body. References to the head referred more to order or primacy, rather than control. If this is the case, then Jesus as Head of the Body is considered first or primary (see 1 Corinthians 15:20). He is the church's beginning, and everything else flows from Him.[7]

ENDNOTES

[1]Leon Morris, *Expository Reflections on the Letter to the Ephesians* (Grand Rapids, Michigan: Baker Books, 1994), p. 29.

[2]The verb *epignoseis* is preceded by the preposition *en.*

[3]William F. Arndt and F. Wilbur Gingrich, trans., *A Greek-English Lexicon of the New Testament and other Early Christian Literature,* by Walter Bauer (Chicago: The University of Chicago Press, 1957), p. 290.

[4]Morris, p. 31.

[5]Ibid., p. 33.

[6]Ibid., p. 15.

[7]Ibid., p. 36.

4

RELATIONSHIPS RECONCILED IN CHRIST

Ephesians 2:1-22

It had been years since they felt this way. The friendship had been close once, but then something happened that caused such a strain on the relationship that it broke. Now, years later, circumstances had brought them together again, and the issue, once divisive, was now resolved. They sat laughing, talking, and catching up on what had happened in their lives over the years, filling the void created by their earlier estrangement.

Reconciliation is that bittersweet experience where one encounters a negative, past conflict and a positive, present resolution. Many issues in life, whether accidental or purposeful, cause strains in relationships. Sometimes these are of such a nature that a separation results. However, time and events often provide ways that bring about opportunities to resolve divisions and reconcile people. This is the message Paul shares in this section. His readers were the victims of two different estrangements: one between themselves and God; and the other between themselves and their Jewish brothers and sisters.

However, because of what God had done through His Son, Jesus Christ, reconciliation had come. This reconciliation is likewise twofold: between themselves and God (see Ephesians 2:1-10); and between Jews and Gentiles (see 2:11-22). Paul distinguished between the Jews and Gentiles by using a direct address toward his readers, referring to them as "you," and to the Jews as "all of us" (2:3). The purpose of this expression is obvious from the context. Paul wants to reveal first how both Gentiles and Jews have been reconciled to God from their sinfulness, and then how this reconciliation brings about a oneness between them.

1. RECONCILIATION BETWEEN HUMANKIND AND GOD 2:1-10

Referring to their previous condition before God's reconciliation had taken place, Paul describes their situation as being **dead in your transgressions and sins** (Eph. 2:1). The latter was the cause of the former, as Paul told the Romans: "For the wages of sin is death" (Rom. 6:23). But what exactly does Paul mean? Obviously he is not speaking literally, as in a physical death. People do not usually write letters to dead people. Paul is speaking of the figurative or spiritual result of sin in one's life.

Death has always been understood to be the result of sin. It was God's warning to the first couple, that if they ate of the fruit from the tree in the middle of the garden, they would die. It was the serpent's questioning the validity of this claim that enticed the first couple to eat the fruit. Since they did not immediately fall over dead, one might conclude that the serpent was right. However, being dead in one's sin encompasses both the physical and the spiritual natures of humankind. Where physical death did not immediately take place, spiritual death did.

Being dead in one's sins is *spiritual* death. Life without God is no life at all. At best, we exist temporarily in a physical state. To be spiritually dead is to live without God's presence. Theologically, this is known as depravity. Depravity, resulting from the fall of humankind and our willful acts of disobedience, influences every aspect of our lives. It is reduced in quality from the original image of God in which we were created. If left to experience the complete effects of our sin, our world would have fallen into a literal hellish decay. But God buoys us up by His grace, preventing the entire decay that the actions of humanity deserve. We may be dead in our sins, but God's grace allows a window of opportunity for any who would so desire to find the deliverance God has provided by which we are once again made alive.

Being dead in one's sins is a *literal* death. It is obvious that God's original intention regarding Adam and Eve was for their continued existence. The Tree of Life in the Garden of Eden would have made this possible. However, once Adam and Eve transgressed God, they were expelled from the garden to prevent their eating from the tree, which would have allowed them to live eternally in their sinful state (see Genesis 3:22-24). The fact that Adam and Eve are no longer with us verifies that what God said would happen actually did happen. God has not changed this message. First Corinthians says, "For as in Adam all die" (1 Cor. 15:22).

Being dead in one's sins is also a *legal* death. In some of our country's prisons, one can find special sections known as "Death Row." This is the area where we keep those inmates who have been sentenced to die as a result of their crimes. They have been tried and convicted, and now, in their condemned state, they await execution. By all rights, unless an appeal or pardon comes through, they are in a "death wait."

Legally, before God, those who are not saved are in a death wait. Their sins have condemned them before the Master Judge. They simply await the performance of God's sentence upon them. However, like the inmates of our prisons, there is always time for an appeal or a pardon by which the sentence can be transmuted.

Paul's description of the Gentiles' spiritual state prior to their salvation is summed up in two words: **transgressions** and **sins** (Eph. 2:1). Even though these are two different words, it is probably incorrect to attempt a distinction between them. They both express basically the same thing and are no doubt used synonymously here. Literally, the words mean "to miss the mark" or "to fall aside." One can best picture the connection by considering an archer shooting at a target. The correct action would be a bull's-eye. However, as the archer shoots, some of the arrows fall short or off to the side. Some reach the target, but not the bull's-eye. It is amid these wayward shots that the unregenerate live, or, as literally expressed by Paul, it is where they "walk."

Both the Apostles John and Paul habitually referred to the way people live by using the Greek word *peripateo,* which literally means "to walk." A form of this word is used eight times in the Ephesian letter (translated "walk" in the King James Version, though not in the New International Version). The expression is not foreign to us, as we often refer to our own experience of living as a "walk of life." Specifically, Paul relates that as Christians they were Christ's handiwork, created for good works, and therefore they should **walk** in them (2:10). In 4:1 they were to walk in a manner worthy of their calling, and 4:17 exhorts them to no longer walk the way the Gentiles walk (in ways presently being considered in this section). They are to "walk in love" (5:2), as "children of light" (5:8), and not as the unwise but the wise (see 5:15). Walking is a good descriptive term for life, as it reveals the past, present, and future of our existence.

Walking reveals the *past* as we leave footprints where we have been, undeniable evidences of the life we once lived. It is good at times to look back at the tracks we have left to be reminded of what Christ has taken us away from.

Walking reveals the *present* as the posture, with stride and speed relating truths of our immediate lifestyle. Some walk with a quick, determined stride, reflecting confidence. Others may be seen shuffling along, dragging their feet, reflecting a not-so-eager attitude. Some may be limping, revealing a wound that needs to be cared for and healed.

Walking reveals the *future* as we can determine a person's destination by the direction presently taken. Where we plan to be tomorrow will most certainly be influenced by the direction we pursue today.

Paul gives three influential reasons why the Gentiles lived in their state of transgression and sin.

First, he says they were following **the ways of this world** (2:2). Paul uses the Greek word *aiona* for **ways,** which literally means "age," or a period of time. In 1:21, this age was presented as being limited in existence, and Paul said that there is another age yet to come. Obviously this describes the present age as that period of time from the fall of humankind until the creation of a new heaven and a new earth. It includes the time we live in now, a time in which the world and its inhabitants are subjected to the temptations and repercussions of sin. Paul writes in 1 Corinthians 2:6 that "this age" is misguided and foolish, having no understanding of spiritual things. There is a god of this age (see below), undoubtedly Satan, who blinds the minds of unbelievers so that they cannot see and accept Christ (see 2 Corinthians 4:4). There is a pattern within this age that entices people to conformity (see Romans 12:2). Paul tells the Galatians that it is an "evil age" (Gal. 1:4) for which Jesus died so that we might be rescued. It is an age that entices even the converted to once again turn their backs on God (see 2 Timothy 4:10). It is an age whose standards and measures are misleading, implying hope where no hope will be found (see 1 Timothy 6:17). These were the patterns and influences Paul saw as instrumental in leading the Gentiles in a life separated from God.

Second, Paul says the Gentiles were following the ways of **the ruler of the kingdom of the air** (Eph. 2:2). This is one of four references Paul makes regarding Satan and his kingdom, though Paul never uses the name Satan within the letter. Paul calls him "the devil" in 4:27, warning the readers not to allow an opportunity, especially through anger, for his sinful influence to make an inroad into their lives. In 6:17 Paul presents him as an adversarial schemer against whom they must protect themselves by way of God's armor. In verse 16 of that same chapter, the reference is to "the evil one" who attacks by launching flaming missiles or darts at the believer. Elsewhere, in 2 Corinthians, Paul calls him "the god of this age" (2 Cor. 4:4) and "Belial" (2 Cor. 6:15), which is a Hebrew word meaning "worthless, useless, good for nothing, base, and wicked." Jesus referred to him as the "prince of this world" (John 12:31; 14:30; 16:11). The inference is obvious. Satan's official position is the ruler of this age of sin described above. It is a kingdom patterned after its leader, with his subjects in obedience to him, rather than to God.

To know the ways the Gentiles formerly lived is to consider the nature and influence of Satan himself. He is an *accuser.* This is revealed in Zechariah 3:1-2, where Satan attempts to demean Joshua the high priest before God (see also Job 1–2). Those who would follow Satan's ways are comfortable bringing allegations against and questions regarding the character of those who endeavor to do the will of God.

Satan is a *liar.* The Greek word for "lying" is the same word from which we get our word *scandal.* Jesus titles Satan a "scandalizer" and the father of lies (John 8:44). It is remarkable to note that Satan rarely tells complete untruths. Apparently he knows we would be quick to discredit them. Instead, he shares partial truths that do not reveal the whole story. Adam and Eve he misled by saying they would not die because of their activity, but would become like God, knowing good from evil. The real truth was that they would die, and while they would receive the knowledge of good and evil, they would not be able to handle it properly. Satan told Jesus, during His temptation in the wilderness, that all that Jesus saw would be His if Jesus would merely bow down and worship Satan. Although it is true that Satan is the prince of this world, the real master is God. Satan's possession is only temporary and without true ownership. Those who would follow in his ways are liars, whether they proclaim outright mistruths or half-truths.

Satan causes *division.* The Greek word for "Devil" is *diabolos,* which means "to divide," "throw over," or gossip maliciously. Satan does his best work by causing splits and divisions among people. His dictum is "Divide and conquer." It has been said that had the Native Americans been able to come together as one massive force, the settlers would never have overcome them, and history would be radically different today. However, because of their tribal factions and inner battles, the United States military was able to battle each small group until they were finally defeated. Satan knows that by keeping people divided, they become powerless. Gossip, pride, and the quest for power and control are his tools to create dissension and derision within the world and church. Those who would follow in his ways cause division.

The kingdom of this ruler (Satan) is described as **the kingdom of the air** (Eph. 2:2). It is difficult to understand what exactly Paul was referring to by using this description. This is the only place in Scripture where Satan's realm is described in this fashion. Paul uses the Greek word *aeros,* which in ancient times carried an understanding of "thick air," as opposed to *aither* or "thin air." The inference could be that Paul is referring to that area close to earth as opposed to the heavens. Philo, a second-century Jewish historian, described this area as the home of entities called demons by philosophers, and angels by the Christians.[1] This would make the domain of Satan and his imps the environment in which we move and breathe. Some would argue that this is the appropriate location since Satan and his demons are spirit, and they must reside within the air, someplace above ground (supraterrestrial), yet under the heavens (subcelestial).[2] Wherever the exact location of this *aeros,* it is the place of the heavenly kingdom wherein are contained the rulers, authorities, powers, and spiritual forces of evil described in 6:12.

Last, Paul says the Gentiles formerly followed **the spirit who is now at work in those who are disobedient** (2:2c). It is important to note that the word **spirit** used here is not a reference to a specific being, but rather an attitude or common atmosphere (see 1 Corinthians 2:12). Some would want to personify the word and relate it to Satan or one of his demons, an "evil spirit," as it were. There are many who endeavor to blame human sin and actions on something or someone else. In an attempt to remain guiltless, they point an accusing finger at the imps and devils that surround them.

Several years ago, comedian Flip Wilson made famous the line, "The devil made me do it!" In like manner, some have developed a Flip Wilson approach in their relationship with God, blaming all of their sinful actions on an outside influence. To do this negates one of the basic tenets of the Christian faith—the fallen state of humankind. Paul refers to this character of humanity in Ephesians 2:3, where he confesses his own guilt as the result of gratifying his own "sinful nature." In truth, we seldom need much enticement or coercion to sin against God. If we were honest, the guilty culprit which causes our disobedience can be seen in any mirror whenever we gaze into it. The Gentiles to whom Paul is writing were at one time guilty of following the prevalent sinful attitudes of their day. The world is adept at promoting and condoning actions and attitudes in opposition to the known will of God. Morality is redefined so that what was wrong is now claimed to be right, and what was right is now considered inappropriate or archaic. The results are often confusing and always misleading. It is only when we allow God to reveal His will and direction for our lives that we have an appropriate replacement for the prevalent actions of the day.

Paul's description of the state and cause of the Gentiles' former spiritual needs would lead one to believe they were an unusually sinful group. However, 2:3 concludes the Gentile/Jew distinction by the inclusive phrase, **All of us also lived among them at one time.** Obviously, **all of us** refers to everyone not included in Paul's original **As for you** (2:1), most specifically the Jews as well. The pronoun **them** also refers back to 2:1—**transgressions and sins.**

Paul mentions two motivations which caused these sinful actions: gratification and following. The object of these motivations is defined as **sinful nature,** literally "the flesh" (*sarkos;* 2:3). In this context, the Greek word *sarkos* refers to our fallen human nature that expresses itself through inordinate desires and appetites. It is these appetities that every Christian becomes aware of in a relationship to God. It becomes most apparent after our conversion, as Paul explains in Romans 7:21-25. It is that nature which strives against the self *(ego)* or mind *(nous)*. It is that rebellious activity which strives against the Holy Spirit (see Romans 8:5). Some of its more "obvious actions" are described in Galatians 5:19-21: sexual immorality, impurity and debauchery, idolatry and witchcraft, hatred, discord, jealousy, fits of rage, selfish ambition, dissensions, factions, envy, drunkenness, and orgies. A distinction is made by Paul between living in the flesh (**sinful nature**) and living by the Spirit. Those who are in Christ have crucified the sinful nature, including its passions and desires; they now walk in step with the Spirit.

Just as Paul describes the prior life of sin that **all of us** (Eph. 2:3) have had—including himself—so does he state the inherent danger of such a life. Because of this nature *(sarkos),* the Jews, like the Gentiles, were **objects of [God's] wrath** (2:3). The strength of this statement can be understood by considering the account in 2 Samuel of Nathan's confrontation of King David regarding the king's adultery with Bathsheba. Using an endearing story of a man forced to give up his only pet lamb that he loved, to a wealthy neighbor who slaughtered it for food, Nathan played on David's heart strings. In a fit of rage, David proclaimed the fate of this despicable man: ". . . the man who did this deserves to die!" (2 Sam. 12:5). Similarly, Paul and all the Jews already had been considered by God worthy of death. The actual sentence simply had not yet been dealt out.

Paul's description carries an atmosphere of hopelessness, but there was help. We all can remember a common scene from an old western movie in which a wagon train moving west falls victim to an angry war party desiring to defend their land. With wagons circled, a battle ensues, with the settlers hopelessly outnumbered. Just when it seems that all is lost and the wagon train, along with its inhabitants, will be destroyed, a bugle sounds, and over the hill comes the cavalry to effect their rescue. Paul's cavalry is announced by the word **but** (Eph. 2:4). It presents a contrast, showing that the situation and expected results are not necessarily final. Just when we would believe both Jew and Gentile will become the fodder of God's great wrath, Paul presents the good news: **But . . . God made us alive with Christ** (2:4-5).

Two attributes of God are credited for this act of rescue: His **great love** and His **mercy** (2:5). Altruism is a difficult thing for people to accept. We remain suspicious, believing that individuals must have alternative reasons for acting as they do. Such suspicion is unnecessary with God because, being perfect and complete in every way, He needs nothing from us that would cause His mercy and love to be extended for ulterior reasons. The beauty of the gospel is found in the fact that everything God has done on our behalf, and all that He has spared us from, is not because of who we are, but *in spite of* who we are. "While we were still sinners Christ died for us" (Rom. 5:8). **God . . . made us alive with Christ** *even when we were dead in trangressions* (Eph. 2:5, my emphasis). No wonder Paul interjects the glorious truth: **It is by grace you have been saved** (2:5). No other word describes the action of God better. **Grace** is unmerited favor extended to humankind by God. By Paul's own description, he, the Jews, and the Gentiles were not only guilty of following their own sinful natures, but as a result were sentenced to be destroyed in judgment for their deeds. God, by His mercy and love, pardoned them and made them alive through Christ (see Romans 5:18-21).

It is important to notice that Paul has made another significant change in the pronouns being used. He began this chapter by referring to the recipients as "you." Having described their original lost state with God, he includes the Jews and himself with the Gentiles, claiming he and the Jews were just as guilty and deserving of wrath. Then he directs his message once again to the recipients, reminding them that **it is by grace** *you* **have been saved** (Eph. 2:5, my emphasis). The shift implies one of the reasons Paul is writing the letter in the first place. He wants these individuals, whom he has never met, to come to an appropriate understanding of their experience in Christ. It was important for them to realize their lost estate before God because of their past sins. It is imperative that they understand the means by which this sin is erased—grace, extended by a loving and merciful God. The words of Paul should come alive to us as well today. These are words we need to hear and of which we need to be reminded. These are words of God's perfect love, His unending mercy, His undeserved grace. We need to be reminded during those times when we do not feel all that lovely or lovable, when our experience in this world has been less than merciful, when we begin to question our worth and find it wanting. We are saved by grace. John Wesley described the workings of God's grace by its channels and expressions.

The *channels* by which God conveys His grace to believers are (1) prayer, both individual and corporate; (2) searching the Scriptures, which includes hearing them as they are spoken, reading them, and meditating upon them; and (3) the sacrament of the Lord's Supper.

The *expressions* of God's grace, Wesley distinguished by way of the function of that grace to the believer. There is a preventing grace, or an extension of God's unmerited favor to humankind prior to salvation that reveals God to the sinful, and also reveals their sin and their need for salvation. There is a saving grace that comes into effect the moment that a sinner realizes the need for deliverance and cries out to God for redemption. This grace works its effects within the individual by justifying, adopting, and redeeming the individual. At the same time, there is a sanctifying grace extended to the penitent that enables one to begin a state of initial sanctification and growth within the grace of God, finding eventual victory over the inner nature of sin. This is climaxed in what is referred to as entire sanctification. The final gracious stage in the believer's pilgrimage comes at death, when God glorifies the individual through the resurrection from physical death.

In Ephesians 2:8, Paul includes the phrase, **through faith** to his testimony of our salvation by grace. By this, Paul reveals **faith** as the means by which God's grace operates in our life. In his sermon, "Salvation by Faith," based on this verse, John Wesley concisely described the workings of faith by which this gracious salvation is obtained, saying "Grace is the source, faith the condition of salvation."[3] He goes on to define this faith in three ways. First, it is a faith in Christ which is more than a mental assent, but a heartfelt belief. Second, it is a faith that acknowledges Christ's death as the only sufficient means of redemption. Third, it is a faith that totally relies on the blood of Christ for atonement, and on its redemption and sanctification in the believer. In light of this faith, Wesley saw a threefold result as it saved one from the guilt of past sins, from fear (by which he means the fear of torment, punishment, and divine wrath), and from the power of sin.

In Ephesians 2:8-9, Paul reminds his readers that their salvation is the result of grace. But now he does not seem as concerned with the recognition of grace as he is with the denouncement of any human contribution. The readers can make no assumptions as to their situation. Salvation comes by God's grace extended to them. It is experienced by their believing in its provision by faith. Just as there can be no mistake about the means of salvation, so is there to be no confusion about what does not bring salvation. First, salvation's origin is not found with us as humans. It is a gift of God. Second, it is not achieved by works. There is no human agency, outside of faith. We are merely the recipients of God's grace.

There is a tendency among people to become confused on this point. We embrace it with our hearts, but it never seems to work in our minds. Those who believe that God's salvation comes to an individual through the process of divine predeterminism understand that we are saved because (1) God chooses us personally; (2) He instills within us an irresistible grace that transforms us from being reprobates to being children of God; and (3) we are made righteous by the righteousness of Christ. However, those who understand salvation as an act of one's free will to embrace or reject God's grace, find it difficult to determine where human freedom ends and God's grace begins. This is a criticism often levied at Wesleyan-Arminian believers. Because Wesleyans believe they can reject God's salvation, critics assume that our embracing it is the result of a constant decision of obedience lived out before God.

The pendulum of this continuum makes a wide swing. On one extreme are the determinists, who would claim an eternal security of God's salvation because they have been chosen by God and He does not change His mind on these matters. On the other extreme, we have the free-will individuals who believe their position in Christ is the result of a personal choice which can be forfeited in the event one does not obediently follow Christ. However, both extremes are in error, as the former has lost a sense of responsibility, while the latter has overlooked the provisions and dynamics of relationship.

Many people become enslaved by a poor understanding of how grace works. They live their lives believing that every choice is a choice either for or against salvation. God becomes this sadistic deity who holds us suspended over the flames of hell by a thin thread. In His other hand is a sharp knife, poised to cut our support at a moment's notice, while He watches for the first opportunity to condemn us to the flames.

The error in this concept is that it calls for maintaining our salvation by what we do. We focus on actions and forget the relationship, an approach Paul speaks strongly against (see Galatians 3:1-14). If this were practiced in marriage relationships, for example, it could mean that the marriage bond might depend on the ability of a spouse to be a perfect helpmate. If that were true, the institution of marriage would have been hopelessly lost centuries ago. However, as we know, our marriage bonds are to be the result of mutual, edifying love, the foundation of a real marriage. It is the same with our relationship with God. It is **because of His great love for us** (Eph. 2:4) that we are saved. Thus, since it is relationship with God that expresses the free will of the individual, and not performance, God's grace allows for a cushion of mercy in our performance. Of course, this latitude does not afford us a license to live as we wish. Paul argues this idea in Romans 6:1-2 by asking, "What shall we say, then? Shall we go on sinning so that grace may increase? By no means! We died to sin; how can we live in it any longer."

There are three words in Ephesians 2:5-6 that are difficult to translate from the Greek with accuracy. They are compound words that have the preposition *with* attached to the front. They describe how we were made alive with Christ, how we have been raised up with Christ, and how we were seated with Christ in the heavenlies. The words imply an experience and relationship that is not easily understood. It is perhaps best explained by the term "already, but not yet." This means that experiencing the kingdom of God here and now has been made possible, but it has not been fully experienced and revealed.

We live in the Kingdom through Jesus Christ and His atonement, though only experiencing a portion of its potential. There is coming a day, however, when all of the Kingdom will be fulfilled and experienced by God's people (see 1 Corinthians 13:12). Thus, in one sense, we already have been raised up in Christ, as God raised Him from the dead. Yet, we await our personal experience of resurrection upon our death. We are already seated with Christ in the heavenly realms, even though we are still here on earth. This is the function of the seal of the Holy Spirit which guarantees our redemption in the end (see Ephesians 1:3, 14). As we tarry here, it is encouraging to know that God's love for us is so great that He has, in effect, already raised us up with Christ and placed us within the heavenly realms. The reason for this action by God is so that He can reveal in the coming ages His grace expressed through Jesus Christ.

Paul would have us understand that our reconciliation is a poem written by God. There is nothing like a well-written poem to inspire an individual. Carefully chosen words brought together by a pleasant meter can express emotions in ways that mere prose cannot. What type of poetry does God write? That question is relevant to this passage as Paul finds a wonderful way of describing the finished product found within the individual who has been saved by grace: **We are God's workmanship** (2:10). The Greek word used for **workmanship,** *poiema,* is the word from which we derive the English word *poem.* It is used only twice in the whole of Scripture—once here and once in Romans 1:20, where Paul argues that the qualities of God's creation of the world give testimony to God and leave humankind without a claim of ignorance concerning God's existence. Now this creative skill has been extended toward God's redeemed so that He might create a "poem" of His revelation. This is a poem that has been **created in Christ** (2:10).

Once again, Paul reminds us of the agency of the Savior. As all of salvation comes to us by way of grace, this grace is extended toward us because of the death and resurrection of Christ. But the influence of Christ's atonement does not stop at salvation; it continues on in the regeneration of the individual. As in salvation, our regeneration is the work of God. The poem (our regeneration and salvation) is designed for a purpose: **to do good works** (2:10). Here is the appropriate place for our activities with God. As mentioned above, works have no place in the *cause* of our salvation. But they do have a significant place as a *consequence* of our salvation. That good work which God performs within us will inevitably have its expression. Works are not the means of our salvation, but the evidence. Here we sometimes tend to put the cart before the horse. Salvation comes not because of works, but rather works come because of our salvation, as we read in the book of James, "Show me your faith without deeds, and I will show you my faith by what I do" (Jas. 2:18b).

The poem is not designed at random, but according to a predetermined plan. We are not saved merely to be rescued from hell and its torment. This would make salvation a cheap form of fire insurance. God has rescued us with a more productive purpose in mind—to do His good will.

A call to God is a call to serve. This has been understood ever since Israel was led out of Egypt. A major Hebrew word found in the Exodus passages referring to Israel's plight and deliverance is *avad.* It is the word used to describe the harsh labor the Israelites were forced to perform for Pharaoh. Yet, it was also used by God as He instructed Moses at the burning bush. God told Moses that it was because of this *avad* forced upon Israel that He had come down. Moses' task was to deliver Israel from their *avad* to Pharaoh and lead them to the mountain where they would *avad* God. It is a play on words, for when *avad* is used in relationship to God, it is understood as worship. Israel's deliverance was from slavery to service, from bondage to celebration. Likewise, as God delivers us from our enslavement to sin, it is with the expectation that we too will come to His mountain to *avad*.

Paul alludes to this idea in Romans 12:1, where he urges the brethren to present their bodies as living sacrifices which is their "spiritual act of worship." The King James Version translates it, ". . . which is your reasonable service." The interchange between worship and service is natural here, since the Greek word used carries the same meaning of the Hebrew word *avad*.

This advanced plan of works is also very specific. God has a definite will for our lives, planned with each individual in mind. He is the one who created us, and therefore He is aware of the individual strengths and abilities we possess. In addition, God graces each of us with spiritual gifts that complement our abilities and enable us to better serve both Him and others (see Ephesians 4:11). One of the necessary tasks of the redeemed is to determine what good works God has created and empowered us to do. By doing so, our lives will retain the order of well-written poems.

2. RECONCILIATION WITH ONE ANOTHER 2:11-22

So far in Ephesians 2, Paul has been dealing with the reconciliation of humankind to God, overcoming the separation of relationship due to our sin. In keeping with this theme, he now moves laterally to discuss the joining together of the faction that had developed between Israel and the Gentiles. This division was secondary to the Gentile's lack of relationship with God. Since they were not "God's people," the Jews of that day enforced a distinction between them which negated any relationship. The Greek word for "Gentile" can also mean "nation," referring to anyone who was not a Jew. In fact, the Jews remembered that during Old Testament times it was the development of illicit relationships between Jews and Gentiles that caused Israel to be conquered and led into exile. The Jews began to live according to the ways of their pagan neighbors and to sin against God. Upon their return from exile, strong rules were established which helped to further the separation between them. But now Paul shares good news to these Gentile people to whom he writes. Because of Christ, they are not only reconciled to God, but are fellow heirs to the Kingdom alongside God's chosen.

a. Between Jews and Gentiles (2:11-13). Paul begins by discussing the distinction between Jews and Gentiles based on circumcision. This had always been a hot topic between Paul and the Jews ever since his conversion. The issue caused a special meeting to be held in Jerusalem at the completion of Paul's first missionary journey with Barnabas, where they enjoyed a level of success among the Gentiles in Galatia. The decision of the early church was that there was nothing wrong with Paul's spreading the gospel to the Gentiles, and that the Gentiles did not need to be circumcised in order to be Christians (see Acts 15). This decision was made by the Christians, not the Jews. As a result, Paul and his fellow Jews often came to disagreement over this topic. Paul's contempt for those who insisted on the physical act of circumcision is evident in his letter to the Philippian church. There he warned the Gentile Christians to beware of the "dogs" and evildoers who are "mutilators of the flesh" (Phil. 3:2). His argument continues that it is the Christian who has the true "circumcision" because we worship by the Spirit, glory in Christ, and put no confidence in any work of the flesh.

Paul's understanding of the function of circumcision to the Christian is explained in a parallel passage in Colossians 2:11-15. Here is a play on words as he uses the Greek word *sarkos,* which means flesh, to refer to the sinful nature as expressed in Ephesians 2:3. He states that the Christian is circumcised by Christ by the putting off of the sinful nature *(sarkos).* Just as the foreskin was removed from the Jew to mark his identity with the covenant, so the sinful nature is removed from the Christian to mark his or her relationship with Christ.[4]

John Wesley, in his sermon "The Circumcision of the Heart," stated,

> The distinguishing mark of a true follower of Christ, of one who is in a state of acceptance with God, is not either outward circumcision, or baptism, or any other outward form, but a right state of soul, a mind and spirit renewed after the image of Him that created it. . . . It is that habitual disposition of the soul, which, in the sacred writings, is termed holiness; and which directly implies the being cleansed from sin, "from all filthiness both of flesh and spirit;" and, by consequence the being endued with those virtues which were also in Christ Jesus; the being so "renewed in the spirit of our mind," as to be "perfect as our Father in heaven is perfect."[5]

The Gentiles were previously separated from Israel because they were not physically circumcised. In fact, the very term "Gentile" was often an expression of contempt by the Jews, as they held the Gentile to be inferior. This contempt can be heard in the way Paul describes their uncircumcised state. They were separate from Christ, excluded from citizenship with Israel (see Exodus 12:43-45), foreigners to the covenants of the promise (see Galatians 3:6-9), without hope (see 1 Thessalonians 4:13), and without God in the world.

The Greek word translated as "without God" *(atheoi)* is used only here in the entire Bible. It was used in the classical Greek and had three meanings: (1) an atheist; (2) impious; and (3) without God's help. Of these three, the second and third definitions are more in keeping with the condition of the Gentiles. They were not atheistic, since their pagan religions included the worship of many gods. It was not that they did not believe a god existed; they just did not know the true God. Therefore, Paul is probably referring to their impious lifestyle and subsequent lack of God's presence in their life.

As he did in Ephesians 2:4, Paul reveals God's intervention into the Gentile's circumstances by describing the cause and relationship that has effected the change: **But now in Christ Jesus you who once were far away have been brought near through the blood of Christ** (2:13). It is a statement revealing stark contrasts. It is a contrast of *time*. Prior to their salvation they were in a lost and hopeless state. But now they are **in Christ.** It is a contrast of *distance*. They who were once separated are now united with God. All of this is unmistakably the result of the sacrificial death of Christ. It was not because of their wisdom, good behavior, breeding, or any good-hearted acceptance by the Jews that had joined them, but because of the blood of Jesus Christ that their entire relationship (both Jew and Gentile) has been changed.

b. Jesus Our Peace (2:14-22). Paul now moves the reader beyond the change that has been wrought in the Christian's relationship with God and others by expounding on how this change was made possible— Jesus **our peace.** The power of this statement must not be lessened. It is in keeping with the entire theme of the letter. The world's salvation is the sole result of God's great love and mercy, expressed through His predetermined plan. Our individual experience of this salvation is the result of God's grace extended to us. We can claim no merit of works. Now, so that Paul's readers will fully understand the renewed relationship between Jews and Gentiles, they must know that it was made possible because Jesus is our peace. This peace has been worked out by a number of influences.

First, God made the two one. During the Middle Ages, a practice known as alchemy was developed by people who believed they could mix various elements together and create gold. Chrysostom, an early church father, saw a type of alchemy in this union—not as Gentiles becoming Jews, but as both Jews and Gentiles becoming something better than they were before. It was as if God had mixed lead and silver and created gold.[6] Paul believed God's purpose was **to create . . . one new man out of the two** (Eph. 2:15). This alchemy of God is the result of the baptism of the Holy Spirit. Paul wrote to the Corinthians, "For we were all baptized by one Spirit into one body—whether Jews or Greeks, slave or free—and we were all given the one Spirit to drink" (1 Cor. 12:13; see also Galatians 3:26-29). This oneness is the fulfillment of the "mystery" Paul claims was entrusted to him (Eph. 1:9) as he explains in 3:6: "This mystery is that through the gospel the Gentiles are heirs together with Israel, members together of one body, and sharers together in the promise in Christ Jesus."

Second, God destroyed the barrier, the dividing wall of hostility. The Temple in Jerusalem was constructed with a number of courtyards. The outermost court was known as the Court of the Gentiles, which was the only area Gentiles were allowed to enter. Further in was the Inner Temple area, raised slightly higher than the Court of the Gentiles and surrounded by a Balustrade. Signs on this wall were written in both Greek and Latin, warning all Gentiles that no one could guarantee their safety against death if they entered the Inner Temple. The Gentiles were allowed to come into proximity with God, but never allowed to get close like the Jews. Gentiles normally entering this outer court were known as "God Fearers" *(sebomai)*. These were men who expressed an interest in serving Israel's God, but were unwilling to be circumcised or observe other regulations of the faith.

There are some who believe Paul is referring to the actual dismantling of this wall, which took place during the destruction of the Temple in A.D. 70. But this would make it impossible for the letter to have been written by Paul, because he would have already been executed at the hands of Nero at least two years earlier. Others have erred in believing that Paul's reference to a wall was the veil in the Temple which separated the innermost chamber, known as the Holy of Holies, from the rest of the Temple. This is the curtain that was torn in half, from the top down, upon the death of Jesus Christ (see Mark

15:38). It is doubtful that Paul was referring to this curtain, as it had no relevance to Gentiles, who could not get near the inner court in the first place. The barrier this curtain illustrated was between the Jews and God because of their sinfulness, and not their breeding. In this passage, the context of Paul's discussion is the separation which existed between two groups of people, not God and humankind.

Rather than a literal wall, Paul is referring to a more figurative wall that divided Jews and Gentiles, namely the law with its commandments and regulations.[7] The wall was not torn down by battering ram or hammer, but by the death of our Lord. **In His flesh** (Eph. 2:15) means that by Jesus' death the means of salvation were procured for which the law had been given.

Humankind has always built walls to maintain separation. We have heard of the Great Wall of China and the Berlin Wall. But there are also figurative walls that have been built over time. Walls built not of stone or brick, but built by ignorance and biases held together by hatred and indifference. Paul's reference to Christ's dismantling the wall is a message for today as we consider the numerous ways we stereotype and label people. Jesus did not just tear down the wall between Jews and Gentiles, but between gender, race, ideology, socioeconomic levels, and more. If we are in Christ, we are all equal. All distinctions must give way to the one overall title for all of God's children—"the Redeemed." As with the Jews and Gentiles of Paul's day, God has combined the many people of this world into one unique and blessed existence known as the church, the body of Christ. There are no walls of separation here.

The result of Jesus' developing the one person out of two, which would dismantle the dividing walls of law and humankind, would be peace and reconciliation. Reconciliation would come about because both groups would be rejoined to God, making it possible for them to be reconciled to each other. This reconciliation would be through the Cross, by which Jesus put to death the hostilities found between them, resulting in peace. The prerequisite to world peace is spiritual peace. Before we can walk in fellowship with other people, we must first walk in fellowship with God. The same death that reconciles us to the Father is that which makes it possible for us to be peacefully reconciled to each other.

In describing the Gentile/Jew situation, Paul uses two terms that were common among the Jews. He claims that Jesus **preached peace to you who were far away** and to **those who were near** (Eph. 2:17). These terms make a distinction between the chosen people of God (the **near**) and the Gentiles (those **far away**). This distinction is expressive of Paul's

85

earlier description of the distance found between the Jews and Gentiles prior to Jesus' coming and their subsequent conversion (see 2:13). What is consistent in this distinction is the message preached to each of them. There was not one message for the Jew and one for the Gentile; both groups received the same message. Just as God promised in Isaiah 57:15-19, He would not always be a God of wrath and judgment. He would also come and dwell with those with humble and contrite hearts. There He would speak peace. Peace to those near and far.

Paul concludes this section with a description of the household God is developing through His fulfilled plan. It is a home built on an unusual **foundation** made up **of apostles and prophets** (Eph. 2:20). Much has already been said of the office of apostle regarding Paul's introduction in Ephesians 1 (see comments in chapter 1 of the commentary). The Greek word *apostolos* simply means "one sent by another."

There are two offices of apostleship expressed in Scripture: the formal office that refers to the twelve apostles; and later Paul, chosen by Jesus. This required certain firsthand experiences by the individual with Christ. However, there is a less formal office of apostleship that referred to a number of people sent by God to establish the church. Barnabas is called an apostle, as were Silvanus and James, Jesus' brother (see Acts 14:14; 1 Thessalonians 2:7; Galatians 1:19). Thus, Paul's reference cannot be restricted to only the eleven remaining disciples and Paul called by Jesus. Rather, Paul is referring to the broader activity of those ministering in Jesus' name by way of a spiritual gift as described in Ephesians 4:11.

It is difficult to prove exactly whom Paul is referencing when he uses the title **prophets** (Eph. 2:20). It could be a reference to those men of the Old Testament who spoke of Jesus' coming, or those gifted individuals described by Paul in Ephesians 4:11 and 1 Corinthians 14. A prophet was always understood as a spokesperson for God, speaking God's very words. They were the only ones who had the right to proclaim with their message, "Thus says the Lord." By Paul's description, the gift of prophecy was to be eagerly sought (see 1 Corinthians 14:1). Prophets spoke to men for their strengthening, encouragement, and comfort (see 14:3). A prophet edifies the church (see 14:4). Paul would rather the people prophesy than speak in tongues, for the one who prophesies is greater than the one who speaks in tongues (see 14:5). Prophecy is for believers (see 14:22), but is instrumental for revealing the presence of God to unbelievers as it convinces them of their sin (14:24). It is the prophets through which God is revealing the mystery of His reconciliation of both Jew and Gentile and the entire universe under Christ (see Ephesians 3:5; Romans 16:26).

There is an important distinction to be noted regarding the building of the **foundation** (Eph. 2:20) for God's household. It is being built out of the message of God as shared by the prophets and apostles. The foundation is not the men but the *message*. It is through the words and truths shared by these faithful individuals that God is now establishing His kingdom. The personal existence found in the wall is **Christ Jesus** and Him only, serving as its **chief cornerstone** (2:20).

When a block foundation is erected, it is built starting with the corners. Great care is taken in laying these first blocks, because they will be the reference points for the rest of the wall. The cornerstone becomes the reference stone from which everything else about the wall is determined. Obviously, this is Paul's understanding regarding Jesus and God's household. In Jesus, the whole building is brought together and determined. If the first stone is placed incorrectly, the entire building can be built incorrectly. Jesus is the perfect and primary cornerstone, and His reference point creates a holy temple for God.

There is an added benefit to the believer. With Jesus as this cornerstone, each believer is being built in Christ to become **a dwelling in which God lives** (2:22). The idea of a dwelling place with God is a unique theme in the Scriptures. It is referred to as a tabernacle.

In the wilderness with the Israelites, God instructed the people to erect a special dwelling tent, known as the Tent of Meeting, the Tabernacle, where God would dwell in His presence (see Exodus 40). The people might witness God's presence, but they could not interact with God when His presence was in the tent. There was a distance maintained between God and His people, a distance that was enforced even during the time of Herod's Temple. Only priests could enter the Holy of Holies, and only at certain times during the year. But then came Jesus.

John, in the first chapter of his gospel, picks up on this theme of dwelling by writing, "And the word became flesh and tented or dwelt among us" (John 1:14, my paraphrase). The Greek word used is *eskenosen,* which means literally "to dwell," but it is taken from the same Greek root word which means tent, dwelling, or body. Quite literally, the passage states that God became flesh and dwelt among humankind in His bodily building. The idea is tabernacle. God, in the person of Jesus Christ, came and set up His tent of flesh. Not separate from the people, but in their very midst.

Later, when Jesus was attempting to console His disciples regarding the news of His inevitable death, resurrection, and ascension back to the Father, He told them not to be troubled or worried, because He was going away to prepare a place for them to come and live with Him (see John 14:2). It would no longer be God moving in among humankind, but now humankind moving in with God: "In my Father's house are many rooms" (John 14:2). Paul echoes this promise by reassuring the Gentiles that they are not only included in this household, but that they are being built into dwelling places where they will live with God who dwells and will dwell with them in Spirit.

Reconciliation is the fulfillment of God's great plan worked out in the life of both Jew and Gentile. Being sinful and separated from God, they were brought back by the death of Christ. Being estranged from each other because of the law, they were brought together into a new existence by Jesus abolishing the law. And now they were being built into **a holy temple** (Eph. 2:21) together with God, founded upon the person of Jesus Christ and the faithfulness of His workers. Such wonderful news and insight is hard to contain, and Paul expresses this as he begins to pray on behalf of his readers in the next chapter.

ENDNOTES

[1]F. F. Bruce, *The Epistle to the Colossians, to Philemon, and to the Ephesians,* The New International Commentary on the New Testament (Grand Rapids, Michigan: Wm. B. Eerdmans Publishing Co., 1984), p. 282.

[2]Samuel Rolles Driver, Alfred Plummer, and Charles Augustus Briggs, eds., *The International Critical Commentary: Ephesians, Colossians* (Edinburgh: T. and T. Clark, 1991), p. 41.

[3]John Wesley, *The Works of John Wesley*, vol. 5, 3rd. ed. (Grand Rapids, Michigan: Baker Book House, 1986), p. 7.

[4]A covenant is a solemn promise made binding by a pledge or vow, which may be either a verbal formula or a symbolic action. Covenant often referred to a legal obligation in ancient times. In Old Testament terms, the word was often used in describing the relationship between God and His chosen people, in which their sacrifices of blood afforded them His atonement for sin, and in which their fulfillment of a promise to live in obedience to God was rewarded by His blessings. In New Testament terms, this relationship (the new covenant) was now made possible on a personal basis through Jesus Christ and His sacrifice of His own blood.

[5]Wesley, vol. 5, pp. 202–3.

[6]Driver, Plummer, and Briggs, p. 61.

[7]Law here refers to the Levitical Code (all God's rules and regulations).

5

PAUL'S PRAYER FOR POWER AND LOVE

Ephesians 3:1-21

A common modern phrase is "beating around the bush." It refers to the tendency of some to take longer than necessary to talk about a particular subject. We have all endured conversations such as this, where the person, instead of getting right to the heart of the matter, begins to describe a number of associated details. This makes the conversation long and tedious. But, sometimes these excursions can be of insightful benefit to the listener.

Such is the case with Paul in this section. Having previously explained in detail the effects of salvation for their present life, he now desires to pray for his readers. But something leads his thoughts away for a brief period, and the reader is taken into a brief description of Paul's responsibilities in ministry. Eventually, Paul returns to his original topic where he prays for his readers a second time.

1. PAUL'S MINISTRY AND MESSAGE 3:1-13

As he did at the end of chapter 1 of Ephesians, Paul again prays for his readers, though not without first taking them on a long discourse concerning his ministry and message. He seems to be excited as he writes, often getting seemingly "sidetracked" onto various subjects that pop into his mind. Ephesians 3 begins with the connective phrase, **For this reason** (3:1), obviously relating back to the theme of God's reconciliation as discussed in the previous chapter. But the phrase merely hangs as a titillation not to be fulfilled for 13 verses. What Paul expresses in the rest of 3:1 carries his interests off on a different topic. The phrase becomes an aid to help his readers recognize his return to his original intent of prayer in 3:14, where he repeats the words again.

The second part of Paul's opening phrase in 3:1 relates an emphatic expression—**I, Paul.** This overemphasis was a literary tool in the original Greek used by Paul on a number of occasions to bring special recognition to an important issue.[1] In 1 Thessalonians 2:18, Paul emphasized his particular part of a letter which was written by more than one person. In Galatians 5:2 and 2 Corinthians 10:1, emphasis is used in connection with a solemn warning. Paul uses emphasis in Philemon 19, where he formally agrees to be responsible for Onesimus's debt, and also in Colossians 1:23, in a manner closely aligned with our present usage, referring to a special call to ministry. Not just any person is about to pray for the Gentiles. Paul, *the God-appointed apostle to the Gentiles,* is about to bow his knee. This emphatic use is probably the motivation for the side road he is about to take in his thoughts. Having emphasized his actions in this way, he no doubt felt obligated to explain why he had expressed himself in this fashion.

Ephesians 3 presents strong evidence that the people receiving the letter may not be as familiar as others are with Paul. Apparently, the recipients' knowledge of Paul comes more from secondhand experience than personal encounter. His statement in verse 2, **Surely you have heard about,** implies that what they knew of Paul came from sources other than himself. The information Paul shares with them in this diversion from prayer is an attempt to fill in the spaces that might otherwise cause difficulty in their understanding of his motivation, authority, and information.

Undoubtedly, there were two different accounts the people would have heard regarding this man named Paul. One account would have told about the zealous persecutor of the church, responsible for the incarceration and death of many fellow believers. The other account would be of his conversion, or at least of the changed man who now spoke authoritatively and eloquently regarding the faith.

As a backdrop to this section, it is helpful to keep in mind Paul's activities prior to his conversion on the Damascus Road; his present statements stand in stark contrast to this prior man. In addition to his persecuting days, Philippians 3:4-6 is helpful as it records Paul's autobiographical sketch of the man he was prior to his conversion. He was circumcised on his eighth day of life into the people of Israel, to the tribe of Benjamin. He considered himself a "Hebrew of the Hebrews," a Pharisee, persecutor of the church, and faultless legalist. But now his description takes a different twist. The zealous "imprisoner" of believers is himself imprisoned. His earlier achievements are of no relevance to his present life. In this parenthetical discussion of the real Paul, he refers to himself by three identities: prisoner (3:1); administrator (3:2); and the least of God's servants (3:7-8).

a. Paul the Prisoner (3:1). The Ephesian letter is known as a Prison Epistle because it was written by Paul while he was imprisoned. He attests to this fact in 3:1 and 4:1, and alludes to in 6:20 by referring to himself as "an ambassador in chains." Traditionally, it has been held by the church that this imprisonment took place in Rome where we know Paul was held in house arrest for approximately two years (see Acts 28:16). However, there are others who argue in favor of an Ephesian imprisonment.[2]

Wherever Paul was at the time of his writing, the issue remains the same: Paul, the once-persecutor of the church, is writing in chains. In our common language, one could say, "What goes around comes around." But Paul sees his experience as something a little more noble than the negative result of his earlier actions. Specifically, he states two reasons for his imprisonment: he is a prisoner of Christ Jesus; and he is imprisoned for the sake of the Gentiles. Being a prisoner of Christ Jesus carries several implied meanings.[3]

First, it speaks *experientially* of Paul's ministry. Paul views it as a part of his ministerial experience. In spite of the fact that ministry seeks the best for humankind, it is often met with opposition. Anyone actively involved in ministry soon becomes aware of this fact. Ministry begets difficulties that must be endured, as Paul describes in 2 Corinthians 4.

Second, being a prisoner of Christ Jesus speaks *spiritually* of what brought Paul to this situation. It was because of his commitment to God's will for his life that Paul so zealously remained faithful to his task. It is an imprisonment of compulsion. Paul cannot see his life in any other terms than to be about the establishment of Christ's church. It is a priestly duty to fulfill God's calling. Therefore, at the conclusion of Paul's third missionary journey, even though he was warned during his trip to Jerusalem of the imprisonment that awaited him there, he was "compelled" to fulfill the ministry laid before him (see Acts 20:22-24; 21:10-14). He is a prisoner for Christ Jesus because his faithfulness to the Lord has led him into this circumstance.

Such an idea seems foreign in today's prosperity-minded Christianity. We spend much of our time proclaiming and expecting blessings as a result of our relationship with Christ, all the time forgetting that the mark of ministry is more often suffering. The example is our crucified Lord. Our illustration is our heritage of persecuted and martyred servants who have been faithful to God to the end. We have forgotten the high honor of suffering for the cause of Christ, trading it for the lesser experience of physical ease. Paul's imprisonment was not a mark of shame, as some of our modern-day ministers experience from their greed and lust, but rather a mark of honorable faithfulness. Paul will conclude this section by requesting that his readers do not misunderstand his circumstances (see Ephesians 3:13). His imprisonment is not to discourage, but to encourage them. He suffered not in vain, but on their behalf and, as such, became their glory. No wonder Paul instructed Timothy not to be ashamed of him as Christ's prisoner (see 2 Timothy 1:8).

Being a prisoner of Christ Jesus was finally a *political* incarceration. Paul's ministry was sandwiched between two political adversaries. Rome was a strongly polytheistic society championing a large list of gods. Both Jews and Christians were monotheists who denied the existence of the Roman deities, claiming their God as the one and only true God. To the Christians and Jews, the Roman religion was pagan. This attitude often brought accusations from Rome of atheism against the church and Christ's followers. Another complication with this rejection of Rome's gods was experienced whenever the emperor was declared a god himself. The refusal to worship him leveled a charge of treason as well as atheism upon the individual, often resulting in death. Throwing Paul into jail because he believed in Jesus Christ would be no hardship to a faithful Roman pagan.

Another opponent of Christianity was the Jews. Christianity was still understood at this time to be an offshoot of Judaism, although heretical in the minds of some. Paul and the other apostles often met with opposition from this side for two reasons: (1) the Christian claim that Jesus was the Messiah and, as such, was God in the flesh (considered blasphemy, an act punishable by death); and (2) the insistence upon faith without the need of observing the law for salvation.[4] Paul's strong development of salvation by grace through faith (see 2:8) replaced the need for the law, except to make people aware of their sin and lead them to Christ (see Galatians 3:24). More than once, Paul was confronted for this belief. Few faithful followers of the law would have lamented Paul's imprisonment. In fact, like the Saul of a few years before, they would have helped to bring it about. The irony of this scene is recognized as those enslaved by the law incarcerate those who are free by grace.

The second major reason Paul gives for being imprisoned was **for the sake of you Gentiles** (Eph. 3:1). Considering the context of this statement, one must be careful not to interpret this too narrowly. This is not a direct statement to the recipients of the epistle alone, but is a general statement relating to all Gentiles.

Paul took his call to the Gentiles seriously, often suffering as a result. His arrest in Jerusalem was based specifically upon his association with those Gentile Christians who accompanied him back to Jerusalem at the conclusion of his third missionary journey. The Jews' accusation against Paul was that he supposedly brought Gentiles into the inner court of the Temple in Jerusalem, therefore defiling it (see Acts 21:27-29). Although Paul's statement in this verse is literally correct, his imprisonment went beyond the charge to be an expression of his faithful work among those God had called outside the tribe of Israel.

There is an interesting side note to Paul's imprisonment for the sake of the Gentiles. When Paul first arrived in Rome, he called for a meeting of the Jewish leaders of the city so that he might speak to them concerning his arrest. In the course of his explanation, he told the leaders that "it is because of the hope of Israel that I am bound with this chain" (Acts 28:20). Obviously, Paul's love for his fellow Jew, often expressed by his habit of entering the synagogue first upon his arrival in each city to proclaim his message, is evident in his imprisonment as well. After all, if he had not been this faithful to share the gospel ("the hope of Israel"), he would not have made as many enemies among his brethren.

Paul's imprisonment stands as a strong testimony to his committed love and zeal for his Savior. The man who a few years earlier was instrumental because of his committed zeal to arrest Christians now finds himself the victim of his zealous love for Christ.

b. Paul the Administrator (3:2-6). Paul's statement in 3:2, that the readers had **surely . . . heard about the administration of God's grace** to him, strongly suggests that neither of them had personal contact with each other; the Ephesians had only **heard about** Paul. The expression appears to be both a statement and a question. It suggests that they should already know the information, but, just in case they did not, Paul plans to inform them. The issue he is concerned with is his God-given responsibility as an administrator of God's grace.

The Greek word *oikonomian* (the New International Version translates it as **administration**), which Paul uses to describe this divine appointment, is a compound word which literally means "house ruler." It is an infrequently used word in the Scriptures that expresses two main ideas.[5] Technically, it referred to a household or estate manager whose responsibility was to oversee the operations of one's home and property (see Jesus' parable of the unjust steward in Luke 16:1-9). This could be understood as a literal or figurative household. In the Christian context, it was understood figuratively in reference to the household of God, or His church. The second main expression of *oikonomian* refers to the control or administration of God's message to humankind. This is more in keeping with Paul's use of the word, as he relates in several of his letters.

When Paul addressed the Corinthian church regarding their divisions, he concluded his correction by stating that people should regard God's workers as "servants of Christ" and *administrators* of God's mystery (1 Corinthians 4:1). Paul referred to his appointment by God as an *oikonomian* in Colossians 1:25-27, where he described himself as a servant, resulting from the *appointment* God had given him to preach the Word of God, which is the mystery. A common relationship is seen between Paul's understanding of his position as an administrator and the item over which he is responsible, namely **the mystery** (Eph. 3:3). Paul has previously mentioned the mystery in 1:9 where he listed it as one of the points of God's revealed salvation plan for which he is giving praise. God had not only made possible the salvation of humankind, but has revealed this potential through what Paul titles "the mystery."

Paul's description of his administration of the mystery can be found in several places in his writings. In Ephesians 3, Paul states that his administration is over the *grace* of God, which is **the mystery.** His position is not one he has assumed, but one that was given to him by God. The purpose of his task is for the benefit of the Gentiles (expressed by the pronoun "you" in 3:2, which obviously refers back to "you Gentiles" in 3:1). The reception of this mystery is the result of divine **revelation** (3:3), which is consistent with Paul's teaching in 1:9.

The reception of **the mystery** (3:3) can be further understood from other passages of Scripture, specifically Colossians 1:25-27 and Romans 16:25-27. In the Romans passage, Paul makes several assertions regarding the mystery: (1) the mystery was hidden from humankind throughout the past ages; (2) its revelation was just now being fulfilled through the prophetic writings by the command of God; and (3) the purpose of this revelation was that all nations (the Gentiles) might believe and obey God. Colossians 1:25-27 follows the Romans expression, though it extends our understanding. The mystery was hidden for ages and generations, but is now disclosed to the "saints" to make known to the Gentiles the mystery which is "Christ in you, the hope of glory."

Returning to Ephesians 3, Paul elaborates that the **mystery . . . was not made known to men in other generations as it** was then being **revealed by the Spirit** (3:4-5). The recipients of this revelation are specifically described as the **holy apostles** and **prophets.** (Both of these could be referred to as "saints," as Paul describes them in the Colossians passage.) The reference to **prophets** is in keeping with the Roman reference to "prophetic writings," though this would imply that the writings were by prophets of Paul's day, and not of those found in the Old Testament. The reference to the **holy apostles** is in keeping with Paul's claim to having received the revelation himself. However, a point of question raised by those who feel that the Ephesian letter was not written by Paul is the unlikelihood that Paul would refer to himself and the others as the *holy* apostles.

Understanding that the mystery is primarily a first-century revelation by God to His called workers within the church, it is important that we come to an understanding of what this mystery revealed. As has been determined from both the Romans and Colossians passages, the beneficiaries of this mystery are the Gentiles. This theme Paul elaborates in Ephesians 3 by using three different Greek words prefixed with the preposition *sun,* which means "with." These "with" words, common in the Greek, become difficult to translate into English. They express a meaning of association. Thus, to Paul the mystery is that through the gospel, the Gentiles (1) are made heirs together *(sunkleronoma)* with Israel; (2) are made members together *(sussoma)* in one body, the body of Christ; and (3) are sharers together *(summetoxa)* in the promises found in Christ.

This description echoes Ephesians 2 where Paul declared that the Gentiles were no longer foreigners and aliens, but fellow citizens of God's household and citizens with God's people. This does not imply that upon believing in the gospel, the Gentiles became Jews. Rather, in Christ there is a new household of God where both Jews and Gentiles become new, related to each other, as well as to Christ. The Jews were sinful and in need of salvation, and yet God in His mercy made them "alive with Christ." The workings of Christ in the individual, whether Jew or Gentile, made them new creations and heirs to a new kingdom.

Although the mystery was revealed in the first century, it is only fully realized in the interrelationship found between Christian Jews and Gentiles. The mystery does not make Gentiles part of the local synagogue, unless the lordship of Christ and His saving grace are also central within the synagogue. The mystery means that Gentiles, who were considered outsiders to the grace and provision of God, are now not only recipients of God's grace, but an equal part in God's planned kingdom of the redeemed in Christ.

In 3:9-11, Paul continues the theme of mystery, but now referring to his task as a humble servant for the gospel. Again he describes it as a message **kept hidden in God** (3:9) in the previous ages. However, it is God's intent that His **wisdom** should be revealed **to the rulers and authorities in the heavenly realms,** by way of the church (3:10). Here we find a number of expressions different than those mentioned earlier in Ephesians 3. God's wisdom is not revealed through prophets, their writings, or holy apostles, but now it is **through the church** (*ecclesia;* 3:10). This Greek term, meaning "the called out ones" refers to all the believers in Christ, or their combined actions. Where Paul before was quite specific as to the office within the church through whom the mystery was to be revealed, he now becomes more general. Apparently, the message of God would be sounded through this new body of believers. The restriction of people through whom this message would come within the church might be intact, but it would be out of the church that God would reveal His great gospel.

Another distinction is seen concerning the recipients of this message. Primarily relating to the Gentiles in the other passages, Paul here refers **to the rulers and authorities in the heavenly realms** (3:10). In several other places in the Ephesian letter, Paul relates to this same area and/or entity. The **heavenly realms** are those areas understood as being beyond our present earthly existence. It is the place from which we are blessed (see 1:3); it is that place where we are already seated with Christ (see 2:6); and it is the location of the malevolent forces associated with this world (see 3:10; 6:12). The **rulers and authorities** are those entities in opposition to God and His church. They are those we struggle against in our spiritual warfare (see 6:12).

The mystery of God is a message once hidden not only from the Jews and Gentiles of old, but from the evil entities and forces beyond this earthly sphere. Its message is now not only for the Gentiles, but for these evil powers and forces. To the Gentile, it is the promise of inclusion into God's kingdom by His grace; to the forces, it is a message that God's eternal plan of salvation has been fulfilled in Christ and is being substantiated by the church (see 3:11). The messenger would be the church as a whole, but more specifically her prophets and apostles. In this operation, Paul was made an administrator to oversee its expression and proclamation.

c. Paul the Servant (3:7-13). Paul's next description of himself is as a **servant** (3:7). Service in the New Testament primarily referred to service to God, which implied service to humankind as well. There were three basic Greek words used in reference to God's service.[6] First there is *leitourgeo,* from which we derive our modern word *liturgy,* meaning mainly priestly service. The priest had the dual functions of representing the people before God and representing God before the people. *Latreuo* was used to describe a detailed service in worship itself, and *diakoneo* expressed mainly help toward other people. "Servant" originally referred to those who waited on tables and did other common and menial tasks. In Acts 6:1-6 is an excellent example of this word, as the early church resolved the problem of certain members not being served by appointing seven brethren to *diakoneo* in place of the disciples.

Of the three words cited above, Paul uses *diakoneo* to describe himself. He is a servant of the gospel (see also Colossians 1:23). Elsewhere, he refers to himself as a servant by whom the Corinthians came to the faith; a servant of the new covenant[7]; a servant of God; a servant of Christ; and a servant of the church (see 1 Corinthians 3:5; 2 Corinthians 3:6; 6:4; 11:23; Colossians 1:25). He also refers to his fellow coworkers as servants (see Ephesians 6:21; Colossians 1:7, 4:7; 1 Thessalonians 3:2).

Paul was placed in this position as a servant of the gospel by the same means by which he became an administrator of the mystery of God—God bestowed it upon him. Paul refers to servanthood as a gift, given graciously by God through the workings of His power. Paul is not a self-made man, nor did he arrive at his position in Christ or the church by His own attributes and means. He is who he is by no other means than that God's undeserved favor was showered upon him. He is able to do nothing in the Kingdom except by the power given Him by God.

We hear the message of a persecuted persecutor expressed: **Although I am less than the least of all God's people, this grace was given me** (Eph. 3:8a). The echo of 1 Corinthians 15:9-11 is sounded unmistakably. Both as an apostle and as a servant, Paul sees himself as unworthy and the lowest and least of all Christians. He had persecuted the church, and, although he had been forgiven by God, Paul apparently is unwilling to overlook his past actions. He who was the persecutor is now the unworthy servant to the persecuted, only because God chose to be gracious to him.

Paul's self-description and self-evaluation are a humble message to all Christians. Care must always be exercised so as to maintain a healthy recognition of one's position before Christ within His kingdom. Two potential errors become evident in the Christian's life.

First is an attitude which places emphasis upon one's own abilities and personality. Because of the gifts and talents we possess, it is easy to become confused in thinking it was these attributes that caused God to call us into His service. The outcome, we believe, is God's benefiting from our abilities. In reality, we must remember that anything we are or become is because of God's unmerited favor, His grace being showered upon us. What we achieve and are able to do is all because God has enabled us by His power through His grace.

Second—and the exact opposite of the first error—is the feeling that I am no one in the Kingdom and therefore can do nothing for God. Here, instead of confusing the credit for what God has done, we give Him no credit at all. Often seen as a statement of humility, our confessions of ineptness are, in fact, denials of God's ministry in our lives. By refusing responsibility and ability, we claim that God has not expressed any grace or power upon us, leaving us as helpless and hapless people.

It is Paul's view, as he describes himself, that Christians need to heed. He maintains the balance between who he was and what God had made him. He knew of his unworthiness, but he also knew the blessings bestowed on him by God. He knew of sin, but, more importantly, he knew of grace. He knew of weakness, but also owned the empowerment that was his as God's gift. We are people not only saved by grace, but gifted, commissioned, and empowered by grace as well.

This grace of servanthood was given to Paul for two reasons: **to preach to the Gentiles the unsearchable riches of Christ** (Eph. 3:8); and **to make plain to everyone the administration of this mystery** (3:9). The two tasks seem to be the same activity expressed in different ways. **To preach** must always be synonymous with the idea of making plain the truths of God. The most gifted of God's speakers will always be those who can make the most complex spiritual truth the most easily understood. **To everyone** is more inclusive than the term **Gentiles,** but only as it does not relate to the Jews and to the "rulers and authorities in the heavenly realms." The word for "Gentile" *(ethnos)* referred to anyone not Jewish. It could also mean nations. **The administration of this mystery** and **the unsearchable riches of Christ** (3:8-9) are one and the same. **The mystery** is the message of God's salvation of humankind, especially to the Gentiles, through the workings of Jesus Christ His Son.

Unsearchable does not imply that we are not allowed to consider these potentials and blessings, but rather that they are so fathomless, so unending that they cannot be wholly sought out or contained. This idea becomes part of Paul's prayer in 3:17-18.

Paul concludes his thought in this section by once again making Christ the central point of the message. God's eternal purpose is **accomplished in Christ Jesus our Lord** (3:11). Paul then goes on to relate that **in him and through faith in him we may approach God** (3:12). Two realities of salvation are implied with this statement.

The first emphasizes Christ. Our salvation was procured by Jesus in His obedient life and subsequent death on the cross. Primarily, there is no other means or hope of salvation outside of Jesus. In Him we find a righteousness that we ourselves could never achieve. This righteousness in given over to us at salvation in what John Wesley referred to as "passive righteousness." We become the righteousness of Christ, as He makes us righteous.

The second expression in verse 12 is directed more toward human agency: **through faith in him.** Here is humankind's responsibility. We are saved by grace through faith (see 2:8). It is not enough that Jesus is righteous and that He died for our sins; we must also respond to this truth by accepting it as fact—fact that is not just a mental assent to a group of expressed truths, but rather a fact that we are willing to embrace with our faith, and to trust with our very eternal existence. It is by the righteousness of Christ and our faith in Him that we can approach God. There is no other means, no other merit, no other way by which we may come to the Father and yet live. Unless we come by the blood of Christ, we have no place before a holy and righteous God.

Moving beyond the necessity of salvation, Paul describes two expressions of favor enjoyed by all Christians who come to the Father through Jesus Christ: **freedom and confidence** (3:12). Though much older, the book of Esther illustrates the experience of a subject coming before a king (see Esther 4:9-11). The privilege was by invitation only. Those who came uninvited were put to death. The only exception was found if the king, in an act of grace, extended his royal scepter toward the intruder. This allowed the subject to approach unharmed. If this were true with sinful kings, how much more would we expect with the King of Kings.

God is unquestionably regent over all. This, and the fact that He is holy, would make approaching God impossible were it not for Jesus. By Paul's words, because of what was **accomplished in Christ Jesus** (Eph. 3:11), we are able to approach God "uninvited." Through salvation (see

Ephesians 2:13), God graciously extends His scepter toward us. We are received, not destroyed. Paul carries through an understanding of this experience by relating that we have freedom and confidence while in God's presence.

In Romans 8:15-17, Paul extends this thought to include the workings of the Holy Spirit within this experience. We were not given a timid Spirit, but rather one of boldness by which we enter before God with such confidence that we are able to express the endearing term "Abba," which is closely equivalent to our modern word *Daddy*. Because of what Jesus has done, we are no longer outcasts, but children with great freedom and confidence to enter before our Father.

Few of us will ever have the privilege of entering the White House unless we go on scheduled tour. To be invited to the Oval Office with the president is indeed an experience of honor. During the Kennedy administration, a rather endearing photograph was taken in the Oval Office of the president at his desk. On the floor in front of the desk was his son, John Jr., then quite a small boy. Completely oblivious of the great honor the child was experiencing, he was comfortable to play in the presence of his father. The man at the desk may have been the president of the United States, but he was also "Dad," and because of this, John Jr. was invited to stay. It is true that God is sovereign of all and, as such, deserves unquestionable allegiance and respect. But He also is our Heavenly Father, who allows His children to come and be comfortable in His presence. What a wonderful joy is ours, to be in Christ.

Paul concludes this section by exhorting his readers **not to be discouraged because of my sufferings**—his house arrest (Eph. 3:13). He shares two reasons for this: (1) his sufferings were for them; and (2) his sufferings were their glory. There is a selflessness expressed by Paul, as he is careful that his circumstances do not in any way destroy his witness and the experience of his followers. Chained in house arrest, he could have—like so many others had—written of his plight to illicit pity. But his words are of glory and suffering for others. Referring to this imprisonment in his letter to the Philippians, Paul stated that his chains served to encourage many to speak the word of the Lord fearlessly (see Philippians 1:14). Others even did so out of "selfish ambition," realizing it would stir up trouble for Paul (1:17). However, he concluded that it did not matter as long as Christ was being proclaimed. Obviously, Paul was a prisoner. But his experience was for the sake of Christ and His church, of which Paul was a prisoner, administrator, and servant.

2. PAUL'S SECOND PRAYER 3:14-21

Having brought his discussion regarding his ministry to a conclusion, Paul continues his original line of thought found in Ephesians 3:1, to pray for his readers. He does this by repeating the phrase, **For this reason** (3:14). Not everyone is in agreement with this, as some would argue that the prayer Paul is about to make is merely a continuation of his earlier prayer found in 1:15-19 and not the development of a new entreaty before God.[8] However, this would require the phrase, **For this reason,** to refer back to 1:15, and would make the purpose of the prayer, once again, a celebration of God's preplanned salvation. The context of the present prayer argues more in favor of the contents of chapter 2 than chapter 1 of Ephesians. There are three main divisions in this section: the introduction (3:14-15); the petition (3:16-19); and the benediction (3:20-21).

Paul's introduction shares the reason, posture, and recipient of his prayer. **For this reason** refers back to the concluding thoughts developed at the end of chapter 2. Specifically, the section begins at 2:19 with the word "consequently." The word suggests a summation or at least an application of what has been stated before. The consequences of Jesus' reconciliatory ministry to humankind are the inclusion of the Gentiles into His family and kingdom. They are now part of the household of God as full members. The reality of this thought has moved Paul to make intercession for these new members on some very specific issues.

The posture Paul expresses is uniquely revealed by the phrase, **I kneel before** (3:14). This is the only place in Scripture that Paul makes reference to his posture in prayer. Scripturally, there is no specific teaching or mandate as to the appropriate position one is to assume while praying. But at least three are mentioned: prostration, kneeling, and standing.

Prostration is understood as lying face down before God. In this position, the entire front of the body is in contact with the ground in an expression of complete submission (see 1 Chronicles 29:20).

Kneeling is understood as being on both the hands and knees, or on the knees alone. First Kings 8:54 describes the kneeling of Solomon during his dedicatory prayer of the Temple, with his hands spread out toward heaven. Kneeling to pray was the common position for Daniel (see Daniel 6:10). It was Jesus' position in the Garden of Gethsemane on the Mount of Olives (see Luke 22:41). Stephen's stoning records two positions during his prayer (see Acts 7:59-60). Apparently he was standing during his petition that God would receive his spirit, and then, having fallen to his knees (which could have been by his choice or the result of his stoning), he continued to pray that his executioners' sins not be held against them. Kneeling was the posture Paul (and those with him) assumed while praying during his last visit with the people from Ephesus who came out of the town to meet him (see Acts 20:36). This action is repeated with the people of Tyre in Acts 21:5. Kneeling is also considered to be the position of honor which will be assumed in the presence of God (see Isaiah 45:23) and at the mention of Jesus' name (see Philippians 2:10).

Standing to pray is mentioned on several occasions by our Lord. In His parable of the Pharisee and publican (Luke 18:10-14), He describes the two as standing while they prayed. In Mark 11:25, Jesus refers to standing while praying when He was instructing about the need to make peace with those one has something against. He describes the errant hypocrite as one who enjoys praying while standing in the synagogue and on street corners (see Matthew 6:5).

Marcus Barth argues that standing was probably the preferred position among Jews, while kneeling was preferred among Gentiles.[9] He cites as his argument that kneeling was the common posture of Baal worshipers. Jews, desiring to distance themselves from this pagan exercise, would have probably refrained from kneeling. In addition, Barth argues that many of the references mentioned in the New Testament regarding kneeling while praying were written about Paul's ministry among Gentiles, and by Luke (a Gentile writer) using phrases that sounded more Roman than Jewish.

The purpose for considering the preference of prayer postures is an effort to answer the question of why Paul would make so unusual a reference to his kneeling. Some would argue that at this point Paul actually knelt to pen these words. However, if Barth is correct in his assertion that Jews stood and Gentiles knelt, Paul's description of kneeling before the Father would be a statement of association with his Gentile readers, and a fulfillment of his claim to align himself with the expressions of his audience (see 1 Corinthians 9:19-23).

Kneeling to pray would later become the accepted practice among Christians. Eusebius, an early church father, described it as a custom proper to Christians. Justin Martyr, also an early church father, saw in the act an expression of humankind's fall from grace.[10]

The recipient of Paul's prayer is expressed as **the Father** (Eph. 3:14). A variation in some other ancient Greek manuscripts of Ephesians have the added words "of our Lord Jesus Christ." These are believed to have been added after Paul to help it align with other portions of the letter, such as 1:3.[11] The addition is hardly necessary to reveal the identity of Paul's reference. His continued description in 3:15 more than identifies the Father as being synonymous with the God who maintains a household of fellow citizens made up of His people (see 2:19), and shares existence with these people in heaven as He has raised both Christ and us from the dead (see 2:6).

The significance of Paul's prayer to the Father is seen in recognizing the supreme position the Father has in the total scheme of creation and its salvation. From the very beginning of this letter, Paul has painstakingly revealed the Father's unique position in the rescue of humankind. It was God who determined and devised the plan by which humankind would be saved, even prior to Creation. It was God who gave His Son, Jesus, to be the fulfillment of this plan by way of His sacrifice. It was God who raised Jesus up from the dead and seated Him in the heavenlies, endued with all power and authority. It is the Father who extends the riches of His kingdom to all who believe by faith, making them full and fellow heirs to all that is His. Paul is praying to Father God, the source of all there was, is, or ever will be.

Paul's reference reminds us of the awesome privilege prayer affords humankind. Perhaps we enter into the activity so often that we have lost the sense of privilege it should engender. It may be easy for us to forget that in spite of our sin we are allowed by grace to speak one-on-one with the Father who is perfect and holy. We may overlook the fact that we who are limited in power have access to enter before the One who spoke all things into existence, and who could just as easily speak again and make all things cease to exist. We may become so accustomed to our activity that we forget how ignorant we are and how all-knowing God is. We may forget that few of us ever will have the unique privilege to be found in the audience of our elected officials, and yet we all have the freedom to come and go at will before the King of Kings and Lord of Lords. No wonder Paul knelt in prayer.

Paul's prayer is to the point, immediately listing two petitions on behalf of his readers (see 3:16-19): (1) that God would **strengthen you with power through his Spirit** so that Christ might dwell within them (3:16); and (2) that they might comprehend the fullness of **the love of Christ** (3:18). Though each request is unique, Paul's prayer is for his readers to receive power—power experienced and fulfilled in a number of ways.

The Greek word for **power** *(dunamei)* is the same word from which the word *dynamite* is derived. Paul is not asking for a minor influence in the reader's life, but one of awesome power. He is praying that God would make the people dynamic. Connected with this request are a number of specifics about how this prayer is answered.

Paul mentions the *source* of this power: **out of his glorious riches** (3:16). The beginning point for any Christian's empowerment can only be God. Paul is not asking the Father to bestow upon the readers human strength, political clout, or financial influence. These are the types of power that humankind seeks and are the products of fallen human nature. What Paul desires for his readers is the dynamic power of God which finds its source only in God.

There is a specific *means* by which this power is relayed: **through his Spirit** (3:16). It is no secret that God uses the Holy Spirit to endue people with abilities beyond their own. It is by the Spirit that we receive certain gifts by which we can do the work of God (see 1 Corinthians 12:1-11; Ephesians 4:11-13). The Holy Spirit enables "fruits" such as love, joy, peace, patience, kindness, and long-suffering, which otherwise would be impossible to obtain, to become evident in the believer's life. The Holy Spirit is also the means by which God bestows upon us wisdom and discernment, direction and rebuke (see John 14). The Holy Spirit would be the source of the power experienced by the disciples in the fulfillment of Christ's commission, as Jesus promised they would receive power to be His witnesses when the Holy Spirit came upon them (see Acts 1:8).

Paul's prayer pinpoints the means by which we receive the necessary abilities to live the Christian life as moral and powerful disciples. Some have lost a sense of this in their quest for other means of influence and effect. We sell out to such limitations as politics, influence, wealth, and popularity. Some forget their purpose before God and go whoring after any number of replacements for His empowerment, only to end up powerless. The means by which we receive power in the Christian life is by the ministry of the Spirit as He bestows upon us those rich abilities that come from the very storehouse of God.

Paul mentions an *abode* for this power: **in your inner being** (Eph. 3:16). Just as it is important for one to recognize the need for God's power, the source of this power, and the means of its distribution, one must recognize where the influence of this power is to be experienced. Christianity is an internal experience. God is far more concerned with what is going on within us than without. He knows that what is happening on the outside of the person is a direct reflection of what is happening on the inside. Humankind has trouble understanding this concept, as we often place our emphasis on the more noticeable of the two, resulting in confusion and hypocrisy.

One of the ongoing struggles Jesus faced while ministering on earth was to get people to look at the inner person instead of the outer appearance. His greatest opposition was the Pharisaical religion which, by Jesus' time, had evolved into a legalistic faith that placed a heavy emphasis upon one's appearance. White robes were more important than pure hearts. Outer actions were prized above inner motives. Jesus wanted His people to realize that it was not what was *without* that was their danger, but what was *within* (see Luke 11:37-52; Matthew 23:25-26). His lessons in the Sermon on the Mount emphasized that it was not the outward action that created the sin, but the inner attitude (see Matthew 6:27-34).

In an age that is always asking for the "bottom line," Paul lists his as the first request. He is asking for this enduement of power **so that Christ may dwell in your hearts through faith** (Eph. 3:17). The Greek word for **dwell** *(katoikesai)* is used only three times by Paul in his writings. It means a permanent dwelling, as opposed to a visit or sojourning. Paul is desirous for the readers to be empowered within so that Christ will permanently dwell there. Here we see the great provisions of grace wrought to their fullest. Realizing our own inability to live a moral and holy life, Paul calls upon God and His resources to make possible what we could never do by ourselves. If by our own strength we endeavor to live for God, we will miserably fail Him and end up apostate. Our task in our relationship is faith, believing in the provisions of our Lord. God's salvation and empowerment make us worthy vessels in which Christ can dwell. In keeping with the meaning of *katoikesai,* this dwelling place must be a home, not a motel room or other temporary lodging.

There is also a personal, life-changing application to be made regarding Paul's final reason for the request. As God works His great power in the inner being of a person, that inner person is changed. This transformation becomes the reflection of the One who is doing the work, just as sin is a reflection of the Evil One. As that power of God is made manifest within us, by way of the Holy Spirit, the resultant nature is the essence of Christ. The beauty of Christ can only shine forth from a heart that has been changed by God, swept clean and empowered. Thus, Paul's prayer request is really a prayer for the cleansing work of God to be done in the individual so that Christ, both in essence and influence, can dwell within as a result of the person's faith.

Paul's request for power here comes from a different perspective than his first request. He adds a precondition that describes the readers and sets an expectation for those who would desire a similar blessing: they are to be **rooted and established in love** (3:17). Here is the figurative foundation for the growing Christian. We can base our relationship with God on a number of things, but love is the foundation.

Some people find their foundation in Christ to be fear. It is true that we should maintain a sense of fear of God, but not as the founding base. The fear we should maintain is understood best by the word *awe*. We are to be spellbound, reverent, amazed at who God is. But these experiences grow out of the realization of God's love for us. Those who base their relationship on fear will come to see God as a vengeful judge who desires their destruction more than their salvation. They have been scared into a relationship with Him, because they are afraid of what He will do to them otherwise. It is the equivalent of making friends with the class bully. You may not be happy to be around him, but it's better than being beaten up. Salvation becomes nothing more than a type of protection. God remains a tyrant, a despot, and—unless the individual discovers love as the foundation to their relationship—an impossible deity to serve. In time, we tire of the threats and sever our ties.

Some people find their basis of relationship with God to be the law.[12] God is a judge who keeps strict account of every thought, word, and deed, judging us harshly for each infraction. There is no tolerance, no mercy or grace. There is a right and a wrong. The right is expected, the wrong punished. The relationship is one of condition—God's telling us He will love us if we keep the rules, while all the time we realize how far short we fall from both His expectations and worthiness of His love. No matter how hard we try, all we hear in response to our efforts is chastisement for our shortcomings and a command to do better. In time, we realize that God's demands exceed our abilities, and we give up, feeling we are hopeless.

But Paul is speaking of a group of people who are **rooted and established in love** (3:17). The basis for our experience is the reassurance that God loves us, even to the point of dying for us. This realization is important if God is ever going to work His great salvation within us. If we do not see Him as God, loving us as His children, we will be blind to His provisions and His true nature. We will not see Him as a God of mercy and grace, but rather as a stern judge and angry despot. We will have no sense of benevolence only malevolence. For God to begin His work in us, we must have a workable understanding of who He is.

Another aspect of Paul's request is the scope of its influence. The first request seemed to remain solely for the Gentiles, but now Paul asks that God's power be experienced by not just them, but by **all the saints** (3:18).

Perhaps we could make too much of this distinction by suggesting that one request is exclusive, while the other is inclusive. It would appear, though, that Paul is being inclusive in both, by reminding his Gentile readers that they are open to the full inheritance of the Kingdom, which includes the power Paul has requested.

Paul's request is for his readers' ability. The Greek word used here literally means "to be fully able." Paul is not seeking any partway measures, no just-get-by attitude. His prayer is for full ability to be given. This is one of the blessings of God's grace. God enables us to experience a full and complete salvation. There are no halfway measures with God. He gives us all that we need to obtain victory over sin, death, and hell. Since He provides us with this full ability, it is obvious that our response can only be full involvement.

A backhoe operator on a construction site was surprised one day by the owner of the company. Being relatively new to his job, the operator was exercising care in his manipulation of the machine. Suddenly the motor, which had been set at half-throttle, roared to life. The startled operator looked behind him to discover that the owner was holding the lever wide open. Shouting above the engine noise, the owner explained to the puzzled operator, "This is the way I want to hear my equipment run." The owner knew the potential of his equipment, and he wanted the full benefit. The same is true with God concerning His children.

Paul's request reminds us of our utter dependence upon God when it comes to doing His will. We are engaged in a supernatural relationship, struggling against supernatural forces and influences. We are seeking victory over issues that have held us enslaved. Obviously the workings and effects of God's ministry requires a strength beyond our own. Paul desires this ability to be known in two ways.

First, Paul prays for his readers to be able **to grasp** (3:18). Originally, the Greek word here was used to refer to wrestlers as they grappled with each other. But in our reading it is meant figuratively, though with the same intensity. Paul's desire is for his readers to have the ability to latch onto an understanding of **how wide and long and high and deep is the love of Christ** (3:18).

Many attempts have been made to explain exactly what Paul meant by this multidimensional description.[13] Some believe it describes the perfect shape of God. Others feel it refers to God's mystery. Others see a description of the entire universe or the holy city. Still others see it as describing the four arms of Christ's cross, or descriptive of specific virtues. In this context, it is apparent that Paul is referring to the figurative measure of **the love of Christ.** No specific dimensions are given because it is an attempt to express the expansiveness of His love. Two realities speak to us. First, as John writes in his first epistle, "God is love . . ." (1 John 4:16b). Second, we understand that one of the basic attributes of God is omnipresence, meaning He is everywhere at once. There are no boundaries to God's presence or existence. If this is true, there can be no boundaries or complete measure of the love of God. There may be dimension, but never limits.

This boundless dimension of God's love is reflected in the second part of Paul's request. He describes this love as **love that surpasses knowledge** (Eph. 3:19). As God is beyond our comprehension, so are His attributes of love. Ironically, Paul makes a seemingly impossible request. He asks that we be given the full ability to **know this love that surpasses knowledge.** How can someone know something that surpasses knowledge? The statement is an oxymoron, a statement in contradiction to itself. However, it can be understood in several ways.

First, Paul could be comparing humankind's ability with God's ability. If left to ourselves, we could never come to an understanding of God's love. But, by God's inspiration, we can receive that which is impossible by any other means. Thus, Paul's request is a request for spiritual enlightenment in the area of love.

Second, we could attempt to understand Paul's statement using the differing definitions of *knowing* as expressed by both the Hebrew mindset and the Greek word. To know (*yada* in the Hebrew, *gnosko* in the Greek) meant more than cognitive ability. It also meant experience or intimacy. Often in the Old Testament the term meant sexual intercourse or intimate knowledge of another. Thus, Paul could be describing an experience by its essence. He is not implying comprehension as much as interaction—allow the people the privilege of experiencing intimately this otherwise unknowable completeness of God's love. The emphasis is on quality, not quantity.

The latter of these two options would seem apparent as Paul states the reason for this request—**that you may be filled to the measure of all the fullness of God** (3:19). Again we discover an apparent oxymoron. How can we as finite individuals contain the fullness of an infinite being? If we were filled with God's fullness, we would explode! What Paul is apparently asking for is our perfection.

Being **filled** carries the idea of fulfillment. Paul's request is that we be completely fulfilled by all that God has for us. The beauty here is found in the reality that this fullness is made possible only by God's enabling us to completely appreciate and experience His love in our lives. Love is the great sanctifier of God. It takes us when we are reprobate and draws us to Him. It covers our sins with the blood of Christ and declares us forgiven. It extends to us the ability to overcome the power of death and sin, and brings us to a completeness that sin otherwise had robbed from us. It fills us and fulfills us. We know it, and yet it is never fully known. We experience it, and yet never in its entirety. It just keeps filling and changing and perfecting its recipient.

The final part of Paul's prayer is his *benediction*. It is a blessing found quite naturally at the end of his prayers in Scripture (see Romans 11:36; 16:25-27; Galatians 1:5; Philippians 4:20; 1 Timothy 1:17; 2 Timothy 4:18b).

One significance of this benediction is its description of God that tends to summarize all that Paul has been saying within the prayer itself. The blessing is extended **to him who is able to do immeasurably more than all we ask or imagine** (Eph. 3:20). This has been the message of Paul's prayer. He is making requests that God work His great power within the believer, by way of the Holy Spirit, so that what is necessary in the believer's life can be done. God is the God whose love goes beyond our ability to measure or fully know. He is the God whose fullness is far greater than we can contain. In other words, the Father to whom Paul bends the knee, in 3:14, is the same God who goes beyond measure and imagination.

The other expression of this benediction is the realized blessing for each believer. This God whose love and fullness exceeds our measure and comprehension is at work within us with His great power. The incomprehensible is understood by experience—not in His fullness, but in His immediacy. The immeasurable finds measure as He fills our beings and completes our lives. That which is beyond is within. That which is within is beyond.

The blessing is found in 3:21: Let **glory** be given to Him **in the church and in Christ Jesus.** The glory is to be expressed within the two means by which God shares His glory. We know the fellowship of God by way of His Son. We know the fellowship of the Kingdom by way of His church. Both of these are God's saving provisions for humankind. What better place to glorify Him than in those places He has provided for our benefit. The glory is not temporal, even as the church and Christ are not limited by time. It is to be **throughout all generations** and all time, even **for ever and ever!** With this, Paul concludes with a hearty agreement of **Amen** (3:21). The word literally means "truly" and is appended to the prayer to attest one's affinity with its claims. It is the same word in the Greek which is used when Jesus taught (see Matthew 6:16; 11:11). It becomes the final attestation of Paul to both his readers and to God to whom he prays.

ENDNOTES

[1] F. F. Bruce, *The Epistle to the Colossians, to Philemon, and to the Ephesians,* The New International Commentary on the New Testament (Grand Rapids, Michigan: Wm. B. Eerdmans Publishing Co., 1984), p. 309.

[2] For further discussion on the imprisonments of Paul, refer to the introduction of this book under "Occasion for the Letter."

[3] Some of the earliest manuscripts do not include the name "Jesus" in verse 1, stating simply that Paul is "a prisoner of Christ."

[4] Law here refers to the Levitical Code (all God's rules and regulations).

[5] Colin Brown, *Dictionary of New Testament Theology,* vol. 2 (Grand Rapids, Michigan: Zondervan Publishing House, 1976), p. 256.

[6] Ibid., p. 544.

[7] A covenant is a solemn promise made binding by a pledge or vow, which may be either a verbal formula or a symbolic action. Covenant often referred to a legal obligation in ancient times. In Old Testament terms, the word was often used in describing the relationship between God and His chosen people, in which their sacrifices of blood afforded them His atonement for sin, and in which their fulfillment of a promise to live in obedience to God was rewarded by His blessings. In New Testament terms, this relationship (the new covenant) was now made possible on a personal basis through Jesus Christ and His sacrifice of His own blood.

[8] Bruce, p. 309.

[9] William Foxwell Albright and David Noel Freedman, eds., *Ephesians 1–3,* vol. 34, The Anchor Bible (Garden City, New York: Doubleday and Company, Inc., 1974), p. 378.

[10] Bruce, p. 93.

[11] Bruce M. Metzger, *A Textual Commentary on the New Testament* (New York: United Bible Societies, 1975), p. 604.

[12] See endnote 4.

[13] Albright and Freedman, p. 394.

Part Two

LIVING THE FAITH

Ephesians 4:1-6:24

In three short chapters, Paul has taken his readers on a theological journey into some of the deepest, most profound truths of Scripture. With euphoric praise, he proclaims God's salvation plan for humankind by which we are made holy and blameless, adopted as children, redeemed from death, and sealed with the Spirit, all through the ministry of Jesus Christ. Paul shares how the great separations in life—between humanity and God, and between people themselves—are brought down so that all people can come together into one household of faith, built upon and united in Christ. There is no longer Jew and Gentile, but rather children of God, heirs to the Kingdom. Those who believe in faith are raised from death to life and seated with Christ in the heavenly realms.

Twice Paul prayed, interceding with specific desires for his readers' spiritual growth and welfare. And, for a brief time, he allows us close enough to his personal life that we hear the clanking of chains as he describes his experience as a prisoner of Christ in faithful ministry to his calling.

Now Paul's writing takes a radical shift, as it does in others among his letters (see Romans 12:1; Colossians 3:5), away from doctrine to personal life and practice. He enters into what is known as *parenaesis* (advice) where he removes his scholar's robe and takes up the shepherd's staff. Now the truths take on a more practical form, as Paul reveals their proper application to life. "Therefore" he says in 4:1 (KJV). One can almost hear him take a deep breath in an effort to revive himself after so hurried a pace in the first half of the letter. The long running sentences, the excitement of the message, and the shift from topic to digression and back to topic again, have created a hectic pace. This has all been shared and explained and prayed for a reason. "Therefore." Therefore, live! Live out these truths in your everyday experiences.

111

A popular phrase today calls people to "walk their talk." Paul was two thousand years ahead of us when he led his readers forward in this application. Repeatedly he exhorts them to *peripateo* in certain ways. The Greek word *peripateo* means literally "to walk," and figuratively "to live." These meanings are interchangeable, as "walking through life" is a metaphor for living. Five times in this section, Paul begins a new application by using this word: "[Walk] worthy of the calling you have received" (4:1b); ". . . no longer [walk] as the Gentiles do . . ." (4:17); "[Walk in] love" (5:2a); "[Walk] as children of light" (5:8b); "[Walk] not as unwise but as wise" (5:15b). Paul concludes his letter by giving specific advice to believers on how to relate to their world—both to the people with whom we live and the malevolent forces from which we were delivered (see 2:2), who continue to attack God's children.

Paul's position in this portion is not taken from some lofty tower of authority, but from a humble home in Rome where he is under house arrest. He is not at ease in this posture, but bound in the flesh. His words are accompanied by the rattle of chains (see 6:19). There is a certain authority which comes from this experience. Suffering begets recognition and respect. There is a sense that Paul, having endured his difficulties for Christ, has a place of respect among those of us who have not experienced the same. His words carry the weight of his chains, the strength of his resolve, the inspiration of his hope, and the unwavering of his commitment to Christ's call. As one who has heard the call of God and known the struggle of life, he has earned the right to speak, and he deserves the respect of our attention.

6

LIVING WORTHY OF YOUR CALLING

Ephesians 4:1-16

Nothing sells a newspaper like scandal, and no scandal is better than one which happens within a socially prominent family. In many cases, the issues surrounding a scandal are not unusual. What makes a scandal newsworthy is when it happens with someone whom we would normally not associate with such behavior. We hold a high standard for our officials which we expect them to keep. Behavior common to the average person is unacceptable. Kings do not get into barroom brawls. Queens do not get drunk in public. Presidents do not shoplift. To do any of these would be to live beneath what is expected of them. If this is true for those of our society upon whom we place great honor, how much more so for the child of God who is heir to His kingdom. Such high and regal honor is bestowed upon the redeemed of God. Therefore, Paul challenges the believers not to lose sight of their responsibility and besmirch their name by acting in a manner not in keeping with who they are.

This section of Ephesians is the beginning of Paul's practical teachings which comprise the second half of this letter. He concluded the first half by praying for his readers to be strengthened, rooted, and established in God and His love. Now Paul moves his readers to consider how to apply these benefits to a specific lifestyle that will reflect the glorious result of God's salvation plan so extensively discussed in the first half of the epistle. He calls on his readers to live a worthy life, expressed by their effort to live in unity with one another.

1. AN IRONIC COMMAND 4:1

There is an irony found in Paul's exhortation when we consider it in light of his opening remark, **As a prisoner for the Lord . . .** (Eph. 4:1). Paul, a Christian, an apostle, and a leading member of the church, is writing while under house arrest in Rome. Such a situation suggests scandal. Was Paul still within his rights to command obedience on the part of his readers, or was he upholding a double standard?

Three times Paul mentions his imprisonment in the Ephesian letter (see notes on imprisonment for 3:1). In 3:1, he states he is a "prisoner of Christ Jesus." Later in 6:20, he is an "ambassador" of the gospel, "in chains." Here in 4:1, Paul is **a prisoner for the Lord.** The key words to consider are the prepositions used by Paul in describing his relationship to his condition. When he states that he is a "prisoner *of* Christ Jesus" (3:1, my emphasis), Paul suggests that he is possessed by Christ and the gospel. Paul sees his incarceration as a result of his being totally consumed by Christ and His will. Anyone less committed would not be found imprisoned for their faith. But in Paul's phrase, **prisoner *for* the Lord** (my emphasis), the word **for** implies purpose or reason, which relates Paul's identity by his task. His present situation has a purpose in God's great plan. Although Paul may not understand it, he is ready to accept it. In both cases, he does not allow his imprisonment to be a detraction, but rather an expression of his life in Christ. It has been said that Paul gloried in his chains as a king would glory in his royal robe and crown. Paul's imprisonment was not the evidence of scandal, but rather of loving commitment.

Paul's challenge to his readers in 4:1 is to **live a life worthy of the calling you have received.** The Greek word for **calling** is *kleseos*. Paul refers to this calling in a number of passages (see 1 Corinthians 4:21; 2 Timothy 2:25; Titus 3:2; Colossians 3:12). In Christianity this calling has two directions.

First, we are called *out from* the world and its sinful lifestyle and ideologies (as Paul has explained in the earlier chapters of this letter). The Greek word for church is *ekklesia* and means literally "the called out ones." Those who are numbered within the Body are those called out from the world to the kingdom of God.

Second, we are called *into* service. This view may be more familiar as we often associate a "calling" of God with a specific office or duty. Pastors, teachers, evangelists, and apostles all have a commission from

God, as Paul relates in Ephesians 4:11 and the longer lists found in Romans 12:6-8 and 1 Corinthians 12:8-10, 28. These are specific positions that are the result of God's extension of grace toward us, empowering us for service in a unique way.

Christians are those called of God, out from the world, into His service. It becomes the responsibility of all believers to live in a manner worthy of this calling by maintaining a distinct separation between themselves and the world, and by faithfully executing those offices and gifts entrusted to them for service. Specifically, Paul challenges his readers to respond to this calling of God by fulfilling three aspects of the faith: celebrate their unity, exercise their diversity, and anticipate their maturity.

2. CELEBRATE YOUR UNITY 4:2-6

Nothing destroys the calling of God more than the inability of God's people to get along with one other. If we have been called out of the world and into the family of God, living worthy of this calling would be to function as family. The quality of a family is measured by how its members relate to each other. When there is harmony, we define the family as wholesome. But when there is an abundance of strife, we define it as dysfunctional, realizing that its purpose is no longer being fulfilled. As the family of God, then, we are to relate to one another in both lifestyle and service.

Regretfully, most of us know of at least one dysfunctional family. While this is sad, most of us also know at least one church congregation which can also be described as dysfunctional. There are far too many churches that are known more for their fights than their faith, their discord than their disciples, their lust than their love. People who bruise and abuse each other are far from living worthy of the calling God has placed upon them. They behave too much like the world, and too little like the offices Paul describes. When this happens to a church, something is missing that needs to be changed.

What often creates conflict within the fellowship of the church is the interaction of its people. It is the church's diversity that creates friction. People moving in different directions at different speeds, fulfilling different tasks, begin to rub each other in the wrong ways. Friction results and temperatures rise.

Paul describes the unique workings of the church as a unified diversity. He describes it as a body with many members, yet still one body (see 1 Corinthians 12:14-31). This idea is an apparent contradiction. We tend to seek unity by sameness and agreement. This is usually the result of everyone's doing the same thing in the same way. But not in God's kingdom. Unity is both created and maintained by each person's faithfulness to his or her unique calling of God.

If we could look inside a car motor while it was running, we would immediately be impressed with its diverse and intricate workings. Pistons slide up and down in the cylinders, rotating the crankshaft. Camshafts turn, causing the valves to go up and down, opening and closing their ports to allow fuel to enter and exhaust to escape. Gears turn against gears in opposite directions, and timed explosions are set off with split-second accuracy, creating noise and pressure. In order for these processes to occur properly, there must be present the appropriate tolerance, or range of variation in the space between the moving and the still parts. Each part performs a unique function, often in seeming contradiction to the others surrounding it, but all function with one purpose in mind: to turn raw fuel into horsepower. Out of its diversity, the motor works in unity.

A comparison can be developed between the running of an engine and the life of the church. For a motor, three specific things are necessary to assure its smooth operation: oil, tolerance, and coolant. In the same way, Paul reveals three specific necessities for the proper operation of the church.

First is the oil of humility and gentleness. Paul's command is for his readers to be **completely humble and gentle** (Eph. 4:2). Oil is used in a motor to reduce the friction caused by the rubbing of moving parts against each other. Without it, the friction would become destructive by wearing away at the surface of the part, producing heat. In time, these negative influences would cause the part to fail and the engine to break down. To prevent this from happening, a thin layer of oil is maintained between the moving parts to prevent them from coming in contact with each other. The surface wear and heat are greatly reduced, assuring the ongoing function of the motor.

Gentleness and humility exercised toward our fellow Christians are means by which we can continue to move in differing directions and speeds without causing undo friction and heat among us. If our actions are buffered with gentleness, our contact with others will likely not be harmful. If our egos are bathed with humility, we will be less likely to become overheated by jealousy or a sense of threat. Dominance is the opposite of these graces and causes us to exert a restrictive force against those moving differently than we are. We collide and restrict, causing damage and heat. Too much dominance, and all other movement slows or stops, and the life of the church wanes.

This idea of humility and gentleness might have sounded strange to Paul's readers since they were Roman citizens. Humility and gentleness were not considered a sign of strength but of weakness in Roman culture. Humility and gentleness were the expression of a conquered people, not of the conquerors. Let the Greeks whom Rome overthrew express humility. Let the Hebrews who had long known subjection to one power or another be gentle. Rome was *the* world power and controller. This was not achieved by being humble or gentle. They were a proud, aggressive people. Being humble and gentle does not conquer worlds, at least not in the understanding of this world. Yet, isn't this the paradox of God's kingdom? Real power is found not in aggression, but gentleness, not in boldness, but humility. It is the meek who will inherit the earth. It is the last who will become first, the least that will be greatest, the servant who will be served. If such teachings are hard for us to understand, how much more so for the conquering people of Rome.

Second, Paul urges his readers to **be patient** with one another (4:2). The metal parts of a motor are made with great precision in regard to their size and shape. Each piece is made slightly smaller than the area in which it will move so as to allow freedom of motion, and to allow lubricant to come between the part and its surrounding surfaces. If the part were made the exact size of its opening, or if a motor were put together without this space, it would not be able to move, and the motor's function would be compromised. This small space is known as tolerance. Patience is tolerance in a relationship. It allows a certain amount of space around a person so that he or she can have freedom of movement. The opposite of tolerance is intolerance, when space is reduced and freedom is restricted. A church or fellowship without patience and tolerance is an association without movement. It does not function or produce. It is frozen and lifeless. In the family of God, there is a need for patient tolerance if we are to assure the free movement of God's people to live worthy of their calling.

Third is the command to utilize the "coolant" of **peace** (4:3). A by-product of a motor's function is heat, created by two influences: friction, as described above, and the heat caused by exploding fuel within the cylinders. If nothing were done to remove this heat, the temperature would continue to rise until it destroyed the lubricants and metals within the engine itself. To counter this problem in most automobiles, a liquid coolant, usually a mixture of water and antifreeze, is channeled through the motor in special chambers. The coolant allows the heat in the metal to be transferred to the coolant and eventually pumped out of the motor into the radiator where the heat is "radiated" away. The cooled water then returns to the motor so that the transfer of heat can continue. The activity of the church can cause a relational heat that in time can detract from the workings of the Body. There is a need to transfer this destructive "heat" away so that the activity of the church can continue unhindered. This is best described as the function of God's Spirit of peace.

Peace can diffuse a tense moment or a potential conflict. It can correct a misunderstanding or soothe a bruised ego. Peace can be the atmosphere that allows us to function comfortably with one another, even amid the hurried activity of a church at full speed. The opposite of peace is discord, the dry conflict that does nothing for the removal of heat, but only assures its continued buildup. Unless the church allows the free-flowing presence of God's Spirit to bathe it with His peace, it will burn out as a result of its own function and inner conflict.

As a car motor finds its sole purpose in creating horsepower from raw fuel, the church finds its sole purpose in the fulfillment of Christ's Great Commission (see Matthew 28:19-20). As much as it is dependent upon diversity of function to produce this oneness, the church can never lose sight of the fact that it is always a single unit. In describing this unity in Ephesians 4:4-6, Paul uses a Trinitarian theme revealing not only the oneness which is to be found within each expression of the church, but each expression of God which is prominent within the church. Paul's distinctions of God are described as **Spirit** (4:4), **Lord** (4:5), and **God** (4:6), the equivalents of which are the Holy Spirit, Son, and Father, respectively. A close parallel of this passage is found in 1 Corinthians 12:4-6, where Paul reveals the diversity of spiritual tasks, and yet their unity in God: "There are different kinds of gifts, but the same *Spirit.* There are different kinds of service, but the same *Lord.* There are different kinds of working, but the same *God* works all of them in all men" (my emphasis). From this Trinitarian description, Paul reveals the inherent unity found in the structure, salvation, and sovereignty expressed within God's kingdom, the church.

Paul has already described the *structure* of the church as the body of Christ, of whom Christ is Head (see Ephesians 1:22-23). Within this Body, which Paul also refers to as "God's household" (2:19) and a holy temple, in which God dwells by way of His Spirit (see 2:21-22). Jesus may be the Head and director of the church, but the Holy Spirit becomes the sinew which holds it together and the vital life source which makes it alive. The

Body's vibrancy is the direct result of the Holy Spirit's moving within its members, instilling life and power. This presence serves as an authentication of the Body. It is what makes the gathering of believers unique from all other gatherings. If there is no Holy Spirit present within a group, it becomes nothing more than a social movement. There can be only one authentic gathering of the Body, and that is when it is brought together under the Headship of Jesus and infused by the presence of the Spirit. Anything else is counterfeit.

The *salvation* of the church is personified through Jesus Christ, the sacrificial Lamb of God. He becomes the focus of our movement, which draws us into a unified direction. Our experience of this salvation is expressed in three words shared by Paul in 4:5: **Lord, faith,** and **baptism.**

The word **Lord** is the title by which we express our recognition of Jesus as the central object of our affections and remembrance. He is our Master. We are His subjects—not because He is a tyrant, but because He purchased us with His blood. As the church recognizes its one Sovereign, its energies and directions are defined and directed into a unified expression.

Faith (4:5) becomes the means by which we relate to our Lord. There are a number of options by which we could endeavor to communicate with Him, but faith is the only acceptable means. It is the way we experience our initial salvation from God (see 2:8). It is the means by which we continue to follow His direction. As Jesus is the central focus of our expression, faith is the central expression of our focus.

Baptism (4:5) is the mark of the faith. From Abraham to Christ, God chose to distinguish His people by circumcision. This scarring of the flesh became a mark of identity to anyone who encountered it. With the coming of Jesus, two radical shifts took place from Old Testament observances: (1) the Passover meal was replaced by Communion; and (2) circumcision was replaced by baptism. The mark of the Christian would not be the removal of the foreskin, but rather the touch of water. Paul saw in this act an expression of testimony (see Romans 6:4), but also a close relation to circumcision. In Colossians 2:11-12, he expresses how in Christ we receive a circumcision that puts off the sinful nature. He claims that this circumcision was not done by the hands of men, but by Christ, ". . . having been buried with Him in baptism and raised with Him through your faith in the power of God."

John Wesley, in his "Treatise on Baptism," describes it as "the initiatory sacrament, which enters us into covenant with God."[1] In addition to this benefit, Wesley adds others: (1) the guilt of original sin is washed away; (2) we are admitted into the church and made members of Christ, its Head; (3) we are made children of God; and (4) we become heirs to the kingdom of heaven. Additionally, he writes that baptism is an outward means of an inner experience, just as outward circumcision was understood to be a means of inward circumcision.

Baptism (Eph. 4:5) is the mark God chose to place upon His church. We benefit by both its identification and administration of God's grace within us. There is no other mark by which this is experienced within the church. We may be diverse in abilities, but we are one in the mark Christ gives us through baptism.

Sovereignty is the essence of the faith. This expression is related to the Father who reigns supreme in all things. He is the designer of our salvation (see 1:4). He is the power by which it was fulfilled (see 1:19). He is the one who in the end will raise us up with Christ (see 2:6). This sovereignty of God is expressed by way of His omnipresence (the ability to be everywhere at the same time). He is not only the **Father of all,** but He **is over all and through all and in all** (4:6). We are unified by the complete saturation of God's presence and influence. There can be no additions or substitutes. There is no need. The one and only true God is sufficient in every circumstance and place. There is no conflict or confusion, only the complete and unified expression of God in all there is.

Recognizing the unity God desires within His church requires our participation and observation. We participate through the expressions of humility, gentleness, patience, love, and peace. We observe as we witness the workings of God within the fellowship in the expression of His Trinity.

3. EXERCISE YOUR DIVERSITY 4:7-13

As I have discussed above, God's call to unity does not come as the result of our being the same, as if we were clones, but from our diverse natures working toward one unified goal. While Paul has called us to recognize the necessity of this unity, he now shifts his challenge to the exercise of the diversity God has given us. This shift becomes apparent in Ephesians 4:7 with the use of the word **but,** revealing a contrast from his previous emphasis. We are one, **but** Christ has made us unique. The instrument of our uniqueness is described as **grace,** which **has been given as Christ apportioned it** (4:7), dividing it out among His people as He desired. Three important insights shout to us from this verse regarding the dispensing of grace.

The first lesson is that the recipients are revealed as individuals (**each one of us**). This is an overlooked reality in the life of the church. Too often we believe that these special graces of God are reserved for a special elite in the church and not for the common believer. However, God leaves no one out of His plan. There are no "common" individuals in the Kingdom. All are fellow heirs with Christ. We are all made worthy of these graces by Christ. If this truth would ever sink fully into our consciousness, the church would be invincible. But the sad reality is seen in our tendency to deny the reception of these graces as a reason for non-participation in certain activities. We approach the occasion with an errant sense of humility, claiming lack of ability, when all along God has given to each of us a specific grace to exercise in His kingdom. Those who claim exclusion would do well to read Jesus' parable regarding the talents (see Luke 19:11-26).

The second essential lesson from Ephesians 4:7 refers to what is received—**grace.** Grace is understood to be unmerited favor. What we receive, we are not worthy of. This is true in any expression of God made to humankind. Since we are totally dependent upon Him for our salvation and righteousness, there is nothing we hold of merit outside our faith in Him. Every expression, no matter how slight or great, that God makes toward humankind is an act of unmerited favor.

The unmerited favor in this context pertains to abilities for service. It is appropriate that God should bestow upon His children such means because He has given them an impossible commission. Not impossible in the sense that it cannot be done, but impossible because it is beyond human ability. Paul's description of our warfare in 6:10-18 tells us that this struggle is not against flesh and blood, but against spiritual forces.

God has placed before His church the superhuman task of battling evil and building the Kingdom. Knowing the impossibility of humankind's ever doing this on their own, He has provided the superhuman abilities to get the job done. It is a comfort to realize that God never calls anyone to a task that He does not provide the means of accomplishing. When we overlook this truth, we end up attempting to do superhuman work by human means, often relying on politics, business, and technology. Guilt, lust, and greed become our motives. The final product looks and smells more like our worldly institutions than the kingdom of God. We endeavor by our own alchemy to spin lead into gold, and all we ever succeed in producing is brass. "Living worthy of our calling" requires the recognition of our gifts and their incorporation into our lives so that we are actively doing God's work, God's way.

The third realization from 4:7 is that these graces are **given as Christ apportioned** them. God's kingdom is not a "one size fits all" enterprise. There is a uniqueness to each person that God complements with His grace. There is no one who knows us better than God. Not even ourselves. We like to believe we know who and what we are about, but at best we live a life of delusion. God created us and, in doing so, knows our particular strengths and weaknesses. Selecting the most appropriate gifts, God augments our existence by supplying what makes our best better and our weaknesses strong.

"We are God's workmanship, created in Christ Jesus to do good works" (2:10). Since this is true, those wishing to know the gifts God has bestowed upon them should make a conscious attempt to discern what these gifts are. A number of questionnaires have been developed to help us discover our gifts. We know that we should seek the insight of mature Christians around us who have had an opportunity to observe us over time. These individuals can be objective about our strengths and weaknesses. Finally, we can do a personal assessment by considering our own strengths. What can you do well? We should also consider our interests. What holds your concerns and attention? What issues heighten your emotions?

Obviously we need to be objective in our quest. We all can think of people who may feel they can sing like birds, but cannot. The same is true of those who feel they have the gift of teaching, and yet cannot keep the class's attention or get a point across. Those truly gifted by God for a certain task or responsibility within the church find not only the ability, but a joy in exercising the gift. There is something very fulfilling in the discovery and use of our gifts. They enable us to experience our faith in a more complete way. As we seek a confirmation of the workmanship God has effected within us, we are rewarded with a deeper satisfaction in our Christian expression.

A final word of insight on this point relates to our yearly endeavor to elect people to tasks within the local church. Seldom is any real consideration given to what God has equipped the person to do. We make our selection on more practical grounds, such as popularity, family history, time of membership, power, control or, in some cases, the fact that they are warm and breathing. The results are catastrophic. We have people who should be teachers, but who never see the inside of a classroom. They are involved in the decision making processes of the administration board. Those with administrative gifts are in the classroom; those who can prophesy are keeping the books; and the bookkeeper is in charge of the nursery. Then we wonder why people approach their ministries with such detached interest. The great news for the church is that every one of us has been given super-abilities, in accordance with his or her personal makeup, to do the work of God, God's way.

As Paul moves along in 4:8, he references a quote to back his claim that Christ bestows gifts on us. However, in doing so, we encounter the problem of where the quote is from. The first option is Psalm 68:18a, which reads, "When you ascended on high, you led captives in your train; you received gifts from men." Two obvious differences stand out when comparing Paul's quote with this psalm. First, the pronouns are switched from first person (you) to third person (he). This changes the direction of conversation from *talking to* the person to *talking about* the person. Second, with regard to the gifts, the psalm makes the subject to be the recipient of the gifts, while Paul's quote makes the subject the one giving the gifts. Assuming Paul meant this reference to be a direct quote, an explanation is necessary for the differences. If he is quoting the psalm, he is obviously taking some liberties.

One explanation holds that Paul is not intending to make an exact quote, but is merely referring to the teaching the verse has to offer. This was a common action done by the Jews of Paul's day when they wanted to use a verse to speak to their own message. It was assumed that the people reading the work were already familiar with the passage and would recognize the difference. In this view Paul was merely following a literary practice of his day.[2]

A second possibility suggests that Paul is quoting the psalm in light of its translation at the time. Two other written sources, the Syriac version of the Psalms, and the Targums,[3] include or refer to the psalm as Paul quotes it (although the Targums make Moses, not God, the victor of the psalm). This suggests that Paul's particular use of the passage was not unique to him. He could have been merely expressing the understanding of his day.

A third explanation for this difference holds that Paul was not quoting from the psalm, but rather an early Christian hymn that took its basis from the passage. Thus it would be a type of Christianized psalm. Though this could be true, as there are other areas of Scripture that reflect early Christian hymns, the argument is one out of silence. Since there are no existing copies of such a Christian hymn, the entire idea is speculative at best. The potential is certainly there, but the evidence is not.

Having presented his reference, Paul obviously felt the need to expound briefly on its application to the Christian context, and most specifically to Christ. In a two-verse homily, he shares what has become one of the church's great questions: What does it mean to say that **he ascended on high** (Eph. 4:8), if it did not also imply that Christ descended into the very depths? From this passage, the Christian belief of Christ's rescue from hades is understood. Christian tradition has taught that while Christ was in the grave, He literally descended into hell and there preached the gospel to those who had perished before His death and were without hope of salvation. The Apostle's Creed expresses it this way: "He descended into Hell."

Paul is quoting from what is known as a war psalm. It describes the victory experienced by a warrior king. The ascent to the heavens was an expression of the king's victory in battle over the lower forces. In ascending, he took with him "captives." This was a common practice of the victorious king in a battle. The return home was with great pomp and pageantry. The king would lead the way with the results of his war brought behind in testimony of his success. The spoils of Christ's war would include a number of things. According to Revelation 1:18, they would contain "the keys of death and Hades." When He took away the curse of death from humankind, the doors of death and hell that once locked away the deceased of our world could no longer be secured. The spoils would also contain the redeemed whom Christ had released from the Enemy. Quite often, people from a defeated kingdom were brought back by the king to serve as slaves, as an expression of his dominance. We who were slaves to sin can relate to the cruelty of an unconcerned and unloving king. But once delivered by Christ, we are brought forward, not as a statement of Christ's ruthlessness in battle, but of His love that overcame evil itself.

Paul moves back to the subject concerning diverse gifts in Ephesians 4:11. The exact number of gifts listed by Paul is a matter of debate. In the Greek, each gift is made distinct by using the direct article *the,* except for the gift of teaching. Teaching appears to be attached to **pastors** as a combined gift. Thus the list would be apostles, prophets, evangelists, and pastors/teachers. However, in other passages Paul refers to teaching as a separate and distinct gift (see Romans 12:7; 1 Corinthians 12:28). Perhaps Paul viewed them as overlapping in activity.

The gift of being **apostles** (4:11) was discussed at length in the first chapter of this commentary under the office of apostleship. Simply stated, an apostle is an ambassador representing Jesus Christ to the world.

An ambassador, when speaking in an official position, serves as a voice of the one whom he or she represents.

Prophets (4:11) are often misunderstood today. Prophecy has taken on the meaning of a fortune-teller that can look into the future, revealing upcoming events before they happen. However, prophecy properly understood is not so much "foretelling" as it is "forthtelling." The authenticity of a prophet was his proclamation: "Thus saith the Lord." A prophet's validity was recognized by whether or not the words proclaimed were true. Often this proclamation took on a futuristic nature, because it required the test of time to verify the claim. However, it was not because the person could see the future so much as the present. Prophecy is the ability to discern present-day situations and project the outcome, based on what one knows about God. The person with the gift of prophecy has an unusual ability to view present situations with spiritual insight.

Evangelists (4:11) are best understood as "good news" people. We have come to understand evangelism as a challenge, since it often makes us talk to people about the wrongs in their lives. Evangelists are known as those itinerant ministers who travel our country holding special services within our churches, stadiums, or tents. But this is far too narrow a view. The Greek word from which we get evangelism is *euangelion,* which means simply "good news."

In 490 B.C., the Greeks and Persians were fighting against each other in what has become known as the Persian Wars. That year, the Persians invaded a plain outside the city of Athens. The Battle of Marathon ensued, with the safety of Athens held in the balance. Tradition holds that once the Greeks won the battle, repelling the invasion, a Greek soldier by the name of Phidippides ran the 22.5 miles from the battle to Athens in order to proclaim victory to its worried inhabitants. The toils of the battle and the long run took their toll, and the exhausted soldier entered the gates of Athens, able only to gasp out the word "Euangelion" ("good news") before falling over dead. The gift of the evangelist empowers an individual to go among those frightened by life's experiences, and tell them good news. The good news is that Jesus Christ has died for our sins.

The word for **pastors** in the Greek language (*poimenas;* 4:11) is the same as the word for "shepherd." There is no more fitting description of this gift and office than that of a shepherd of sheep. Jesus referred to himself as the "Good Shepherd" (see John 10). Later, when He reinstated Peter from his previous denials, Jesus instructed him to feed His sheep and take care of His lambs. These are the acts of a shepherd, to care for the flock of God.

We have become increasingly confused with the job description of the pastor today. To the unenlightened, the pastor is seen as one who does nothing but preach for an hour on Sunday, enjoying a one-day workweek. To others, the pastor becomes the one who is to do everything that the congregation feels is the pastor's responsibility, plus whatever the congregation happens not to do. (After all, that is what the pastor is paid to do, right?) To those who specialize in modern church life, the pastor's office is described as a business manager of a company, or a rancher. The list could go on ad infinitum. It would do us all well not to attempt to improve on the description given to us by Christ. He is the Good Shepherd who takes care of His sheep. It is the task of those He empowers to be involved in this same way.

Teachers (Eph. 4:11) is self-explanatory. They are people who are given special abilities to share information so that others come to understand it. This should never be misconstrued as a mere sharing of facts. It has been said that a teacher's work is not done until the student is changed. The goal of Christ's teachers is not to share information, but to institute inner transformation. The message must always have application. Application must be coupled with invitation. It is a wonderful privilege for one to not only share the truths of God, but to see it become fruitful in the life of the student. Sadly, many fall short of this high calling by limiting their function to the mere sharing of information. We hear it expressed by students and teachers alike. The reason for their attendance at seminars, small groups, and Sunday school is "to learn more about Jesus." In reality, our purpose is not to help people know more about the Savior, but rather to know the Savior in a life-changing experience. Those with the gift of teaching are enabled to share the awesome truths of God with life-changing effectiveness.

Having shared his list, Paul begins to expound on the reason for the gifts. It is in this passage that we find the awesome power of the English comma. The earliest Greek manuscripts of the Bible were written in what is known as continual script, meaning they contained no breaks between letters, words, or paragraphs. There was no punctuation to separate sentences or clauses. Picture this page as one continuous line of characters all hooked together without spaces or marks. Readers were dependent upon their understanding of Greek grammar to determine where the sentences ended and what phrases were to be separated from others by commas.

This discernment is not always as clear as we would like it to be. A comma placed in one location or the other can radically change the emphasis of the text. Specifically, in 4:12 there is a distinction found in the translation offered by some Bibles regarding whether a comma should be placed between the words **people** and **for,** or whether it should be left out. If the comma is used, it makes Paul's statement a threefold responsibility for those who have received the gifts. The gifts were given (1) to prepare God's people; (2) for works of service; and (3) to build up the body of Christ. This is the interpretation given by the King James Version, among others. The problem with this interpretation is its shift of responsibilities.

Apparently, Paul is instructing only those with these gifts, so that their task is to do all the work of the Kingdom. The others not gifted are left off the hook. It encourages a wide division between clergy and laity. Since the gifts Paul lists are associated mainly with specific *offices* in the church, it was understood that the proper execution of these offices was to do the work of the church including the watching over of a rather idle laity. However, this does not seem to be in keeping with Jesus' emphasis upon His desire for all people to be actively involved in ministry to one another, including the proclamation of the Word. It also does not square well with the Protestant movement, as one of its basic tenets is the priesthood of all believers.

More recently, interpreters of the Bible, such as in the New International Version, have removed the comma. With the comma removed, the list of responsibilities for the gifted is shortened to one task: **to prepare God's people for works of service** (4:12). Now the activity of service is placed upon the laity, and the gap is closed. The gifts are given not to preclude the laity, but to include them.

The result of this preparation of God's people for service will be experienced in a number ways. First, it will result in **the body of Christ** being **built up,** developing a **unity in the faith** and **knowledge of the Son of God** (4:12-13). Here again, we find Paul's recurring theme of unity by way of diversity. As each Christian is responsible to live worthy of his or her gifted call, the Body benefits by being built up, not torn down. Second, the application of these gifts and their fruition will result in our maturity in Christ. We will gain **the fullness of Christ** (4:13).

This fullness can be described by both experience and expression. By *experience,* we encounter the fullness of God's grace and mercy when everyone is acting responsibly with their gifts. Paul's "body" analogy shared in 1 Corinthians relates how a body without a foot or hand is incomplete. If a whole is the sum total of its parts, then the lack of any part detracts from the entire experience of the body. The *expression* of fullness relates more to maturity. The Greek word used by Paul *(telios)* is used often to mean perfection. It does not suggest an errorless ability, but a sense of completeness, lacking nothing, without shortfall.

One way of understanding the meaning of perfection as described by *telios* is to consider some of the great masterpieces of art on exhibit today. Many have stood marveling at the smile of "Mona Lisa" or the brilliance of Van Gogh's "Sunflowers." As the artist came to the end of his work, how did he know when to quit? At what point would a continuation of painting have detracted from the picture instead of adding to it? What touch of the brush made it complete? *Telios* implies the Master Painter has touched us with His brush in an act of final creation. The fullness of who we were created to be has been realized.

4. ANTICIPATE YOUR MATURITY 4:14-16

Now Paul moves on to describe the experienced results of this diverse unity. Once the gifts of Christ are shared, recognized and utilized, it is left for the Body to anticipate its workings to come to completeness within their fellowship and individual experiences. The results are shared in one phrase: They **will no longer be infants** (Eph. 4:14). The Greek word for **infants** means "immature," which stands in contrast to *telios* mentioned above. The evidence of this immaturity is expressed by their present experience, namely being blown here and there by every teaching and deceit.

James writes of this in his epistle (see James 1:6-8) in the context of faith. Maturity in Christ comes from asking Him for wisdom, but it must be asked for in faith without doubt. The sense of the words are lost in English, since James is not speaking of whether we believe in Christ's existence, but whether we want to remain committed to following Him. If that commitment is not determined, then we are blown in any direction by the next interesting concept that is shared with us.

There is a care that must be held by the believer to discern God's truth from the variety of half-truths and lies encouraged by the world. Like a child, if we remain naive, we can come to believe anything, which could easily end in our destruction. Maturity takes away our naiveté and enables us to recognize truth. The church and its people can be steered in wrong directions, costing them dearly in lost opportunities and souls. It is the mature individual who can discern the things of God from those which are not.

The history of the United States includes a number of gold rushes which have resulted when someone found the valuable ore in a specific spot. Prospectors have scoured the hills and valleys of our nation in search of the "mother lode." One of the challenges which quickly separates the professional from the mere novice is presented by iron pyrite. This mineral has become known as "fool's gold" since its close similarity to the original has tricked many would-be millionaires. As much as the mineral may look like gold, it is really quite common and, therefore, worthless. Coming down from their claims, prospectors would excitedly turn the results of their work over in anticipation of a wealthy reward. Many have placed their future on the worthless, having confused it for gold. The same can be said of the immature and their walk with God.

The opposite of being blown around and deceived is growing up into Christ. This will be accomplished by **speaking the truth in love** (Eph. 4:15). We need to hear this statement and take its message under advisement. Rarely do we find **the truth** and **love** coupled together in our experience. There are many who are faithful to speak the truth, but they do so in such a way that they harm whomever they share it with. They become candles attracting moths. The light is there, but, if encountered too closely, only serves to destroy. Truth is shared by these for less-than-noble reasons: to denounce, ridicule, control, etcetera. The truth of God should only be shared within the environment of love. It is like the letter *q* in the English language. *Q* is never used by itself, but is always accompanied by a vowel, most often the letter *u.* Those who would share truth without love only succeed in destroying the message.

On the other hand, there are those who would emphasize love at the expense of truth. Truth can be harsh. It can tell us things we would rather not hear, or reveal things we would rather not see. There can be a negativity with truth that encourages us to downplay it in favor of love. But love without truth is an empty sentiment. It has no base or strength. Truth without love is a tyrant. Love without truth is a lie.

ENDNOTES

[1]John Wesley, *The Works of John Wesley*, vol. 10, 3rd. ed. (Grand Rapids, Michigan: Baker Book House, 1986), pp. 188–201. A covenant is a solemn promise made binding by a pledge or vow, which may be either a verbal formula or a symbolic action. Covenant often referred to a legal obligation in ancient times. In Old Testament terms, the word was often used in describing the relationship between God and His chosen people, in which their sacrifices of blood afforded them His atonement for sin, and in which their fulfillment of a promise to live in obedience to God was rewarded by His blessings. In New Testament terms, this relationship (the new covenant) was now made possible on

a personal basis through Jesus Christ and His sacrifice of His own blood.

[2]Samuel Rolles Driver, Alfred Plummer, and Charles Augustus Briggs, eds., *The International Critical Commentary, Ephesians, Colossians* (Edinburgh: T. and T. Clark, 1991), p.112.

[3]The Targums is a compilation of interpretive translations of the Scriptures recorded over time by the Jews. These writings were more flexible and expressed more of a paraphrase than a literal translation. They were a reflection of how the passage was understood by the people of that time.

7

LIVING NO LONGER AS GENTILES

Ephesians 4:17-32

A s with most people, one man was fond of reminiscing about his childhood, recalling a number of memories, especially of his father. Not being a Christian man, his father had attended a revival service with the family in a small Nazarene church. While there, the Spirit of God spoke, and he opened his heart to the Lord for salvation. Upon returning home, the father, convicted of some of his previous habits, went to his large rack of pipes and tobacco humidor and, without a moment's hesitation, threw them all away. His son estimated it was a rather expensive sacrifice. But what impressed him long after his father's death was the clean and complete break his father made from his previous lifestyle.

Paul continues the practical application of the Christian lifestyle that he began in our last section. Having impressed the importance of unity among believers, he now moves to a more personal consideration of individual behavior. In a command that would call his readers to deny themselves, Paul argues that since they are children of light, they should no longer lead lifestyles like the Gentiles. As his readers were Gentiles, he is challenging them to become radically different. This attempt would be made possible as they were willing to gain victory over their sensual appetites, which were normally given freedom and indulgence.

In perhaps his strongest expression in this letter he instructs the readers that a clean and complete change must be made from their previous lifestyle as Gentiles. Twice he has described their previous condition, as a contrast to what God had done in their redemption (see Ephesians 2:1, 11-12). Now it is not in relation to what God had done, but what they must be willing to do: . . . **you must no longer live as the**

Gentiles do . . . (4:17). This is no mere suggestion, but a command. Paul makes a threefold emphasis: **I tell you this, and insist on it in the Lord, that you must . . .** (4:17a). We hear the authority of Paul, an apostle of Christ to the church. These are not his words, but Christ's. This is not an optional exercise for his readers, neither then nor today. Those who have been made new creations in Christ must live as new creations, and not as they once were. However, they must be careful they do not limit Paul's instruction to just behavior. His concern runs deep, into the very essence of who we are as people. He speaks of our foundational starting point with Christ, revealing the fallacy of our former view and the superiority of our present experience.

1. THE GENTILE LIFE DESCRIBED 4:17-19

What is foundational in Paul's description of the Gentiles is his consideration of their starting point in relationship to life and God, namely their thoughts. How do the unconverted think, and how do these thoughts influence their values and behavior? The thought process that Paul is concerned with is what influences his readers in their understanding of God. To appreciate this, it helps to realize that any attempt by humankind to think of God is limited at best, just as Paul said regarding the Gentiles.

Anything we ever know about the reality of God comes to us by way of revelation. It is only as God reveals himself to us that we see Him as He intends. When we endeavor to think of God on our own, we define Him in our image. Without revelation, humankind is left to its own limited understanding of God and this world. The reason for this, in Paul's view, is twofold: We have a hardened heart of sin, and this sinful heart causes us to live in ignorance of spiritual things. This passage sounds much like Paul's description of humanity in Romans 1:18-32, where he explains that the world is on a continual spiral downward into deeper depravity.

One result of the Gentiles' living in this way is that they **live . . . in the futility of their thinking. . . . are darkened in their understanding and separated from the life of God** (Eph. 4:17-18a). **Futility** of thinking is an empty, wasted effort. It is an attempt to discern the undiscernible. What we know of God must first come from God. Our understanding of Him is the result of His revelation to us, and not our own comprehension of Him. To think our way about God only results in the humanistic, pagan idolatry that has been devised over the centuries with various cultures. Since we can develop no true thoughts of God, our endeavors to do so result in empty activity.

To be **darkened in their understanding** (4:18) expresses the unclear vision they have of truth without God revealing it. Darkness is the absence of light. It is nothingness, awaiting something to come and fill its void with substance. Used in relation to our minds, without the truth being revealed, we have only the darkness of our own ignorant concepts to fill their void—ignorant concepts as illustrated by the mythologies of Greece and Rome. They vainly attempted to explain reality with human terms. The same is true today in our humanistic mentality whenever we attempt to explain the workings of life by our own perception. Even the Christian does not have complete clarity in understanding the truths of God, as Paul expressed to the Corinthian church, "Now we see but a poor reflection" (1 Cor. 13:12).

To be **separated from the life of God** (Eph. 4:18) is the truth that we can never reach God through our mental processes. Our greatest thoughts are God's most simple. We tend to distort both His image and our own, making Him less than He really is, while elevating ourselves above our true station. The Gentiles, like all people without God, attempted to reason their way through life. This resulted in an empty, darkened, estranged experience.

A second area of the Gentiles' experience resulting from their hardened hearts relates to their sensual activities, or what the New International Version translates as **sensuality** (4:19). The picture is unsurprisingly perverse. Sensuality and religion are closely related within us. This close tie can be seen in the ancient religions which were extremely sexual in their orientation. There is an obvious spiritual hunger within humankind, but since it is so closely related to our sexual drive, the two desires become confused. By observation alone, it appears that the more godless a society becomes, the more sexually active and perverse the people grow. This is an act of compensation, attempting to pacify the inner spiritual needs with a sexual substitute. Since sexuality fails to meet the spiritual need, we are never satisfied, driving our desires to a more aggressive immorality. This is not to suggest that sexuality is merely a perverted spirituality. Both the spiritual and sexual appetites within humankind are normal and necessary. Their perversion results whenever we attempt to substitute one for the other.

In Paul's description, this substitution has taken place as they gave themselves over to sensuality instead of spirituality. Their hunger drove them to a wide variety of base acts, which only left them hungering for more. The most obvious influence to the region was the worship of Artemis (see Acts 19:24-29), whose temple and worship was a source of great pride at Ephesus. The temple was considered to be one of the seven wonders of the world. Artemis was the Greek equivalent of the Roman goddess Diana. Though served by eunuchs as her priests, she was worshiped by a fertility cult which exercised a number of perverse practices. No doubt this is the challenge Paul is addressing to his Gentile readers. Their background led them to be dependent upon their own creative, human thinking, rather than God's revelation to develop their understanding of deity. Their inner hunger for God, confused with the similar drive for sex, became a confused expression of worship.

2. THE CHRISTIAN LIFE CONTRASTED 4:20-24

Worship and perversion were considered one and the same to the darkened and ignorant Gentiles. But Paul speaks against this whole line of thinking by reminding his readers, **You, however, did not come to know Christ that way** (Eph. 4:20). Their understanding of Christ had come from above, not from within. Their relationship to Christ was to be spiritual, not sensual. As Christianity stood at the opposite end of the spectrum from the pagan religions, so must the life of Christ's followers.

At this point, Paul once again expresses some uncertainty due to his lack of familiarity with his readers. Just as he was unsure in 3:2-6 of their understanding of His ministry, he now suggests uncertainty about the full experience of their own conversion and subsequent training. **Surely you heard of Him and were taught in Him in accordance with the truth that is in Jesus** (4:21). With this uncertainty, it appears Paul expected them to have a particular awareness about the new change in their lives as a result of their conversion and discipleship. He lists three specifics that they "surely" had been taught: (1) with regard to their former way of life, they were to **put off your old self, which is being corrupted by its deceitful desires** (4:22); (2) regarding their way of thinking they were **to be made new in the attitude of your minds** (4:23); and (3) in relation to their nature, they were to **put on the new self, created to be like God in true righteousness and holiness** (4:24). A parallel passage is found in Colossians 3:5-10.

The contrast is stark between the **old self** and the **new self** (Eph. 4:22, 24). The old self is being **corrupted** while the new self is being **created.** The influence upon the old self is its **deceitful desires,** while the influence of the new self is the **true righteousness and holiness** of God. The use of the adjective **true** implies a contrast being made with that which is false. False righteousness and holiness would be a lifestyle reflective of their lewd and perverse worship. It has been said that people will never rise above the leader that leads them. It must be equally true that our morality and purity will never exceed that of the god we follow. If our ideal of morality is only a self-perceived deity who acts like us, or at least accepts our indiscretions, our moral direction will only sink to the depth of depravity determined by our own lusts. But if our inspiration comes from a revelation beyond ourselves, from God who is holy and perfect, then His standard will lift us to a new height. This, however, will require a new attitude in our thinking—one that does not develop God in our image, but rather allows Him to reveal His image to us.

In a similar passage (see Romans 12:2), Paul exhorts his readers to no longer conform to the pattern of this world, but to be transformed by the renewing of their minds. The word he uses for "transformed" is the same from which we get the modern term *metamorphosis*. This is a word describing the miraculous change that takes place inside a cocoon of a moth or butterfly. It enters the cocoon as a caterpillar, and emerges as an adult species. The change within the cocoon is profound, influencing each part of the insect in its entirety. What emerges is radically new and different from what went in. The analogy holds true for the Christian: we may come to God very much in our old nature, but it must be with a desire to be changed from what we are to what we shall be. This is not a rearranging of attributes, or simply a dusting off and fixing up. This is a complete and total change wrought within the individual which renews and transforms from the inside out, into the holy image of God.

3. THE SPECIFIC COMMANDS GIVEN 4:25-32

A parishioner caught up in the inspiring words of his pastor shouted out a number of "amens" to affirm the truths being proclaimed. But, as the minister became more specific in what was meant and how the truths should be applied to daily life, the man grew more and more quiet, until he sat silent in his pew. Noticing the difference, his pastor asked him at the door why he had lost his enthusiasm for the message. The man answered hesitantly, "Because you quit preaching and began to meddle."

In the remaining eight verses of this section of Ephesians 4, Paul quits preaching and "begins to meddle." He has preached a number of profound truths relating generally to the need for change in the minds and morals of his people. Now he minces no words, and speaks specifically regarding their behavior as it is lived out in everyday life. He speaks of some very practical and specific expressions in the Christian life that reflect a life different than that of the Gentiles.

Paul commands that the person in Christ must **put off falsehood and speak truthfully** (4:25). Falsehoods are a contradiction to Christ and His way. Some people lie so much that their own dogs would not answer their call. Lying is the sign of a darkened mind, of a person who cannot deal with reality or assume responsibility. We express outwardly what is happening within. But Paul emphasizes the severity of the wrong by reminding the readers of their interrelatedness to the Body. Lying damages us and our relationships. Let everything else be proven false in the world, save the statements and claims of the children of God.

Paul tells them that the person in Christ must be in control of his or her anger. **Anger** (4:26) has been a confusing expression for the Christian. It is often seen and denounced as a sinful trait that should be erased from the believer. We attempt to rename it by more spiritual terms such as "righteous indignation" or "spiritual fervor." In reality, we cannot empty ourselves from anger anymore than we can empty ourselves of any of the other emotions God has created in us by which we relate to the world.

Anger is not a sin, though it can be used in a sinful way. Paul notes this distinction when he quotes Psalm 4:4: **In your anger do not sin** (Eph. 4:26a). The prohibition is on the improper use of the emotion, and not the emotion itself. Anger is basically a defense mechanism built into us to protect us in life. Without it, we would be overtaken in no time. The trick to anger is to know when its expression is appropriate or sinful. One way to make the discernment is by distinguishing between its constructive and destructive effects.

A constructive effect of anger is when it corrects a wrong. People who are opposed to certain social issues will find that anger is a motivation to speak out, protest, and actively become involved in the process that will bring change for the better. A spouse or a parent unhappy with a behavior may endure it until moved with dissatisfaction to protest and demand a change. Anger expressed out of genuine concern and in constructive ways that bring about positive change is appropriate. However, those expressions of anger that result in harm or destruction are not appropriate. If our anger is destructive, then we have sinned. If our correction of a child results in abuse, we have sinned. If a disagreement with our spouse or other person results in physical harm, we have sinned. If our protest of an abortion clinic results in the loss of life, we have sinned. The Christian is one who recognizes the necessity of anger and exercises it appropriately as the tool it was created to be.

Paul mentions one improper use of anger—anger that is held onto over an extended period of time: **Do not let the sun go down while you are still angry** (4:26b). While anger may be productive, extended anger is destructive. Grudges, an unforgiving spirit, and noncooperative attitudes are all expressions of confused anger. Anger allowed to fester over time becomes bitterness. Bitterness influences the entirety of a person's life. By holding on to the anger, we endeavor to hurt the person continually until we are satisfied. The problem is that we are never satisfied. Bitterness is like an ocean. No matter how much water flows into it, it never gets enough. No matter how many times we express our anger in a grudge, it will never be enough. Eventually, the anger destroys the one harboring it and, therefore, it is a sin.

Grudges and bitterness are divisive tools used often by Satan. One of his traits is to cause a schism or division among God's people. Schisms follow the military dictum, "Divide and conquer." Unforgiving anger becomes the cutting horse of this demon. Like a skilled cowboy, the angry person rides this bitterness in and out of the church, separating people from each other. In some cases, the angry person may single out an individual and drive him or her away from the herd. Other times, the person will cleave the group in two, or take smaller groups away so he or she can allow anger to slowly devour them—**Do not give the devil a foothold** (4:27). The sobering truth that embittered people need to hear is that their actions are not of God, no matter how justified they may feel. It is the beginning toehold by which Satan scales the walls to enter into the fold (see John 10:1).

"Idle hands are the Devil's workshop!" This age-old adage appears to be the expression of Paul's next instruction: **He who has been stealing must steal no longer** (Eph. 4:28). Stealing is an expression of non-productivity that takes away from the person and the group as a whole. Work was important to Paul. He was a tentmaker and used the craft to supply his needs while in ministry (see Acts 18:3). He held a strong work ethic by expressing in his letter to the Thessalonians the necessity of employment for our daily needs: "If a man will not work, he shall not eat" (2 Thess. 3:10). Paul attests to his own hard work (see 1 Corinthians 4:12) and, although in a more figurative context, claims the right of a worker to receive his wage (see 1 Timothy 5:18; see also Luke 10:7; Leviticus 19:13b). To steal is to shirk one's responsibility in life. It takes away the usefulness of the individual, causing deep damage to the inner person. It also takes away one's ability to help others. Those who can be productive should be, so that they can aid those who are unable.

Unwholesome talk is unacceptable (Eph. 4:29). We are not even to allow it out of our mouths. Many things can come under this term. Quite often we see it as profanity or vulgarity and strive to prevent its use. However, there is a broader application than this if we are to consider the opposite of Paul's parallel exhortation, **but only what is helpful for building others up** (4:29). In this verse, **unwholesome** means anything that does not build up others. Now the words slander, gossip, ridicule, insult, and mocking become relevant. The issue with Paul is not so much what is said as how it affects those who hear it. Words can be a positive force or a destructive blow. Jesus warns us of the misuse of words against one another. To call a person a fool results in the danger of hell's judgment (see Matthew 5:22). Jesus also warns that every careless word uttered in our lifetime will be brought before us so as to make us accountable (see Matthew 12:36). Our conversations then should be influenced by the needs of others, what they need to hear to help build them up and encourage them. People should benefit, not suffer, from our conversations. The old teaching, "If you have nothing good to say, then say nothing at all," if followed today, could quite possibly plummet our world into silence.

Paul's final admonition, **Do not grieve the Holy Spirit of God** (Eph. 4:30a), is almost a repetition of his admonition against the sinful use of anger. Everything that results from abusive anger can result in the potential grieving of the Holy Spirit. Again, Paul makes reference to the Spirit's task as a seal to the believer for their redemption just as he stated earlier in 1:13-14. But now he warns that certain activities will bring pain to this Spirit, grieving Him as a result of our actions. We are to get rid of all negative, sinful expressions such as **bitterness, rage and anger, brawling and slander, along with . . . malice** (4:31). In their place, we are to **be kind and compassionate to one another, forgiving each other, just as in Christ God forgave** us (4:32).

Paul's strong commands to make a clean break from our past lifestyles and character is an undeniable duty and responsibility before God. Our task is not an option, but a requirement. It is not to be a change on the surface, but one that affects the thoughts that inspire us and the urges that drive us. It requires us to shift from relying on *our* thoughts of God, to receiving and relying on *God's revelation* of himself. It requires us to refuse a sensual substitute for the reality of worshiping a holy and righteous God. It is a metamorphosis that is evident in our outward expressions as our daily actions relate His beauty in the lives we live.

138

8

LIVING A LIFE OF LOVE

Ephesians 5:1-7

Few themes enjoy as much popularity in our world today as love. Numerous songs, books, plays, and movies are written with this theme in mind. Its popularity suggests how important this emotion is to us. We need love in our lives, both as an experience and as an expression. Paul is concerned that his readers' expression of love be found appropriate.

The Greeks were very interested in the expression of love—so much so that they had four different words for it that distinguished its various expressions. *Storge,* though not found in the Bible, refers to the affection one might hold for a nonhuman object or animal. For instance, the emotion one feels toward a pet may be described as *storge. Eros* is romantic love and is best understood by our modern term *erotic.* It is the attraction stimulated primarily by a sexual desire. *Phileo* refers to brotherly or sisterly love. *Agape,* though broad in meaning, can best be understood as perfect love, or that which is expressed by God. *Agape* is the word used most often for "love" in the Scriptures, and is the word Paul writes in his command, **Live a life of love** (Eph. 5:2a).

1. BEING IMITATORS OF GOD 5:1-2

It has been said that imitation is the greatest compliment one can give to another. We are rarely interested in imitating individuals we despise or discount. It is the heroes of life that we most wish to emulate, whether as a child with a bed-sheet cape, or as a young adult patterning after a parent. In the phrase, **Be imitators of God,** the Greek word Paul uses for imitators (*mimeitai;* Eph. 5:1a) is one the people of Ephesus would relate to easily. It is the same word from which we derive our modern term *mimic*. The Greek plays were presentations in which actors would put on masks of heroes and gods, and portray them to their audience. Obviously, those who could best express their roles were acclaimed the better actors. Paul begins this passage by exhorting us to portray a likeness of God.

Actually, Paul's command is unique in several ways. It is the only time in all of the New Testament that this expression is specifically made. Patterning after the likeness of God is implied in many ways throughout Scripture, but not in so direct a command. Paul shares commands for imitation in other passages, but not of God. To the Corinthians, his exhortation was for his "children" (converts) to imitate him (1 Cor. 4:16). Later in that same letter (11:1) he encourages the Corinthians to "follow my example, as I follow the example of Christ." In writing to the Thessalonians, Paul expands his list of people to be imitated to include not only himself, but his companions as well (2 Thess. 3:7, 9). In 1 Thessalonians 1:6, he commends his readers for doing this very thing, as well as the imitation of "God's churches in Judea" (1 Thess. 2:14).

The imitation of God is influenced by our relationship with Him. As suggested above by Paul to the Corinthian church, their spiritual relationship to Paul should be a motive for their emulation of him. Now, the ultimate command is given. We who are **dearly loved children** of God (Eph. 5:1) should reciprocate this love by imitation.

Love that results in imitation is a very natural thing, although it is not always for our best. There is a story of a father whose young boy loved him very much. The father became involved in some rather inappropriate behavior at a local gathering spot. One wintry day, he began to make his way to this haven of iniquity to enjoy its favors. As he trudged through the snow, he heard a small voice from behind, pleading with him to wait. Turning, he saw his boy coming through the snow leaping from one footprint to another. The boy cried out, "How can I follow you if you take such big steps!" Realizing the wrong of his life, the father went back to his son, picked him up and carried him home, never to walk to that place again. Our motivation for being imitators of God is the result of His love expressed to us. Much like the child, this emotion compels us to pursue our Father in whatever the circumstance.

Paul summarizes the means of achieving this imitation by giving the command to **live a life of love** (5:2a). As I have discussed previously, Paul uses the Greek word for "walk" *(peripateo)* which carries the figurative meaning to **live** or direct your life. Since God loves us, this love should be evident in our own lives, expressed in all that we do. It should influence us into the unmistakable image of God, as we make ourselves available to love's life-changing influence. The example of this openness to God's love is found in Jesus Christ, His Son. We should live this life of love **just as Christ loved us** (5:2). The ultimate expression of this love is found in Christ's sacrificial death on our behalf (see John 15:13). Paul says that Christ **gave himself up for us as a fragrant offering and sacrifice to God** (Eph. 5:2). Paul uses two Greek words to describe this sacrifice of Jesus: **offering,** which is *prosphoran;* and **sacrifice,** which is *thusian.*

Prosphoran refers more specifically to the gift that was brought to the Temple for the sacrifice, while *thusian* refers more to the act of sacrifice itself. This twofold expression illustrates well our response to God's love that will result in our imitation of His likeness. As *phosphoran* suggests, we must be willing to see ourselves as a sacrifice given totally to God, for His pleasure. The sacrifice of objects required their death and destruction. One did not bring a lamb to the Temple with the intention of returning home with it. The sacrifice was consecrated and surrendered to God. We will never obtain a likeness of God until we become totally surrendered to Him. We sing this truth often in our churches: "But we never can prove the delights of His love until all on the altar we lay."[1]

Thusian, the second reference to sacrifice, relates to what should be the end result of our efforts. Originally, *thusian* related to the smoke resulting from the sacrifice, which produced an aroma. The basic understanding of the primitive mind, in regard to sacrifice, was that it became the means by which earth-dwelling humans presented their gifts to heaven-dwelling gods. No matter how many times they would throw a slaughtered ram into the air, it always seemed to find its way back down. But, once burnt with fire, this same offering was transformed from its solid state into a vapor that ascended into heaven, to be enjoyed by the deity to whom it was offered.

Like the aromatic smoke that arises from the altar, so should our actions and attitudes be to God. What He receives from our lives should only be that which is pleasant and well pleasing to Him. Our surrender and subsequent living should always be seen as an action before God, and thereby tempered with a resolve to make our lives pleasing.

2. REFUSING SIN 5:3-4

Now that he has given the positive ideal of imitating God, Paul begins to address specific expressions that this imitation must not include. Paul's list of prohibitions could be understood as a personal instruction of what individual Christians should refrain from, as well as a corporate lesson on what the church should not allow in its expression.

A necessity for the early church was to determine how it should govern itself, especially in determining what was acceptable behavior and what was not. Several examples of its experiences in this area can be gleaned from Scripture. Jesus taught that anyone having a problem with an offending individual should take a multistep approach toward its correction. After a series of personal confrontations with witnesses present, the final attempt involved confrontation by the church. If the person was still unwilling to be compliant, they were to treat him as an outcast (see Matthew 18:15-17). In the very early days of the church's existence, we find a judgment against dishonesty pronounced by the Holy Spirit upon Ananias and his wife, Sapphira, who endeavored to lie to the church regarding the actual price of a piece of property sold (see Acts 5:1-11). By example, and coupled with Peter's strong statement of disfavor for the act, the Holy Spirit struck them both dead.

In several places, Paul exercises his authority regarding unbecoming behavior in the church. To those who proclaim a false or corrupted gospel, he proclaims an eternal condemnation (see Galatians 1:8-9). Regarding an incident of immorality within the Corinthian fellowship, he proclaims judgment, commanding that the guilty man be handed over to Satan so that his sinful nature might be destroyed (see 1 Corinthians 5:1-5). Later, in Paul's second letter to this troubled church, we find a third ruling expressed by Paul, quite possibly in reference to the incestuous man, calling for the complete forgiveness and comfort of the individual so that he is not overcome by sorrow (see 2 Corinthians 2:6-8).

Paul is specific in stating that inappropriate actions are not to be tolerated. Ephesians 5:3 expresses this strongly by not allowing even a hint of these acts to be found within the church. Verse 4 is more general in its prohibition, but no less accepting: **Nor should there be. . . .**

The church has always been challenged with the responsibility to police its ranks. Realizing that we deal with a fallen people at various levels of regeneration, it can be difficult to determine when grace should be applied or judgment pronounced. The pendulum swings broadly here, and the church has been found guilty of both excesses. If the church becomes too restrictive, attempting to respond to every infraction or unchristian expression, it soon loses its ability to reach a world lost in sin. The church becomes like a hospital that refuses the sick in order to keep its rooms sterile and clean. On the other hand, if the church becomes too lenient, and does not deal with sinful behavior, it loses its identity and influence with the world it desires to change. If the world can make no distinction between itself and the church, of what merit is the church's message? This extreme makes the church a hospital that fills its rooms with the sick, but fails to heal because it cannot determine who is diseased and who is healthy.

The church must maintain a healthy balance between expectation and reality. If it has no goal of holiness to challenge the people, and no sense of relating to the human situation, it will always err to one extreme or the other. Its determinations need to be buffered by grace and love. Its judgments must take into account the desire of the heart. Its understanding must be conditioned by an awareness of ignorance. In everything, the church must be buoyed up by the influence and power of God's love.

Paul begins his list of inappropriate behavior by bringing together three examples in 5:3: **sexual immorality, impurity,** and **greed.** He lists these same vices in 1 Corinthians 5:9-10 as well, except he replaces "impurity" with "robbers." **Immorality** (Eph. 5:3) is expressed by the Greek word *porneia,* from which we get our modern word *pornographic.* It refers, in a general sense, to any sexual indulgence outside marriage. We have little difficulty in understanding this idea today, since we have the benefit of two thousand years of Christian influence in our present moral definitions. However, Paul's lesson may have found some rather surprised readers in his day.

The sexual sins among the pagans of Paul's day were a little more limited. Incest would have been considered wrong, as Paul expressed to the Corinthian church in 1 Corinthians 5:1. But other practices were determined more by gender than by act. There was a discrepancy between what was allowed for men and what was expected of women. For example, adultery was prohibited to the wife, but not to the husband, unless he was involved with another man's wife. The infraction was seen not so much as an immoral behavior as it was an infraction against the rights of another man.[2]

Fornication was accepted as a natural experience. Cicero expressed this viewpoint when he wrote contesting anyone who would prohibit a man from having intercourse outside marriage: "He is at variance not only with the license of what our age allows, but also from the customs and concessions of our ancestors. When indeed was this not done? When did anyone ever find fault with it? When was such permission denied? When was it that which is now lawful not lawful?"[3]

One could understand from this quotation how controversial and radical the Christian faith would have been within the pagan world. However, Paul was not willing to give in to popular practice or belief. It was not the opinion of humankind that was important here, but rather the will of God. In this regard, the beginning stages of the dismantling of our double standards can be seen. Christianity has always seen the equality of men and women with regard to morality. We have just been slow in living it.

Impurity is expressed by the Greek word *akatharsia* (Eph. 5:3). It is the negative form of the word *katharsia,* which means "clean or pure." By adding an *a* to the beginning of a word, the Greek people made it negative, expressing the complete lack of what the original word meant. Thus, *akatharsia* literally means "the lack or absence of cleanliness or purity." The word is rather broad in its application, and seems to take in whatever is left over beyond *pornea.*

We must be careful in considering the word **greed** (5:3) that we do not make its definition too narrow by modern understanding. Usually related to wealth or property today, the Greek word for **greed** was often used in a more general sense in Paul's day. This word, *pleonezia,* expressed the idea of being insatiable, not being able to be filled or satisfied. When applied to all our experiences in life, it becomes especially alarming when related to immorality and impurity. The sense of Paul's statement seems to be that not only are the immoral and unclean acts of humankind not to be tolerated, but our insatiable appetite for these should not be allowed to go uncontrolled.

Paul explains why: **Because these are improper for God's holy people** (Eph. 5:3b). Again, the radical nature of this statement might escape us in our day and age, since we are so far removed from the common practices of the pagan people of Paul's day. We need to remember that a "holy person" could very well have been a male or female prostitute in one of the temples of their pagan gods. A hearty appetite for perverse sexual experiences could have been interpreted as a very holy lifestyle, given the right situations. In keeping with his exhortation in 4:17, to "no longer live as the Gentiles," Paul continues to prohibit any suggestion of pagan lifestyle and worship that could become confused with the Christian faith. Such actions might have been popular before Christ came into their lives, but they could no longer even be hinted at within the church.

It is interesting that this entire prohibition comes to us in the context of love. It is because we are loved of God, and because Jesus Christ loved us by dying for us, that we are to become imitators of God and not enter into immoral acts, feeding our insatiable hungers. Yet, it has become ever more prevalent today to validate our immorality by the excuse of love's influence. The teenage couple driven by their passions and infatuations become intimately involved because they "love" each other. The adulterous individual often explains his or her actions by claiming to no longer love the spouse, and to have found a new love in a new companion. Perhaps the real problem which faces our society, with regard to our immoral behavior, is not so much a lack of love, but rather a confusion about with whom this love is to be expressed. If our love is first directed toward God, all of our other excuses fall away. "God's holy people" are those who love God with a whole heart, mind, and soul. Because of this, any perverted expression of love toward others is a perversion of our love for God.

Paul's next list of prohibitions refers mainly to verbal expressions that are not to be a part of the believer's life. The context implies that Paul is now prohibiting from the mouth the same kind of immoral actions that are expressed by the body. **Obscenity, foolish talk or coarse joking** should not be exercised (5:4). The root word Paul uses for **foolish talk** is the same Greek word from which we derive our modern word *moron*. Paul is not prohibiting the good-natured fun that people have with puns or exchanging jests. He is addressing the error that results when such communication takes a downward turn, and uses ideas and situations that are not in keeping with the Christian lifestyle or its expression. After all, if an act or behavior is inappropriate for us to become involved in physically, it is just as inappropriate for us to enter into verbally. This prohibition would again be a particular challenge to the people of Ephesus; a play from that area expressed that it was a common practice of the people of Ephesus to speak in this way.[4]

The opposite behavior of these prohibitions is **thanksgiving** (5:4). This is not to imply that the only thing Christians can converse about is their thankfulness for God and His salvation. Instead, Paul is setting the perspective so we remember that instead of being involved in such sinful practices, we should use our tongues to express thanks for what we have received from Him.

3. REFUSING TO PARTNER WITH THE DISOBEDIENT 5:5-7

Paul shares three things of which his readers **can be sure** (Eph. 5:5) with regard to people who willfully become involved in the wayward behavior discussed above: (1) they have no inheritance in the Kingdom; (2) they are idolaters; and (3) God's wrath comes upon them. Paul's judgment sounds harsh and insensitive. Today, Paul would be denounced for his lack of sensitivity toward the needs of these people and their right to express themselves in these different ways. What we tend to have is an insensitivity toward judgment. We do not like it expressed, so we deny its validity, calling it insensitive and errant, unenlightened and ignorant. But Paul has no apparent reservations about what he is writing, and minces no words. We hear the apostle speaking to the church. His indictment strips the guilty of their inheritance, their God, and His mercy.

Perhaps we can best understand Paul's other statements by considering first his claim that those who are involved in these various acts of immorality are idolaters; **. . . such a man is an idolator . . .** (5:5). His charge appears to be out of place for we would seldom equate sexual immorality with the raising up and worshiping of idols. However, the actions of these people can be considered idolatrous in at least two ways.

First, they are idolatrous because their acts were done in the course of idol worship. As has been mentioned before, idolatry was closely related to sexual expression and experience. Fertility rites were often performed in an attempt to manipulate the god(s) to act on behalf of the worshiper. Thus, what was considered immoral sexual activity in the eyes of the Christian could be understood as a common worship practice at the local temple of Artemis. Their coarse talk and idolic conversation would be unacceptable to God, since it was both morally wrong and broke His first commandment, listed in Exodus: "You shall have no other gods before me" (Exod. 20:3).

Second, their actions are idolatrous because they elevated certain human activity to a level of priority above God. This is an ongoing challenge with Christians today as we endeavor to order our lives so that God is given the uppermost concern. However, there are certain issues that challenge our allegiance to God because we deem them either more desirable or important than obedience to His will. Typically these are activities that deal with our survival or more basic needs. Our appetite for sex can be as compelling and overpowering as our appetite for food.

When what we experience in life takes precedence over what God tells us we should be doing, we have just replaced God with our desire. Now we serve the appetite, and not the Father. The results of replacing God with something else in life is just as much an act of idol worship as any pagan bowing before a wooden figure.

Paul states the grim reality that no one who practices these sins **has any inheritance in the kingdom of Christ and of God** (Eph. 5:5). To hear Paul express that these individuals will be barred from the Kingdom and will be under God's wrath is a sobering reminder of the reality of sin and its influence. So far in the letter, Paul has shared the wonderful news of God's great salvation plan and how it has made possible our inclusion into the Kingdom as children of God and fellow heirs to the Kingdom. As wonderful as this message is, there is the equally important message that those who do not accept this provision will be judged by God and will experience His wrath. We may want to lighten the message, but truth will not allow it. We may want to widen the possibilities, but God's holiness will demand adherence to what is perfect and just. As much as these words become a stern warning to those who would be tempted to enter into these activities or condone their practice in our fellowships, it should be a reminder of the deadly important task of the church to proclaim God's salvation plan to all who are caught up in their idolatry.

Paul's final statement in this passage is a summation of all that he has said: **Therefore do not be partners with them** (5:7). His last word brings us back to an earlier observation brought out by Paul's instructions. The passage was not written just to the individual people of the church, but to the church as a whole. Just as the individuals needed to be discerning and careful, so must the church. Here is Paul's call for the "called-out ones" to maintain this identity. They were to maintain a distinction between themselves and the world around them. By this distinction, the truth would become self-evident above the human foolishness propagated at the local temples.

There is a temptation with love to overlook certain shortcomings in an attempt to assimilate people into a group. There are always areas of difference which are not primary and that can be adapted, but this is not to what Paul is referring. These are the nonnegotiables of human behavior in regard to sexuality. These issues cannot be explained away as a difference in worship preferences or personal opinion. These actions and words are in direct conflict with the person of God, and one's involvement in them contradicts the image we are commanded to imitate. Love for God compels us toward Him and one another. We must be careful in this experience that we do not compromise the original concern by a secondary interest. To paraphrase John Wesley, in matters of doctrine and our faith, we should desire unity. In matters of opinion and preferences, we should express liberty. In all things, we should exercise charity. What Paul has expounded upon in this section are matters of behavior in keeping with the doctrine or beliefs of the church. In these, there can be no compromise.

ENDNOTES

[1]John H. Sammis and Daniel B. Towner, *Trust and Obey: The Singing Church* (Carol Stream, Illinois: Hope Publishing Co., 1985), p. 321.

[2]Leon Morris, *Expository Reflections on the Letter to the Ephesians* (Grand Rapids, Michigan: Baker Books, 1994), p. 156.

[3]Ibid.

[4]Morris, p. 158.

9

LIVING AS CHILDREN OF LIGHT

Ephesians 5:8-14

W hile going to college, I worked as a security guard in an old factory. As no one, except I, worked in the building during the night, all the lights were turned off but for a few small light bulbs suspended by wires far enough apart from one another that you were more in darkness than light. During the summer, the building became a shelter for bats, which added an interesting twist as I walked my rounds.

Moving through the dimness of the long rooms, I would catch sight of movement coming quickly out of the gloom and past me at close proximity. It was unnerving, as you never knew when—or from where—the winged creatures were coming. Needless to say, I came to have an appreciation for each light bulb I passed, as it afforded me a small measure of comfort, illuminating my surroundings.

Perhaps it is our limitations in the dark that make us so uneasy. Equally so, it is these limitations that make the darkness a refuge for those who do things not acceptable to the seeing public. No doubt, this is why we associate good with light, and evil with darkness. As in his prior, ongoing commands for appropriate living, Paul now challenges his readers to live as those whose deeds are made evident by the light. The Christian responsibility is to shun the deeds of darkness and embrace those activities of the light.

1. BEING LIGHTS FOR THE LORD 5:8

In a number of places in Ephesians, Paul makes a distinction between his readers' previous situation with God and their present relationship. In 2:1, he states that they were dead. But in 2:5, Paul says that they have been made alive in Christ. In 2:13, he describes them as being far away, but brought near by Christ. And in 2:15, Paul says they were Gentiles, but are now made into new persons by Christ. In our present passage Paul states, **You were once darkness, but now you are light in the Lord** (5:8a).

Darkness and light have long been used in the figurative sense to describe right and wrong, good and evil, righteousness and unrighteousness. The two Greek words Paul uses, **light** *(phos)* and **darkness** *(skotos),* have been used to reflect these moral contrasts since the time of the early Greeks. In fact, in the Greek mind it was considered the responsibility of a judge to bring the dark deeds to light. *Phos* means literally "light," but figuratively it describes life, salvation, happiness, and righteousness. *Skotos* means literally "darkness," but figuratively it describes the opposite of *phos.* Darkness is the arena of evil, where sin and wrong are performed. Light is the arena of all that is good, and reveals the wrongs found in darkness.

The Old Testament described light as an attribute of God. It is His garment (see Psalm 104:2). His presence was indicated by light (see Exodus 13:21; Psalm 89:15; Daniel 2:22). In fact, He is the origin of light that shines out from Him (see Psalm 4:6; 44:3). To humankind, light is salvation (see Psalm 27:1), which is missing among the ungodly. They grope in the darkness because their light goes out, or is taken away from them (see Job 12:5; 18:5; 38:15).

In the New Testament, the disciples are described as light bearers as they reveal God to the world. By Jesus' own words, He describes them as "the light of the world." They were to let their light shine so that the world could see their good deeds resulting in the glorification of God (see Matthew 5:14-16). Their anticipation for the returning Christ included having their lamps lit (see Luke 12:35). It is the Gospel of John that develops the theme of light and darkness the most. John described Jesus as "the true light that gives light to every man" (John 1:9). Jesus was life, and this life became the light of all humankind (see John 1:4). But even though this light (revelation) shone from Him, the people who dwelt in darkness did not understand it (see 1:5). Light was therefore the nature of Jesus. He did not reflect it, or look like the light—He *was* the light. Even Jesus, warning His disciples of His upcoming death, encouraged them to "walk while you have the light." By doing so, they would put their trust in the light and become "sons of light" (John 12:35-36). In his first epistle, John shares the message he has heard with his readers that "God is light; in Him there is no darkness at all." If we claim to walk with God, yet live in darkness, we lie. But if we walk in the light as God is in the light, then we indeed have fellowship which results in our purification from sin (see 1 John 1:5-7).

Another interesting development regarding light and darkness comes from a reference outside the Bible—a writing known as "The War Scroll" from the Dead Sea Scrolls. The Dead Sea Scrolls are a compilation of scrolls and pieces of writings done by a Jewish sect known as the Essenes, who lived in an area northwest of the Dead Sea, in the village of Qumran. These individuals lived from roughly 100 B.C. until A.D. 68, writing a number of enlightening pieces of literature, which they stored in clay jars and hid in caves. The Essenes were a very strict, separatist group who emphasized a pure and holy lifestyle in preparation for the coming of the Messiah. The War Scroll describes a battle between the "sons of light," who are described as Jews from the tribes of Levi, Judah, and Benjamin, and the "sons of darkness," who are the armies of Edom, Moab, Ammon, Philistia, and Assyria. The scroll assures the reader of victory for the sons of light as it describes the plans for a holy battle for God.[1]

Paul's description of the unsaved as being in **darkness** (Eph. 5:8) is very much in keeping with the biblical theme. But his expression is not to reveal the change that has been wrought within these people, but to command them, since they are children of light, to **live as children of light** (5:8b). After all, as he asks in 2 Corinthians 6:14, "What fellowship can light have with darkness?" Again, we find Paul using the Greek word *peripateo* ("walk") in its figurative form meaning "to live" or so regulate one's life.

We find a threefold message expressed in this command. On one hand, it is a personal exhortation for each reader to assume responsibility to live appropriately. On the other hand, Paul is speaking to the church with regard to what is expected of it as the body of Christ. Another application is Christianity's expression to the world. As Christians take seriously the Lord's command to allow their lights to shine within the darkness, they will impact the darkness which surrounds them. In this way, Paul's exhortation to expose the "dark deeds" (see Ephesians 5:11) relates to those deeds done within the fellowship as well as without.

2. MANIFESTING THE FRUITS OF LIGHT 5:9

Living as children of light required the recognition of the **fruit of the light** (Eph. 5:9), which comes from living in the light. There are three fruits listed: **goodness** *(agathosune),* **righteousness** *(dikaiosune),* and

truth *(aleitheia).* This reference reminds us of Paul's other list of fruits which result from the Spirit's ministry within us (see Galatians 5:22-23). In fact, one variation of this passage found in other early Greek manuscripts attempts to replace the word for **light** *(photos;* Eph. 5:9) with the word "Spirit" *(pneumatos).* Even though this variant is found in the oldest existing manuscript we have of Ephesians,[2] scholars believe this was merely an attempt by other scribes to associate Paul's mention of fruit with his Galatian description of the fruits of the Spirit.[3]

The idea of **fruit of the light** helps relate the attributes of this revealed truth of God. But beyond goodness, righteousness, and truth, living as children of light has other evidences: It "makes everything visible" (5:14). Just as a ceiling light reveals the contents of a room when it is turned on, so does the light of God when it is shown within the dark confines of this world. It allows us to see instead of stumble. But this illumination of the world and its deeds is not always positive, for light exposes those things that the world would rather keep hidden. Jesus said that because of this light, there will be nothing done in secret by humankind; it will all be revealed and made known (see Luke 8:17). He also taught that people who desire to do evil will prefer darkness because light reveals their evil deeds. Thus, they will hate the light and stay in the darkness. Those who love truth will live in the light so that what they do may be easily seen, because what they have done, they have done for God (see John 3:19-21).

Thus living as children of light has a positive and negative aspect, depending on the perspective one holds. To the Christian, it is a positive experience as it enlightens one's way through this dark world, revealing the dangers. It is also positive in that its influence in our life, which produces fruit, brings glory to God as we reveal His likeness to the world and one another. The negative aspects are found in its influence upon the world. Being unenlightened and darkened in their understanding (see Ephesians 4:18), those who are not following God, in His light, spurn and react against its shining upon their life and deeds.

When my son was small, he did not like his bedroom light to be turned on when he was first awakened. The uncomfortable feeling he experienced while his eyes adjusted to the brightness would cause him to cry out, "You're burning my eyes out!" The same is true in the moral world. It is no wonder that the church often finds itself at odds with the world over issues. Our revelation of God's righteousness "burns their eyes out." It should be no surprise to us that there is a tendency for the world to react to the church with persecution. Our light is a hurtful thing, because it requires them to adjust from the darkness to the light, as well as condemns them in their activity. Their reaction is defensive. Yet, we seem surprised by this. We errantly believe that our opinions and influences, since they are good, will be readily accepted, as though people are all quasi-Christians and simply need to be reminded of what they really want to know.

Sin makes us dark. It darkens our minds and our hearts. It makes us desire the shadows and gloom of this world, and any infusion of light into this environment will be looked upon as an intrusion. This should not prevent us from being faithful to shine our lights, but it should help to keep us mindful of the controversy our illumination will cause in this world. After all, Jesus told His disciples, "If the world hates you, keep in mind that it hated me first. If you belonged to the world, it would love you as its own" (John 15:18-19a). The fruits of the light have a varied taste. To those in the light, they are sweet and delectable. To those in darkness, they taste bitter and are detestable.

3. FINDING WHAT PLEASES THE LORD 5:10

Paul attaches the command, **and find out what pleases the Lord** (Eph. 5:10), to the end of his exhortation for the people to live as children of light. The appendage does not appear to be an additional exercise, as much as an experienced result of living as children of light. The implication is the enlightenment which results from this lifestyle is a revelation of God's good pleasure upon His children. It is a blessed benefit of holy living to discover what makes our Heavenly Father smile.

Paul, in writing to Timothy, makes special mention of one enlightened action that "pleases the Lord." It is in regard to the proper care of widows by their children and grandchildren. These offspring should live their faith so as to care for these spouseless ladies by supporting them in their needs. This, said Paul to Timothy, "is pleasing to God" (1 Tim. 5:3-4).

The prophet Micah wrestled with our attempts to please God (see Micah 6:6-8). The context deals with sacrifices for our sins and the decision about what the appropriate gift should be. The suggested options include year-old calves, thousands of rams, ten thousand rivers of oil, and one's firstborn. Micah's response is from an entirely unexpected direction. It is not from the aspect of making propitiation for our sins, but rather living a life so that propitiation is not required. According to Micah, God has revealed to us what is good, and what He requires of humankind: to act justly, to love mercy, and to walk humbly with God. The messages of Paul and Micah seem to be the same. What is pleasing and good to God is not the exercise of our sacrifice, but of His righteousness in our lives. It is not the constant return for deliverance from habitual and continued unrighteousness, but the outward daily exercise of that image of God that enlightens the world. True, we need always remember that we are people who tend toward sin, and that confession is often a part of our spiritual lives. However, what pleases God is a life lived in holiness before Him and the world, as we reveal His glory and help those stumbling in darkness to see.

4. AVOIDING AND EXPOSING DARKNESS 5:11-14

Paul now approaches the opposite side of his command by stressing what living as children of light does not involve: **Have nothing to do with the fruitless deeds of darkness** (Eph. 5:11a). The obvious understanding would imply that life in darkness is no longer an option. However, this leaves the church with the challenge of how exactly this command is to be followed. After all, the church finds itself established in the midst of a darkened world. The people we are to be reaching dwell in darkness. Their activities are those that work within and are hidden by darkness. So how does the church do its work and still refuse darkness?

Some have interpreted this as complete separation from the world. The darkness is kept well away from the people who inhabit the fellowship. The light is contained and not allowed to shine out to the lost, for fear that it will be adulterated by their activities. This was apparently the attitude of the Pharisees of Jesus' time in regard to the sinners of society. They kept themselves away from the sinful so as to maintain their purity. Jesus was just the opposite and caused confusion by His actions. Instead of being separate from them, He fellowshiped with them, entering their homes and eating at their tables. Matthew 9:10-13 illustrates Jesus' activity, as He ate in Matthew's home among other characters of questionable ethics and morality. Jesus responded to the Pharisees' displeasure by telling them that His purpose in coming was not to be cloistered with the righteous, but to reach out to the unrighteous. He then referred them to a teaching developed out of the Micah passage cited above—that mercy is preferred above sacrifice.

Discovering what pleases the Lord involves being among the lost of society. Jesus ministered to the needs of the lost and allowed them to touch Him (see Luke 7:36-50). In His High Priestly Prayer found in John 17, Jesus prayed for His disciples, and subsequently the church, that the Father would keep them in the world, but protect them from the Evil One (see John 17:15). The inference is obvious. The place of the church is in the world, ministering to it, revealing God's glory and their sin. Having **nothing to do with the fruitless deeds of darkness** (Eph. 5:11) means exactly that. It is the **deeds** that we are to be separate from, and not the people who commit them. There is no call of God to holiness that is achieved at the expense of the lost. Purity by indifference is phariseeism. Purity which involves ministry to the lost is holiness.

Juxtaposed to Paul's exhortation for separation from deeds of darkness is his command to **expose them** (5:11). Again, we can understand this activity as it relates to both the church itself and the world in which it dwells. Exposing acts of darkness within the fellowship is a theme repeated from 5:3-7. It is the church's responsibility to police itself and maintain an appropriate Christian expression to the world (see notes on 5:1-7). Paul instructs Timothy and Titus that this exposing activity is a particular responsibility of both the teachers and elders within the church (see 1 Timothy 5:20; 2 Timothy 4:2; Titus 1:9, 13; 2:15). These acts of darkness, because of their despicable nature, should not be a part of the fellowship. In fact, Paul instructs, they should not be mentioned within the fellowship. This is not an instruction to prohibit any reference whatsoever; it is profitable for the church to consider what is wrong with society so that it can voice a counter-message.

What Paul is warning against is any mention of the activities as though they hold merit. Just as there should not be a "hint" of immorality among the brethren (see Ephesians 5:3), so there should not be any consideration of the world's darkness that would give it validity. This is a temptation for the church that is often found on the opposite end of the spectrum from the phariseeism discussed above. Instead of separating entirely from the world, the individuals of this persuasion consider those activities of the world they think will enhance the church's ministry. There is a grave danger in this action as many of the things that appear benign are really destructive. After all, even Satan can appear as an angel of light (see 2 Corinthians 11:14).

A normal attraction these worldly influences have is in the area of pragmatics. North American culture places a strong emphasis on the practical. We gravitate to those things that "get the job done." Our dictum is, "If it works, do it." However, there are a number of practical things that may work very well, but whose ethical and moral applications are wanting. Ministry within the church is not a means to an end, but rather the end itself. The "bottom line" for our consideration is not the result of our ministry, but the quality of ministry—quality that reflects the teachings and directions of God. Ministry should result from our discovery of what pleases God, and not what impresses the world.

In the egg industry, eggs being processed for the market pass through what is known as the light test. As the eggs make their way down a conveyer, they pass in front of a strong light that enables an inspector to determine the quality of the egg contained within the shell. If the egg is substandard, it is removed from the conveyer so that it is not passed on to the consumer. Ministry within the church should be given the same scrutiny. Everything we do should be scrutinized by the light of God. Paul tells us that this light exposes everything, the good and the bad. By this, we can make certain that what we are doing in the church is in keeping with lifestyles appropriate for people walking in the light.

Exposing the dark actions of the world is an awesome responsibility that requires a special sensitivity. Light has many abilities and, if used wrongly, can harm instead of help. Light can create a warm, attractive atmosphere, or it can shine with an intensity that causes as much blindness as the dark. It can be an illumination that enables us to see, or a laser strong enough to burn through steel. How we shine the light of God into the world will be determined by our attitudes and motives. If our intent is to denounce and judge the world, the beam will, no doubt, be intense and harmful. If it is to enlighten and attract, then our expression will be one that enables those in darkness to be drawn into the light.

Pilots flying at night enjoy a beautiful experience. They float along above the world, passing over towns and cities with their various arrays of light. To maintain night vision, it is usually quite dark in the cockpit. On some nights, this darkness is increased by the lack of moonlight. But even on those crystal-clear nights, a special challenge exists for the pilot, as it is sometimes difficult to determine the horizon—where the sky meets the ground. House lights at a distance, especially in a rural area, can appear as stars. There are other lights of importance. Towers have bright flashing strobes or blinking red lights that say, "Stay clear." Other planes have lights that say, "Here I am." But out of all these different lights—many blinking, many quite bright—there is one that catches the pilot's eye. It shines white, green, white, then green. This is the beacon located at the airport to which the pilot is flying. Out of all the others, this light beckons home. It calls the pilot out of his or her darkened environment, into the lights of a well-lit runway. This is how our light needs to shine in the world, as an attractive beacon revealing the location of home, a special light that shines a message obvious to those who see it—that, by following it, they too can come in out of the darkness.

Of course, there is another light that at times should be shone, and that is the illumination that dispels the shadows and darkness which would hide evil's activity. Certain buildings have security lights that—if ever there is a question about the activity taking place within an area—can be turned on and will shine with the intensity of daylight. There are times when evil attempts to devise activities that, though seemingly hidden, play havoc with the inhabitants of this world. There is even an attempt at times for these "evil workers" to enshroud their activities in darkness, and then argue that it is really light, so that their activities will be accepted. However, it only takes the brightness of the true light to reveal the inconsistencies of the fake.

Sometimes, the church needs to shine with an intensity that reveals the evil works and methods of the Enemy as he endeavors to hide in the solace of his dark world. However, this light should be shone not only to reveal the Enemy, but also to reveal our God. Too often we expose the evil workings of the world without revealing the alternatives of God's kingdom. The result becomes nothing more than back-door advertising.

This mistake is often made in dealing with our entertainment industry. A movie, song, book, or other medium is produced that the church finds particularly offensive. The church responds by expressing its disfavor and describing what it finds offensive. The producers take this protest and use it to their favor by eliciting interest through controversy. Suddenly what may have been a minor work has become a best-seller. The church has done nothing more than promote what it is against. As we reveal the wrong of this world, it must be done with an emphasis on the right so that it will shine with a greater beauty and attraction than what the world can offer. Otherwise, we defeat our own purpose.

Paul concludes this section by quoting a three-line poem: **Wake up, O sleeper, rise from the dead, and Christ will shine on you** (Eph. 5:14b). The origin of this quote is difficult to determine. There are no verses in Scripture close enough in structure to lay claim as its source. Several explanations have been made, of which the most attractive are those that see the quote coming from a no-longer-existent hymn of the early church. Marcus Barth believes it is an old baptism hymn sung by the witnesses of a baptism as the person was raised up out of the water.[4] This would be in keeping with the testimonial interpretation of baptism as described by Paul in Colossians 2:12. One commentator suggests that the hymn was not so much a baptism song as it was a song used to encourage people away from a life of sin.[5] Perhaps it was the equivalent of our present-day invitation hymns used in concluding a worship service.

Whatever the origin of the work, the message is inspiring to any who would give consideration to the light of God's revelation in this world. It is a call out of our sinful stupor (see Romans 13:11; Proverbs 6:6-11). It is a call to experience the resurrection from our sins. For we were once dead, but God has made us alive in Christ, and has raised us up with Christ (see Ephesians 2:4, 6). It is a call of assurance, that the light that has come into the world will shine upon all who turn to Him. As John wrote, "In him was life, and that life was the light of men" (John 1:4).

ENDNOTES

[1]Charles F. Pfeiffer, *The Dead Sea Scrolls and the Bible* (New York: Weathervane Books, 1969), pp. 77–84.

[2]F. F. Bruce, *The Epistle to the Colossians, to Philemon and to the Ephesians,* The New International Commentary on the New Testament (Grand Rapids, Michigan: Wm. B. Eerdmans Publishing Co., 1984), p. 374.

[3]Bruce M. Metzger, *A Textual Commentary on the Greek New Testament* (London: United Bible Societies, 1975), p. 607.

[4]William Foxwell Albright and David Noel Freedman, eds., *Ephesians 4–6,* vol. 34a, The Anchor Bible (Garden City, New York: Doubleday and Company, Inc., 1974), p. 574.

[5]George Stoeckhardt, *Ephesians,* Concordia Classic Commentary Series, Martin S. Sommer, trans. (St. Louis: Concordia Publishing House, 1952), p. 235.

10

LIVING WISELY

Ephesians 5:15-20

A father and master woodsman was instructing his son in the art of hunting. As they made their way through the woods, the experienced hunter would pause to make an observation of what to seek and what to avoid. Limbs and sticks lying on the ground were to be stepped over so they would not snap underfoot. Stones were to be avoided, as their unevenness could make a rattling noise against one another, or cause the person to stumble. With each step, the foot was to feel what was underneath before the person's weight was allowed fully on it. All the time, the eyes were to look ahead, observing the areas beyond the present position. The father moved smoothly, silently through the woods, continually encouraging his son to be stealthy. His son, not having mastered the skill, stumbled and crunched his way along, seemingly ignorant of all his father was teaching him.

Be very careful . . . how you live (Eph. 5:15a), is literally written by Paul, "Watch how you walk!" Like the hunter, Paul realized the importance of moving with care through this present world, which presents a number of figurative snags and holes to catch and trip up the careless person. His exhortation to be **careful** is expressed by the Greek word *blepo,* which literally means "to watch, to be aware, on the alert." It is the word used to describe Jesus' exhortation to His disciples in Mark's gospel, when He answered their question about when the end of time will come: "Be on guard! Be alert! You do not know when that time will come" (Mark 13:33). Paul's word for **live** *(peripateo)* is the same that he has been using since 4:1, and means to walk or direct one's life. Like a master to his son, Paul encourages a care and discernment in life as we make our way through its various traps and challenges. This lesson is taught by negation, which contrasts what we should not do with what we should do. Our care in walking should not be as unwise, but wise; not as fools, but as discerners of God's will; not as drunkards, but as those filled with the Holy Spirit.

Wisdom is an important quality in the Christian's life. It is what prevents us from making mistakes or committing sin. Previously, as Paul exhorted his readers to walk in light rather than darkness, he now challenges them to live their lives under the influence of wisdom or, more specifically, the revealed and experienced will of God.

1. MAKING THE MOST OF EVERY OPPORTUNITY 5:15-16

Paul says in his Ephesian letter that the care of our steps in this life should be influenced by wisdom; live **not as unwise but as wise** (Eph. 5:15). The contrasting terms are developed by using the same root word *(sophos)* for "wisdom." (The opposite of wisdom, *asophoi,* is used only here by Paul.) Wisdom is understood as the ability to discern the true and right and make sound judgments and decisions based upon this insight. With Paul, this ability is not something developed naturally within humankind, but is the direct result of God's provision to humankind. It is one of the benefits of redemption as God lavishes wisdom upon us in association with other pleasures (see 1:7-8). It is one of Paul's specific requests in his first prayer on behalf of the Ephesians when he asks God to give them the "Spirit of wisdom and revelation" so that they may know Him better (1:17). Wisdom is the understood result of the Father's revelation of the mystery which, although known by God from the very beginning of time, is now being revealed to His followers (see 3:9). Paul's command is closely repeated in Colossians 4:5, though with an emphasis on relating to those outside the faith: "Be wise in the way you act toward outsiders; make the most of every opportunity."

The Old Testament has much to say about wisdom, especially in Proverbs 1 through 9. Here wisdom is described as a woman to be sought after and desired by everyone (see Proverbs 3:13-18; 4:6; 9:1). Those who do so are blessed (see 8:34). Those who find wisdom find life and receive favor from God (see 8:35). In contrast, those who fail to find wisdom harm themselves and love death (see 8:36). Where an exhaustive study of this theme would go beyond our purpose, it is significant to realize that the Old Testament understanding of being wise and being a fool does not necessarily refer to one's intelligence, but to his or her belief in and relationship with God.[1] Psalm 14:1 states, "The fool says in his heart, 'There is no God.'" Atheism is understood to be foolishness. The opposite understanding is that the wise individual believes in God, and benefits from this belief. Paul's command to the Ephesians should speak a word of encouragement today, when so many are doubting the existence of God. "Be careful how you live, not as unbelievers but as believers in God."

The context of Paul's concern for wisdom is in relation to application. Their wise living is to be expressed in their stewardship of time by **making the most of every opportunity** (Eph. 5:16a). This expression is influenced by another observation: **The days are evil** (5:16b).

There is an urgency in Paul's statement. There is an urgency of quality of time, as Paul suggests the immediate need of the Christian's influence in the world, to counter the teachings and influences the world relays to its people. Realizing the error of the world and its society, wisdom should compel Christians to service with the understanding that they may be the only voice in opposition to the status quo. In this spiritual battle in which we are engaged (see Ephesians 6:12-18), we must be willing to take advantage of every opportunity made available to us in order to counter the errors of our world.

There is urgency also because the window of opportunity afforded the church to bear an influence is coming to an end. A sense of this urgency is found in Paul's second letter to Timothy (chapter 3) where he describes the terrible times of the last days. People will be more involved with their sin than they will be interested in God's Word. His instruction to Timothy to have nothing to do with this attitude (see 2 Timothy 3:5), implies his belief that this experience will become a reality within Timothy's lifetime. In chapter 4, he charges Timothy to "preach the word" and be prepared at all times to "correct, rebuke, and encourage," for the time will come when humankind will no longer desire sound doctrine, choosing their own desires instead (see 4:2-3). In a sermon on this same verse, John Wesley described the Christian's attitude as "saving all the time you can for the best purposes; buying up every fleeting moment out of the hands of sin and Satan, out of the hands of sloth, ease, pleasure, worldly business; the more diligently, because the present 'are evil days,' days of the grossest ignorance, immorality and profaneness."[2]

Making the most of every opportunity (Eph. 5:16) requires vigilance in our stand, realizing that the growing evil within the world will demand our time and energies at their ultimate ability, while realizing the narrowing of our opportunity to serve.

2. AVOIDING FOOLISHNESS 5:17

The word **Therefore,** that begins this sentence (Eph. 5:17), implies a summation of the earlier verses regarding walking wisely in this world.

It applies this wise walking with three negative commands and one positive. The first of these negatives is directed toward foolishness.

Paul's negation of foolishness is not an exact repeat of his command for wisdom in 5:15. He uses a different Greek word, which places more emphasis on insight into the wisdom of God than its application. *Aphrones* ("foolish") is the negative form of *phroneo,* which means to think or form an opinion. To be *aphrones* is to be without thought or opinion. Since Paul is concerned with the will of God (**but understand what the Lord's will is** [5:17b]), his exhortation is for his readers to not be without an understanding of God's mind.

Albert Einstein once said, "I want to think the thoughts of God; everything else is details." One of the great blessings made possible to God's people is the disclosure of His design and desire for our world and our lives. This is the task of the Holy Spirit—to reveal God to the believer (see John 16:13-14). Our task must be the open and accurate reception of this expressed will so that it becomes effective in our lives. Where it is the task of the Holy Spirit to make the revelation possible, we must be willing to hear what He has to say.

John Wesley, in a sermon preached on the topic of enthusiasm, gave insight into the discernment of God's will.[3] He cautioned that this is an area of considerable abuse by those who would claim to be led by the Spirit when they really are not. Wesley had reservations about what he called an "extraordinary manner" by which people received the will of God. By this he meant visions, dreams, strong impressions, or sudden impulses of the mind. While he admitted that God revealed himself by these means in times past, and can still do so today, the likelihood of this happening is probably less than we would like to admit. Too often, what we proclaim to be "divine revelation" is merely individual preference. We are misled by pride, imagination, and impulse to proclaim something as important to God which in reality is unworthy of Him.

Wesley's reservation regarding the will of God discerned by the individual believer does not mean he totally denied the possibility of its being known. However, he stated that such discernment would not come from dreams, visions, impressions or impulses, but rather by studying the Bible. Herein can be found what is "the holy and acceptable will of God." In those instances where we cannot find a specific statement from Scripture to enlighten our understanding, Wesley encourages a discernment from the general understanding of God's will for us; namely that "I should be holy and do as much good as I can." This is further determined by one's reason and experience. Experience reveals to us what potential we have for doing good in our present situation. Reason enables us to consider what potential good we can do in the future if we take a certain direction. By considering these, we can determine to an extent what God's will is for our lives.

Overarching this process is the assumption that the Holy Spirit will be doing His part. Where the actual involvement by the Spirit may be somewhat masked and undiscernible, His actions may bring to us a memory of other issues that bear an influence on our consideration. He may place our understanding of things in a stronger light. He may give us a stronger sense of conviction either for or against certain possibilities. Finally, He may bestow upon us a special sense of peace and love that makes one aware of His presence in their decision.

Wesley viewed this understanding toward God's will as the "plain, scriptural, rational way to know." However, he also was aware of how infrequently this approach would be taken in preference to the more emotional and enthusiastic means. He warns us that to do so places one in danger of breaking the third commandment by taking the Lord's name in vain, as it "betrays great irreverence toward Him." In short, Wesley felt it would be better if a person, instead of asking what the will of God is in a particular area, would ask, "How can I know what will provide for me my greatest improvement; and what will make me most useful?" To do so places "the matter on a plain, scriptural issue, and that without any danger of enthusiasm."

Christians today find themselves somewhere between Paul's exhortation to not be ignorant of the will of God, and Wesley's caution to not confound it. There is danger in ignoring either one of these precautions. To not seek God's will allows us to waste many precious years of potential for God's kingdom, to the detriment of everyone we may have influenced for Him. On the other hand, we risk the trivializing and distortion of the faith because of our personal interests and carnality. The prophets of old were recognized by their proclamation, "Thus says the Lord." Their validity was determined by their accuracy. If what they said became true, they were accepted. If not, they were rejected. Perhaps this litmus test could serve to caution us in our zeal in finding God's will for our lives.

3. AVOIDING DRUNKENNESS 5:18

Paul's second negation in directing us how to walk wisely is found in a prohibition against drunkenness. This has been a useful text against alcohol usage in the church. While it does not prohibit the use of alcohol, it does specifically address the sin of excess. Intoxication is not a sign of one's walking wisely in the faith. Drunkenness, from Paul's perspective, leads to a reckless lifestyle. Sadly, we are far too familiar with the effects alcohol has on the individual, family, and society. The addiction to the drug can become so strong that those involved in it are willing to sacrifice everything for its influence. They live in a constant stupor, impaired by the drug's numbing effect and its tortuous demand. All sense of responsibility dissipates. What controls the person is no longer the individual, God, or even societal norms, but the drug. Is it any wonder that Paul not only warns against intoxication, but encourages the controlling force within the individual to be the Holy Spirit?

One cannot read this section of Ephesians without reflecting upon another time when the infilling of the Holy Spirit was presented in contrast to being drunk. On the day of Pentecost, the disciples, having been filled with the Spirit of God, came tumbling out of the Upper Room consumed in the ecstasy resultant from their experience. Upon being observed, some believed their claims of spiritual influence while others suspected too much wine (see Acts 2:13).[4]

Paul's prohibition may be closely related to a confusion by the people between legitimate worship practices and drunkenness. Many of the pagan cults of the day utilized alcohol as part of their celebration, allowing for inebriation and its effects as part of the "religious" experience. Bacchus, the god of wine, was understandably worshiped by excessive drinking. The cult of Dionysus observed the use of alcohol as a means of increasing one's unity with the divine world.[5] Perhaps some had attempted to bring this into their Christian observance as a means of experiencing God more fully. However, as Paul points out, there can be no adequate replacement for the presence of God active within the believer in the form of the Holy Spirit.

Experiencing the spiritual in life is a central need for humankind. If we do not have a legitimate experience of God, we attempt to imitate it by other means. Activities that encourage a sense of euphoria are often sought. Drugs, alcohol, and sex are all prime choices. As any society moves farther away from a relationship with God, the exercise of these practices increases, often in an addictive and perverted expression. Where these may help one encounter something similar to a religious experience, there is no legitimate replacement. Drugs are a disappointingly poor substitute for the personal interaction God has made available to His children.

Whereas both wine and God can give one a warming euphoric sensation, the two can hardly be confused. Drunkenness dulls the senses, where God's presence heightens them. Drunkenness places one in a stupor, where God enlightens. Drunkenness drains one of dignity and purpose; God gives dignity and purpose. Drunkenness kills; God gives life. Drunkenness takes away our sustenance; God provides our needs. Drunkenness makes us stagger; God gives us direction. The contradictions seem endless, and yet we are usually blind to them.

One of the great attractions of drunkenness is its provision as a means of escape from life's harsh realities. We are not always able to overcome the challenges of life, and must often experience the results. Those unable to do so retreat into a drunken stupor. While this does nothing to overcome the challenges of life, it gives a false sense of removal from the circumstance so one does not have to deal with it. The Holy Spirit is given as an answer to many of our needs and crises in life. Jesus lamented over how often He desired Jerusalem's inhabitants to come to Him like chicks to a hen, that he might protect them and care for them (see Matthew 23:37-39). Yet they chose not to. Paul's exhortation away from alcohol and back to the Spirit is very similar.

4. SPEAKING WITH PSALMS AND HYMNS 5:19-20

Paul shifts his focus from the negative to the positive. Earlier in this section, he prefaced all that we were to do by what was not to be done. He now begins with an affirming command: **Speak to one another with psalms, hymns and spiritual songs** (Eph. 5:19a). This is not to imply that a negative had not been given. In 4:29, he teaches that "no unwholesome talk come out of your mouths." Instead they are to speak only what will serve to build one another up. In 5:4, Paul prohibits obscenity, and foolish and coarse talk, but encourages expressions of thanksgiving.

It is doubtful that Paul is setting a precedent in telling us to live as if in an opera, relating to our brothers and sisters in Christ through songs instead of conversation. According to Colossians 3:16, the singing of psalms, hymns, and spiritual songs were a means by which "the word of Christ" would dwell among the people. It is difficult to determine if Paul is making specific references to the types of music for a purpose, or if it is an attempt to express an encompassing idea toward music.

The difficulty lies in any effort to make a distinction of how these three terms differ from each other. No doubt, **psalms** (Eph. 5:19) is in reference to the contents of what we know as the book of Psalms. This book contains the worship songs of the Hebrew people, utilized in their worship over the centuries. These were used by the early Christians in their worship as well. **Hymns** (5:19) could potentially refer to the early Christian songs composed for the purpose of worship and the expression of faith. Acts 16:25 states that Paul and Silas were singing hymns at night while imprisoned in Philippi. A possible example of a hymn is found in Ephesians 5:14. **Spiritual songs** (5:19) were possibly those songs that, by their nature and content, were not used so much in public worship, but found their popularity within Christian homes as the people fellowshiped with one another. These songs would be edifying to both God and humankind.[6] Perhaps an early illustration of this can be found in David's Psalm 108:3: "I will praise you, O Lord, among the nations; I will sing of you among the peoples."

Whatever their particular content, origin and use, it is obvious that songs in their various expressions held an important influence over the lives of the early Christians—an influence that Paul wanted to encourage. "You have songs of the faith to sing, sing them to one another!" The church has a vast wealth of music and songs from which it benefits. Every possible style can be found within its history. The reality of music's importance in the life of the believer is still measurable today, with the number of Christian singers and musicians producing recordings, sheet music, and concerts for the edification of all. The church's music is filled with her faith. God's Word is put to music, as is also the church's experience. By singing our songs together, we testify of our faith in God, as well as our experience of His grace. Speaking to one another in this way serves to build us up.

But this sharing in song is not to be restricted to our fellow believers. We are told, **Sing and make music in your heart to the Lord** (Eph. 5:19b). The use of music in worship among God's people has always been a common experience. David's skill as a musician is well known, as are the many contributions he made to the book of Psalms. The Psalms themselves either speak of music used in worship, or exhort us in its use. Psalm 108, one of David's psalms, states, "I will sing and make music with all my soul" (verse 1). He claims he will "awaken the dawn" with the playing of his lyre and harp (108:2). Psalm 105:2 instructs us to "sing to him, sing praise to him; tell of all his wonderful acts." Psalm 98:1 tells us to sing a new song, to shout for joy and burst into jubilant song, to make music before the Lord with harps, singing, trumpets, and the ram's horn. It concludes by recognizing that creation itself makes music in praise of God as the rivers clap their hands, the mountains sing, and the sea resounds. Jesus himself sang a hymn with the disciples before leaving the Upper Room for the Mount of Olives (see Mark 14:26). Paul shares a brief insight into early Christian worship in 1 Corinthians 14:26, where he describes the coming together of the brethren, where "everyone has a hymn. . . ." His exhortation to the Ephesian readers is in keeping with the traditions of those who worship God.

The command to sing and make music carries with it an internalized expression that this melodious practice should take place in the heart. There is a sense of genuineness expressed. Paul is not looking for an empty practice to be continued, but that an expression of the faith be found in the people's worship in song. Though perhaps not as much then, the heart now is understood to be the central point of our emotions. Paul's direction is one that calls for a genuine expression of an inner experience.

Paul's phrase, **always giving thanks to God the Father for everything** (Eph. 5:20a), is either a direction for the content of their song, or the focus of their worship, whether in song or not. Here we find an echo of 5:4, as Paul had already given the command to give thanks. In the parallel section in Colossians 3:16-17, the same call is made for thanksgiving and for it to be done in the name of the Lord Jesus Christ. Everything we do, we should do in the name of Jesus, even giving thanks to God. The reason is twofold. First, since Jesus is our intercessor, we can only come to the Father by reliance on Jesus Christ and what He has done for us. Second, since it is in Jesus that all the provisions of God for our salvation and subsequent life are fulfilled, there is no one better by whom to come before the Father with our praise and thanksgiving than His Son.

In this section of the Ephesian letter, we find the call to live carefully and wisely before God. To do so requires a faith in His existence that makes us wise, as opposed to being fools. It requires that we have a sense of God's will for our lives in what is recorded through His Word. It compels us to seek the filling of the Holy Spirit so that our experience of God may be complete and correct. It challenges us to interrelate in praise of God and to one another through song, and most especially to Him with thanksgiving through Jesus Christ. It is to live wisely—to live in God while God lives in us. It is to sing songs of praise to each other and to God himself.

ENDNOTES

[1]Gerhard Von Rad, *Wisdom in Israel,* James D. Martin, trans. (Nashville, Tennessee: Abingdon Press, 1972), p. 64.

[2]John Wesley, *The Works of John Wesley,* vol. 7, 3rd. ed. (Grand Rapids, Michigan: Baker Book House, 1986), p. 67.

[3]Wesley, vol. 5, pp. 473–75.

[4]In the New Testament, Pentecost primarily refers to the event when the Holy Spirit was given to the church; this occurred on the day of Pentecost. The Greek term *Pentecost* comes from means "fiftieth" or "the fiftieth day" and is literally the fiftieth day after the end of the Passover. It is also known as the Jewish Feast of Weeks, a day that is part of the Jewish observances, and was the beginning of the offering of first fruits.

[5]William Foxwell Albright and David Noel Freedman, eds., Ephesians 4–6, vol. 34a, The Anchor Bible (Garden City, New York: Doubleday and Co., Inc., 1974), p. 580.

[6]George Stoeckhardt, *Ephesians,* Concordia Classic Commentary Series, Martin S. Sommer, trans. (St. Louis: Concordia Publishing House, 1952), p. 238.

11

GUIDELINES FOR RELATIONSHIPS

Ephesians 5:21–6:9

O ut of the many commands Paul has shared with his readers regarding the appropriate behavior of Christians, there are few as far-reaching and influential as the need to submit one to another. Paul's shift in Christian practice moves to specific relationships within this world. Having just exhorted his readers to wisdom in the last section, he now challenges them to three of life's arenas where Christians will need to practice submission if they are to practice appropriate Christianity. These areas of life include relationships with spouses, children, and masters or, more appropriately today, employers.

1. SUBMITTING TO ONE ANOTHER 5:21

It was a beautiful German Shepherd, still very much a pup, though its size betrayed this. Its owner exhibited great patience as he endeavored to train the dog in obedience. Commanding the animal to "sit and stay," the owner would walk away. As he did, the dog would instinctively get up and follow. Each time, the master would return the dog to the original spot and repeat his command. Eventually, the dog understood what its owner desired, and remained sitting while the man walked away. Having walked a short distance, the owner stopped and looked back at the perplexed canine. Giving a short call, the dog immediately ran to its master, and together they continued down the street.

There was more than a simple command learned in this exercise between man and beast. A relationship was defined. If the dog and owner were to continue to relate to one another, it would require the dog to recognize its submission and its master's dominance. Though the dynamics of relationship are different, humankind must realize the need for mutual submission if we are to function as a society. As much as we may resist it, the inescapable fact remains that for any people to coexist, a sense of submission must prevail.

Paul begins this section with the generalized command, **Submit to one another out of reverence for Christ** (Eph. 5:21). The key word **submit** is a compound word in the Greek *(hupotassomenoi),* which means to be under command or order.

Mutual submission is an important reality for the church if it is to function as it should. Jesus taught us both by example and word that the path toward greatness in the Kingdom is by becoming a servant to the least (see John 13:4-17; Matthew 20:26-28). Paul speaks of submission in his earlier letter to the Galatians by commanding, "Serve one another in love" (5:13). First Peter 5:5 commands young men to be submissive to those who are older, and commands everyone else to exercise humility toward one another because God opposes those who are proud, but extends His grace to the humble.

Submission to one another should be motivated out of reverence for Christ. The Greek word for **reverence** (Eph. 5:21) is *phobos,* from which we derive our English word *phobia.* Where *phobia* carries a negative connotation inferring an uncontrollable fear, *phobos* also expresses the meaning of awe, reverence, or respect. To fear God is to capture the experience of the Israelites at the foot of Sinai, or earlier at the Red Sea, when they were privileged to see His awesome expressions. In reverence, one steps back, realizing the power of God, while at the same time desiring to stay and relate to Him. We recognize our sin, while at the same time our longing for deliverance. *Phobos* is what made Moses hide his face before the burning bush (see Exodus 3:6). *Phobos* is what caused Isaiah to lament his unworthiness before God in the Temple (see Isaiah 6:5). It is what made Peter entreat our Lord to depart from him because he realized his sin (see Luke 5:8). It is the experience of John on the island of Patmos when he encountered his vision of the risen Christ, and fell as though dead before Him (see Revelation 1:17).

Reverence is the recognition of God as the exalted deity He is. It is to see in Him His worthiness, while recognizing our own unworthiness. Fearing God is to hold Him at that appropriate distance that marks a distinction between Him and ourselves. Fearing God is to show a respect rightfully due one that is perfect holiness, love, and justice. It becomes a motivation which helps to lead the Christian in the appropriate response to God.

The influence of *phobos* also affects our relationships with one another. As we allow our relationship with God to influence our behavior, it becomes apparent in our daily expressions. Jesus' command to His disciples, having washed their feet, was that they should do likewise. He had set an example for them to follow (see John 13:12-15). Out of respect or reverence for Him and His desires for us, we should in turn exemplify this submissive posture.

Another area that exemplifies the humble nature of Christ is found in Philippians 2:5-11. Paul introduces this section by saying, "Your attitude should be the same as that of Christ Jesus." He did not consider equality with God something to be demanded, but rather became a servant in human form, obediently following the Father's will, even to death. The implication behind this and many other passages in Scripture is that if humble, reverent obedience was appropriate for Jesus, how much more so for those who follow Him. Our obedience to Christ's example should be motivated by reverence, and not compulsion.

Though Paul calls upon his readers to be submissive to one another, it is not a mutual, but rather a reciprocal, exercise. The same expressions are not required of all. Instead, different groups are to reflect submission in different ways. Wives are to "submit to your husbands" (Eph. 5:22), while husbands are to "love your wives" (5:25). Children are to "obey your parents" (6:1), while parents are to raise children wisely (6:4). Slaves are to "obey your earthly masters" (6:5), while masters are to treat slaves with consideration (6:9). There is a mutual submission, but not a mutual act. Like Paul's earlier expression of unity found in diversity (see 4:1-13), mutual submission is manifested in a variety of obedient expressions. Paul's specific directions given to each group are echoed in Colossians 3:18-25, though in a much more abbreviated form. What is most obviously missing is his analogy of the relationship between Christ and His church, on which he elaborates in our Ephesian section.

2. BETWEEN WIVES AND HUSBANDS 5:22-33

There are four instructions Paul lists in this section of Ephesians for wives in relationship to their husbands: (1) **Wives, submit to your husbands as to the Lord** (Eph. 5:22); (2) Husbands are to be **the head of the wife as Christ is the head of the church** (5:23a); (3) **Wives should submit to their husbands** as **the church submits to Christ** (5:24); and (4) Wives **must respect** their husbands (5:33).

In our present culture, we have become quite sensitized to the topic of women's rights. A significant part of this movement is dedicated to raising the position of womanhood to a higher, more respected level than that previously experienced within our culture. The movement has not come without its controversy. To hear Paul's words, **Wives, submit to your husbands as to the Lord** (5:22), seems out of place. In fact, it is scriptural teachings such as these that have often caused the Christian faith to come under attack as an obscurant and sexist religion. The problems result more from a limited interpretation of the Scriptures than from their actual teachings. In reality, the Christian faith has much to say about equal rights among the sexes.

There is no specific mention of submission in 5:22. It is a phrase without a verb which literally states in the Greek, "Wives, be unto your husbands as to the Lord." Where submission may be implied, the verb meaning "to be submissive" *(hupotassetai)* must be borrowed from verse 21 or 24. There are some later Greek manuscripts that actually inserted the word in verse 22, but these are not considered as accurate. Though the word **submit** may not be present, the context strongly implies that Paul intended for wives to be submissive to their husbands.

The idea of women being submissive to men is quite old within both the Christian and Jewish faiths. Its first expression is found in Genesis 3:16, where God proclaims the results of His judgment against the disobedient first couple. The wife's attraction will be to her husband and "he shall rule over you." Paul develops this understanding in his first letter to Timothy as he relates his expectations for women in the faith (see 1 Timothy 2:9-15). Their appearance should be modest and decent with a testimony of good works. They are to be quiet and fully submissive, not giving instructions to men, because that would put her in a place of authority. The reason for these restrictions is twofold: (1) Adam was created first; and (2) Eve was the one deceived by the serpent. Paul's teaching is consistent on this topic as he writes to the Corinthian church instructing women to remain silent in church and under submission as the law requires (see 1 Corinthians 14:34).[1] To Titus he says that the older women should teach the younger women to be subject to their husbands (see Titus 2:3-5). Peter, in his first letter, instructs wives to be submissive to their husbands, even if they are nonbelievers, because this action could serve to convert the unbelieving spouse (see 1 Peter 3:1-5). He saw in the submission of women, expecially of those women in the past, a holy beauty.

However, with Paul, women's submission is not to be understood in the context of grace as bestowed on humankind by Christ. There is no first or second at the foot of the cross. Submission may be important in the daily expressions and workings of the church, but in Christ, "there is neither Jew nor Greek, slave nor free, male nor female," for all are one in Christ, as Paul wrote to the Galatians (3:28).

Paul's analogy of the marriage relationship and Christ's relationship with His church, presents **the husband is the head** *[kephale]* **of the wife as Christ is the head** *[kephale]* **of the church** (Eph. 5:23). Paul has previously mentioned this relationship with the church in 4:15-16. In 1 Corinthians 11:3, he develops this headship idea as a multi-leveled hierarchy. God is the head of Christ; Christ is the head of man; and man is the head of woman. But he also depicts Christ as the head over all the universe (see Ephesians 1:22; Colossians 2:10).

Being **the head** (Eph. 5:23) carries two different meanings. Though commonly held as the director or controller today, in biblical times the center of one's control was considered to be in the bowels of the person. **Head** carried not so much the idea of control as it did *primacy.* The head was first, and as such received emphasis. Being first it was also *the source* for what was to follow. Thus, Paul's interpretation of the garden experience of Adam and Eve states that man was the superior individual because he was created first (see 1 Timothy 2:13). Jesus is referred to as the "firstfruits" of the church (see 1 Corinthians 15:20-24). Headship, understood as being the first, calls for those who come after to follow the example of the one who has gone before. Thus, as Jesus dwelt among us, died, resurrected, and ascended to the Father, He sets the way by which the church is to follow Him. Applying this understanding of headship to the marriage relationship would imply that the husband was to take the lead and by example, lead his wife along in the walk of life. The wife's submission would be to follow him, not because he is the superior sex, but because he is the first.

Headship is also understood as administrative, or that which brings everything together in organization: **. . . Christ is the head of the church, his body . . .** (Eph. 5:23). Paul referred to this in 4:16 where he states that the entire church is held together by the head (Christ) via ligaments into one body. In that passage, headship suggests orchestration and direction. All that is diverse about the church is unified through the person of Jesus Christ. He is the unifying head that directs. To have a director assumes that there are those who are directed; otherwise we have anarchy. If an orchestra does not recognize the authority of its director, every musician will play what he or she wants. The result would be far from harmonic. If the church is not willing to listen to Christ, our diversity will never become unity.

In relation to Paul's analogy of the church being many members yet one part (see Ephesians 4:7-13; Romans 12:4-5), marriage has also always been seen as the combination of two made into one (see Ephesians 5:31; Genesis 2:24). As in the church, the marriage relationship requires a unifier to bring the man and the woman together. By Paul's instruction, this unifier is the husband. If the wife is not willing to follow the directions of her husband, matrimony soon becomes pandemonium. However, as we shall see in later consideration, this headship of the husband does not come automatically, but must be the result of the fulfillment of responsibilities by the husband himself. Christ is head of the church by virtue of His being its Savior. His death has established Him over all (see Ephesians 1:19-23). Thus, as the church submits to Christ as the firstfruits to follow, and the head by which we are all brought together, so wives should be submissive to their husbands.

Paul adds to this statement in 5:24 the inclusive phrase **in everything,** which implies that this teaching is not merely to be applied to matters of the faith. We know from other experiences that we run into trouble when we endeavor to make a distinction between what is "spiritual" and what is "secular" in our lives. For the Christian, there is no distinction between the two. The lordship of Christ comes over the entirety of our human experience. Those who attempt to isolate areas and activities apart from the faith are on a rough road to destruction. Marriages that distinguish between marital and individual experiences are on the same highway. The two become one; any attempts to divide this relationship by distinction are destructive.

The first three verses, directed to wives, become distorted if they are not considered in light of the verses which follow. While the submission to one another may not be mutual by means of the same expression, it is mutual in the sense of responsibility. Any attempt to interpret this section with a "Me, Tarzan; you, Jane" mentality distorts the first three verses, and must completely deny the instructions that follow. Wives are to submit to their husbands; **husbands** are to **love your wives** (5:25). In Paul's instructions to the husbands, he presents two ways by which this love is to be expressed: **as Christ loved the church,** and **as their own bodies** (5:25, 28).

Loving one's wife as Christ loved the church can be summed up by one word—sacrifice. Paul states it as, He **gave himself up for her** (5:25). Here is a love that leaves self-gratification out of the relationship. Jesus, in order to express His love for the church, came among us to die. In His own words, he came not to be served, but to serve and to give His life as a ransom (see Matthew 20:28). The husband's love for his wife should exemplify these same attributes. His life should become secondary; the life of his wife becomes primary. His interest is in her and her well-being. Jesus' sacrificial love for the church was done with an end in mind, and that was her fulfillment. He died **to make her holy, cleansing her by the washing with water through the word** (Eph. 5:26). He died to be able **to present her to himself as a radiant church, without stain . . . or any other blemish, but holy and blameless** (5:27). Such a thought should humble every husband.

Who we are as husbands is directly reflected by our wives. Their beauty in holiness is directly related to our sacrificial love or the lack thereof. Thus, if the husband is fulfilling his responsibility in the marriage relationship, it is to the wife's own benefit to submit to her husband, since he only has her best interest in mind. However, if the husband is not fulfilling his part, the wife should still continue in submission so that he might be saved (see 1 Peter 3:1-2). Wives are called to submit to their husbands, but husbands are called to die!

Loving our wives as our own body implies care and nurture. As Paul states, **No one ever hated his own body, but he feeds and cares for it** (Eph. 5:29a). Paul's statement must be taken in a general sense, as specific exceptions to this statement can be found. Emotional disorders with self-destructive tendencies reveal that there are people who are unhappy with themselves. This self-loathing can become the fertile ground for discontent, which subsequently is taken out on the spouse. If we do not like what we see in the mirror, we endeavor to change it, even by the most destructive of means. How we feel about ourselves will influence how we treat those around us.

One major area of self-dissatisfaction results from a perfectionist mentality, which actually destroys the person in an attempt to meet a self-imposed concept. Perfectionists are people seldom, if ever, satisfied with life, and especially with themselves. There is always something out of place or not correct. Exercised within marriage, this unforgiving spirit places demands upon the spouse that do not allow for acceptance. Perfectionists set standards they can never attain, and berate their spouses for their continued failures. The spirit is beaten, the self-esteem crippled. In place of a woman of beauty, the wife can become a defeated individual who sees nothing good about herself.

As destructive as this is to the psyche of the wife, there is another self-hating influence that destroys many women physically. Men, in general, place heavy emphasis upon performance. If emotionally they feel weak or threatened, they often attempt to compensate by becoming physically aggressive. We usually term this behavior "macho," and while its tough appearance might suggest a strong individual, it is a sign of a frightened person attempting to cover what he wants no one else to see. The shame of this insecurity is its effect upon wives. The threatened husband defends his psyche by exerting his physical strength. In place of a lady of beauty and holiness, we fined a bruised and bloody victim. Some people do hate themselves, and their wives are often the evidence of this fact. There is nothing Christian about a woman who has been beaten emotionally or physically. There is nothing manly about making victims out of our wives.

The responsibility of the husband is to love his wife by caring for her, nurturing her, feeding her just like Christ does the church. As a healthy church is a testimony to our Lord, so a healthy wife is a testimony to her husband. The concept of two becoming one is central to our understanding of this section. As husbands, if we truly believe that we are one with our wives, then whatever we do to them is equivalent to doing it to ourselves.

Paul concludes this section by listing the two expressions of submission side by side: **Each one of you must also love his wife . . . and the wife must respect her husband** (5:33). This is a somewhat unusual summary as it emphasizes the "self-care" expression of love at the cost of the "sacrificial" expression which emulates Christ's love for His church. Also, the word for **respect** is the same Greek term Paul used in 5:21 *(phobos)* in relation to the general church's attitude toward Christ.

Overall, the relationship between a husband and wife is one developed through submission. The wife expresses this by submitting to her husband, the head of the body their relationship creates. The husband loves his wife sacrificially so that she may be made holy and beautiful. The husband loves his wife beneficially by caring for and nurturing her as he would his own body.

There is a strong message about the relationship between Christ and the church in this section that should be considered briefly. As Paul builds his analogy for marital relationships, he also develops an understanding of how Christ relates to His church.

First, he tells us that **Christ loved the church** and expressed this love when he **gave himself up for her** in death (5:25). He did this with one purpose in mind, that the result of this sacrifice would develop a church that was pure and holy. This purification is done by **the washing with**

water through the word (5:26). John Wesley understood Paul to be referring to Christian baptism, "the ordinary instrument of our justification," where "the virtue of this free gift, the merits of Christ's life and death, are applied to us."[2] The function of the Word brings to mind Jesus' prayer for His disciples where He petitions the Father to "sanctify them by the truth; your word is truth" (John 17:17). Jesus' love for the church is revealed through His sacrifice. This sacrificial love is not only exemplified by His death on the cross, but also in His ongoing work with the church to make her beautiful. As God, He could easliy demand us to come up to His standards. But His desire for the church is fulfilled by His interaction and giving. The church is made beautiful by the sacrifice of Christ—it is blemished and marred by our own unwillingness to surrender. When we take control of the church in our humanity, it loses its splendor. When we surrender this control to Christ, we are truly made beautiful.

Second, Jesus relates to His church by feeding it and caring for it. Here is Paul's oft-used analogy of the body with its many members. As we form the body of Christ, He is careful to provide for us the sustenance necessary for a healthy and vibrant life. Christ feeds us in several ways: by the Word of God that becomes as milk to newborn babes (see 1 Peter 2:2) or a meaty meal for the mature individual (see Hebrews 5:13-14); and through our Lord's Communion. In this meal of remembrance, we not only commune with Him and the saints of the church, but we also eat of His flesh and drink of His blood. It is a spiritual meal meant to sustain our souls as we thankfully remember what Christ has done in sacrifice for us.

As we become one with Christ, He becomes the Head of the Body which we corporately create. All of our diverse gifts and abilities are brought under His divine control and direction. He directs us to perfection, as we play before Him and the Father the blessed symphony of the redeemed. This reality Paul calls a **profound mystery** (Eph. 5:32), suggesting its depth goes beyond human comprehension. Christ relates to His church in sacrificial love, benevolent care, and as the unifying Head.

3. BETWEEN CHILDREN AND PARENTS 6:1-4

Paul now moves away from the spousal relationship to the next level within the family: parent and child. As we have seen in the previous section, Paul's call for subjection to one another is mutual in the command but not in the expression. As it was true with husbands and wives, it is also true with parents and children. Paul commands,

Children, obey your parents in the Lord, and **Fathers, do not exasperate your children** (Eph. 6:1a, 4a). Fathers are to train and instruct their children in ways so as not to turn them away in anger and frustration.

The Greek word for obey, *hupakouete,* is used by Paul to describe what a child's response to parents should be. It is a compound word which literally means "to come under hearing or under one's voice." It paints a picture of a person submitting to a voice of authority. Since teaching is central in Paul's mind in this section, his lesson of submission is for the child to listen willingly to what the parents have to say. The command echoes the Proverb writer who instructs his "son" to keep his commands and not forsake his mother's teachings (Prov. 6:20).

The phrase **in the Lord** (Eph. 6:1) is debated as it is not found in some Greek manuscripts. Its inclusion in the text makes possible an exception for children whose parents are not Christians. These parents might require something of their children that would bring the children into conflict with their faith. Apparently Paul is leaving a provision for these children to disobey such an order without invoking condemnation. If the phrase is left out, as some manuscripts suggest, then no exceptions would be allowed regarding the obedience of children to their parents, whether Christian or not. However, as Paul does not elaborate on this issue, its application remains somewhat speculative.

In the parallel passage found in Colossians 3:20, Paul gives the same command, but with a more abbreviated reason. The child is to obey his or her parents "in everything" because it pleases the Lord. The Ephesian passage does not include the inclusive term "in everything," but it does add a more descriptive reason for obeying by quoting from the Old Testament—it fulfills the fifth commandment. It can easily be argued that Paul's reason in Colossians is synonymous with the one listed in Ephesians, since keeping God's commandments always pleases Him.

There are two places in the Old Testament where the Ten Commandments are listed: Exodus 20:3-17 and Deuteronomy 5:6-21. In quoting the fifth commandment, it is obvious from the words used that Paul is referring to the passage in Deuteronomy that includes the phrase, "so that it may go well with you in the land the Lord your God is giving you." Paul does not quote the extra phrase in its entirety, but edits it to say **that it may go well with you** (Eph. 6:3). He also changes the reference "the land the Lord your God is giving you" to **on the earth** (6:3). Since Paul was writing to Gentiles instead of Jews, the reference to the Promised Land would be irrelevant. His editing gives the passage a more Gentile expression. Paul states that keeping this commandment carries the promise of reward from God. An exception to this might be argued citing Deuteronomy 5:10, which proclaims the second half of God's response to people who obey Him. He promises to punish the people who hate Him to the fourth generation, but to the ones who love Him and keep His commandments He will show His love to a thousand generations.

At this point, Paul turns his attention specifically to the fathers. His statement to the child was in relation to both parents (see Ephesians 6:1). No doubt, this is done because of Paul's position regarding the husband's responsibility as the head. If the marital relationship is a single body made out of two and unified by the headship of the husband, it is not too far of a stretch to include the children as part of this extended body. Thus, where the father is head of the marital relationship, it is reasonable to infer his responsibility over the children as well.

One reason for Paul's specific instruction to the fathers is based upon social influences. Women were normally not educated in his day, and it fell to the man to educate both his wife and children. Support for this understanding can be found in Paul's instruction for women to remain quiet in the church as it was disgraceful for them to speak. If they had a question, they were to ask their husbands at home (see 1 Corinthians 14:34-35). It is believed that what was happening in their worship services was that anytime a question arose, wives would call over to their husbands for explanation or verification, since women did not sit with their husbands. This communication was obviously causing a distraction in the church, and Paul wanted the practice stopped. The husband was to do his instructing at home. Obviously his responsibility carried over to the children.

The command for the father to follow is twofold: **Do not exasperate your children,** and **bring them up in the training and instruction of the Lord** (Eph. 6:4). Paul's prohibition to the father needs to be heeded carefully. Literally, the word **exasperate** means "to make angry or resentful." Colossians 3:21 states, "Fathers, do not embitter your children, or they will become discouraged." Sometimes in our zeal to do right, we create a tragic wrong. It is an awesome responsibility to raise children, especially when one considers their spiritual training. If taken too lightly, children may grow up without any spiritual interest at all. If taken too sternly, we may succeed in moving children away from the faith, creating young men or women whose only intention is to separate themselves as far and as fast as possible from the church and its God. Either attempt creates a terrible result.

Perhaps the greatest cause of an exasperated child is inconsistency— "Do as I say, not as I do." Our best means of learning is by following an example. Long lectures, stern warnings, sound beatings, and hours of church services will not replace what hypocrisy removes. If we want our children to grow up like Christ, we must first be what we want them to be.

Closely aligned to inconsistency is irrelevance. Our children will naturally embrace what we feel is important in life. Some have erred in making a distinction between the activities of the week and the activities of the church. The lifestyle expressed at home may not be immoral; it is just not spiritual. Christian training, for some, means making sure the children are in the church every time the doors are opened. But, unless what is proclaimed in the church is followed up in the home, the children find little reason to hold it as important. When this irrelevance becomes evident to the parent later in the child's life, a correction is attempted which only appears contradictory, and the child rebels.

Children naturally want to please their parents and be a part of their parents' lives. In our instruction, we must be certain that it is possible for them to do this, or they will become frustrated. Nothing makes us as angry as an unmet goal. This anger we usually refer to as frustration. It is the feeling we experience when we are late for an appointment and the person driving in front of us is traveling at a snail's pace. The same feeling is developed in children whose parents set impossible goals for them to attain: perfect grades, spotless clothes, impeccable behavior, perfect manners, angelic attitudes. In their attempt to please the parent, they are consistently shot down because, no matter how good they are, they still lack something. Psychologists have long determined that our understanding of God is influenced by our understanding of our parents. If children only see a father who is an impossible taskmaster, never satisfied with their attempts and unforgiving of their failures, they will project this same understanding onto God. Their frustration toward their earthly father becomes frustration with their Heavenly Father.

The submissive task of the father in a family is to become an excellent instructor of his children. This is a task often surrendered to the mother. Some men see it as a task which is beneath them. After all, they are too busy with "men things." This is where Paul's message of mutual submission speaks loudly. If we want our children to be submissive to us in obedience, we must be submissive to them as instructors. This requires being among them, communicating with them, listening to their questions and thoughts, taking time for them out of our personal schedules. A man who lives by the adage, "Children should be seen, and not heard," will someday resent the silence he has created.

Before departing from Abraham to destroy Sodom and Gomorrah, God ponders whether or not He should confide in Abraham what He is about to do to the cities. It is in this consideration that God reveals the reason for choosing him, as we read in Genesis: "For I have chosen him, so that he will direct his children and his household after him to keep the way of the Lord by doing what is right and just" (Gen. 18:19). God's expectation for His men has not changed.

The command for the father is to raise the child **in the training and instruction of the Lord** (Eph. 6:4). Paul uses two different words in this phrase that carry a very similar meaning. *Paideia* means to instruct or discipline. *Nouthesia* means to instruct or warn. Both refer to educating, but from slightly different perspectives. *Paideia* emphasizes advancement in training. This is the more positive of the terms in that it encourages progress by consistency and support. It carries the understanding expressed in Deuteronomy 6:7, where God instructs the Israelites to consistently teach His laws whether at home or outside, sitting or standing, in the daytime and at night.[3] Discipline, in this sense, means to do something continually or habitually—to be disciplined in one's devotions and life.

Nouthesia suggests a more corrective type of instruction: "Spare the rod and spoil the child" (see Proverbs 13:24). This passage does not suggest severe corporal punishment, but does imply discipline, taking responsibility to keep them on the right path. Paul's command implies that both aspects of training are necessary in raising our children to fear the Lord. There must be instruction that encourages children to take upon themselves certain life disciplines that, when exercised consistently, promote appropriate behavior. On the other hand, there must be that corrective influence that turns the child back from a wayward direction that would lead to destruction.

A shepherd's staff can be used in two ways. On one end is the crook which allows the shepherd to pull the lamb toward him away from harm. The other end is used upon the more unruly animals that refuse to heed the shepherd's care. This end is used to prod or negatively enforce the shepherd's will by striking the sheep. While Paul's command is not a dictum for physical punishment, it is a statement confirming that proper instruction requires the exercise of both positive and negative reinforcement for those ends we wish to achieve.

The final part of Paul's instruction to the fathers is the need to train the child in the **instruction of the Lord** (Eph. 6:4). In our zeal to follow God's will and assure our children will follow God in their mature years, we must be careful not to confuse our will with God's. Many lessons are taught that have nothing to do with God and everything to do with how "religious" we are. Teaching our children convictions that are not in tune with Scripture will do little to draw them to God. Often, our children are raised more versed in our religion than they are in the will of God.

Many have poured their lives into their children, only to have them rebel in their teens and set off on a different course. Feelings of failure and heartbreak set in. Proverbs 22:6 becomes the anchor in these times, as it requires one to wait upon and trust in God's promise. If we train up our children in the way they should go, we trust God to call them to himself so that their faith might be made complete. If we have been faithful in providing the foundation in their lives for God to work, God will be faithful in calling our children, even in their rebellion. Have faith in God and His promises. Our efforts are not done in vain when they are done in the Lord.

4. BETWEEN SLAVES AND MASTERS 6:5-9

Paul now turns his attention to the last of the three social relationships in which he calls for mutual submission. Wives are to be submissive while their husbands show love. Children are to be obedient while fathers carefully instruct. Now he says, **Slaves, obey your earthly masters with respect and fear, and with sincerity of heart** (Eph. 6:5a).

Although it is looked upon negatively today, slavery was an accepted practice in biblical times, even among Christians in Paul's day. Where he never speaks against slavery, he does share a number of instructions regarding the Christian's part as both a slave and owner. In 1 Corinthians 7:21-24, he instructs the believers directly. He says that if they were called by Christ while a slave they are not to be concerned about their station in life, but to continue therein. If, however, the possibility arises for their freedom, they should take advantage of it, all the while remembering that any person who is a slave in coming to Christ becomes Christ's freedman. Any free man coming to Christ becomes His slave. For both have been bought with the price of Christ's blood. We are no longer our own.

Closely associated with this continuation of slavery as a Christian, is Paul's letter to the slave owner Philemon on behalf of Onesimus, the runaway slave. Paul had converted him and now sends him back to his owner with a letter of reconciliation. Paul encourages Philemon to receive the man as he would Paul. He is to no longer consider him as a slave, but as a man and a brother in Christ (see Philemon 15-21).

In his letters to Timothy and Titus, Paul has instructions for the slaves, but not for the masters. To Timothy, Paul states that the slaves are to show full respect to their masters so that God's name and teachings will not be slandered (see 1 Timothy 6:1-2). If their master is a Christian, the slaves should not slack off in their duties, but serve them even more, since it is a Christian brother who will benefit from their service. His message to Titus instructs slaves to be subject in everything, with a desire to please their masters (see Titus 2:9-10). Specifically he mentions that they should not talk back, nor should they steal anything. Obeying this standard will show that they can be trusted and will make the teachings of God our Savior attractive.

Peter shares some similar information about the slave/master relationship (see 1 Peter 2:18-25). Like Paul, his instructions are for submission and respect on the part of slaves, whether they have good or bad owners. Whether they are abused for no reason, or for doing good, they are to bear up under it, realizing that suffering under unjust pain is commendable to God. Peter believed they were called to this particular station in life. Since Christ has already set the example by suffering for them, they should follow Him and endure the punishment.

Ephesians and Colossians include not only instructions for the slaves but for the owners as well. Colossians 3:22 through 4:1 is a parallel passage with Ephesians 6:5-9. Paul tells his readers that slaves are to **obey your earthly masters** (6:5). The Greek word for **obey** *(hupakouete)* is the same Paul used for children in our previous section, and means literally to be under command or orders. His description of the "master" is literally "the flesh lord." By this, Paul makes a distinction between their earthly master *(kurios)* and their heavenly Lord *(Kurios)*. By making this distinction, it becomes obvious that Paul was not making a general rule for all slaves and owners, but rather for those who are children of God.

The obedience of the slave is to be expressed in three specific attitudes: **respect and fear, and with sincerity of heart** (6:5). The first two attitudes make up a phrase used by Paul elsewhere in Scripture: "fear and trembling." He uses it to describe his attitude in coming among the Corinthian people (see 1 Corinthians 2:3). It is descriptive of the way the Corinthian people received Titus, whom Paul had sent to them (see 2 Corinthians 7:15). It is the attitude we are to assume in working out our salvation before God (see Philippians 2:12). Coupled with the description of single-hearted devotion, it relates Paul's view that the slave's service should be primarily as one would serve Christ. In fact, he says this in so many words, **just as you would obey Christ** (Eph. 6:5).

Because of the lack of slavery today, it may be tempting to pass over this section with the feeling that its message is irrelevant. However, what Paul has to say regarding the service of workers and the treatment of masters is timely given our modern work ethic. It gives us insight as to how we should work for our employers and how our employers should treat their workers. In spite of the presence of wages, the message is still the same. The Christian worker has a twofold responsibility as he or she obediently fulfills an employer's expectations.

First, work well at all times, and not just when you are being observed in an attempt to win favor. In an age where the attitude is to get by with as little effort as possible, Christians should be giving their best to their employers, even when not being observed. Such an attitude reflects integrity, which brings honor to God. Our ethics should not change from church to job. Our effort for our employer should be based upon receiving God's approval, not the approval of others. This integrity will be found unmistakably in the product of our efforts. Many have bemoaned the quality of our modern industry. Warnings that one should not purchase items manufactured on certain days of the week, because of low worker interest, underscore this concern. In our work ethic, we have lost something of the individual expression we should desire to make within our tasks.

Several years ago, the cleaning of Michelangelo's frescoes on the ceiling of the Sistine Chapel was undertaken. As the workers carefully removed the buildup of dirt and stain accumulated over the centuries, they marveled at some of the treasures the grime had hidden. Among these unseen portions of the paintings were fingerprints of the artist left unnoticed through time. Now they stood in testimony to the painter's identity. Here was the evidence that the master artist had done the work. A part of his identity remained with the product. What fingerprints of our lives do we allow as evidence of our work?

Second, our service should be done **wholeheartedly** (6:7), as if serving the Lord, not humankind, because we know God rewards those who do good. During the Middle Ages, the churches of Europe were opened to the craftsmen during the week, as a place to ply their trade. Tinsmiths would work their metal. Cobblers would make their shoes. All within the walls of the church. The purpose was to inspire the tradesmen to realize that their daily lives, even their occupations, were to be done before the Lord. Christians cannot be comfortable with a "get by" attitude. They should give their employers their full attention and best effort. What we do for our bosses should be with the same attitude that we hold in serving the Lord. It may never result in a raise or promotion here on earth, but it will result in a reward from God (see Matthew 16:27).

Paul's command to the **masters,** to **treat your slaves in the same way** (Eph. 6:9), is a command of reciprocation based upon one's expression to the Lord. The master is to treat his slaves as though he were serving the Lord (see 6:7). They are not to be threatened, because the Christian master must remember God is **both their Master and yours** and that **there is no favoritism with him** (6:9). As Paul tells the Galatians, in Christ there is neither "slave nor free" (Gal. 3:28).

During one of Job's lengthy discourses, he expresses this truth with regard to the potential mistreatment of his servants (see Job 31:13-15). He realizes that if he willfully did such a thing, he would be going against what is right, because God created both him and his servants in the womb. In society, we make many distinctions between people, but these distinctions fall away before God. Paul's instructions to the master speak as well to employers today. Our treatment should be fair and humane. We dare not trade off humanity for productivity. No person is of such insignificance that he or she should be sacrificed by poor conditions or unfair practices. How a Christian employer treats his or her employees should exemplify one's love for Christ. If employers are cruel to their employees, what does this say about their relationship to Christ?

Submission. In an age of individualism, that word is not well received. Yet, its necessity in today's society is seen every time we fail to practice it. Wives, husbands, children, parents, employees, and employers all stand to benefit by following this mutual, but unique, relationship ordained by God.

ENDNOTES

[1] Law here refers to the Levitical Code (all God's rules and regulations).

[2] John Wesley, *The Works of John Wesley*, vol. 10, 3rd. ed. (Grand Rapids, Michigan: Baker Book House, 1986), p. 191.

[3] See endnote 1.

12

BEING STRONG IN THE LORD

Ephesians 6:10-20

T
he typical western theme has become familiar to us all. The town is in peril from a group of notorious desperados who prove too much for the good townfolk. Powerless against the desperados, the townfolk are forced to live under their evil control until, by some remarkable fortune, a stranger comes to town, who, though he is a maverick of questionable character, has a compassionate spirit for the townspeople. This mysterious individual stands up to the bad guys, running them off. The minister of these towns is usually typecast as some frightened, mousy individual who is completely inept and scared of his own shadow. The implied message is that only evil can combat evil. But, according to Paul in this section, this claim could not be farther from the truth. The Christian is not only empowered by God, but enabled to fight the very forces of evil that would make even the toughest of Hollywood's heroes run and hide. As Paul explains this provision of God to his readers, he reveals that we are given protective armor for our battle, as well as weapons to inflict spiritual harm upon the enemies of God.

Two major points are developed in this section: (1) Christians are in a battle against opponents far greater than themselves; and (2) if they plan to win the battle, Christians must rely on provisions beyond their human capabilities. Neither of these themes is unique to Paul. The Scriptures, especially the Old Testament, are filled with accounts of God's people going to war against God's enemies. But even the most formidable foes found in the Scriptures pale in comparison to those Paul now lists. These are not Canaanites or Hittites. They are not even the dreaded Assyrians, the mere mention of whom brought terror to the hearts of people. The enemies are not human, and the means of combating them are not of human contrivance. Their warfare will be dependent upon a much higher means.

1. PUTTING ON THE FULL ARMOR OF GOD 6:10-17

To begin the battle, the Ephesians must recognize the need for strength beyond their own. The source of this strength is none other than God himself. They are told, **Finally, be strong in the Lord and in his mighty power** (Eph. 6:10). This phrase could be translated, "Strengthen yourself in the Lord. . . ." It carries the sense of a command for the preparation of battle, a command often repeated in the Scriptures (see Joshua 1:7; 1 Samuel 30:6; 2 Samuel 10:12; Psalm 27:14; Zechariah 10:12; Haggai 2:4). Paul also instructs the readers of other letters to be strong. In 1 Corinthians 16:13, he lists several expressions the Corinthians should seek: watchfulness, tenacity, courage and strength. In 2 Timothy 2:1, he instructs his "son in the faith" to be strong in the grace of Jesus Christ.

Specifically in Ephesians, God's strength and its importance for the believer is mentioned in both of Paul's prayers. Ephesians 1:19-20 relates that part of what Paul wants his people to know is the power of God that was manifested when He raised Jesus from the dead and seated Him at His right hand, above all other powers and principalities. Paul's prayer in chapter 3 calls for, among other things, the reader to be strengthened by God's power by way of the Holy Spirit (see 3:16).

The purpose for needing this power is to enable us to **stand against the devil's schemes** (6:11). The Christian's opponent is not human (**flesh and blood**), but rather **the rulers . . . authorities . . . the powers of this dark world and . . . the spiritual forces of evil in the heavenly realms** (6:12). Paul is describing two distinct spheres from which evil assails the church and her people. The **dark world** implies those malevolent forces that we have come to experience within the confines of our world— demons that attack, tempt, and possess. The second realm is an area beyond our present orb, **the heavenly realms.** Satan himself is implied here, as it is he that apparently holds the ability to dwell beyond the confines of this world. The account of Job mentions Satan as being among the angels who present themselves to God, apparently in heaven (Job 1:6-7; 2:1-2). He also is present at the right side of the angel of the Lord, during the judging of Joshua the high priest (see Zechariah 3:1).

In addition to being strengthened by God for battle, the Christian is also in need of good equipment. Through allegory, Paul describes the necessities of spiritual warfare as those implements of war common in his day. It is contrasted with the young boy David some centuries before as he prepared himself for the Lord's battle against Goliath the giant (see 1 Samuel 17:38-40). Having convinced King Saul of his ability to do battle, even as a boy, Saul dressed David in his armor, encasing him against the weaponry of the giant. But David took the armor off because it was too cumbersome, choosing instead his sling and five smooth stones. But our Enemy is not a mere giant of Goliath's stature. His weaponry is far more destructive and powerful. Even Saul's great armor would be of no help. As the battle is against spiritual enemies, so must the weaponry be spiritual.

Twice the readers are instructed to **put on** this **armor** (Eph. 6:11, 13). Paul gives two reasons why it should be worn: (1) so that the Christian can **stand against the devil's schemes** (6:11); and (2) to enable the Christian to stand his or her ground **when the day of evil comes** (6:13). The two instructions focus upon the intermediate and the ultimate. The **devil's schemes** suggest the ongoing affront Christians experience in their daily lives as Satan tempts and challenges us in our walk with God. The ultimate focus is in view of the coming end, an obvious reference to the last days when Satan will be doing all-out battle against the people of God. Thus, the armor is not for just one special occasion in the Christian's life, but is an everyday necessity if we are to ever withstand the Enemy.

The Greek word for armor *(panoplia)* is used only one other time in the New Testament, in Luke 11:21-22. In his letter to the Romans—though a different word is used in the text—Paul instructs his readers to put on the "armor of light." The particular pieces of armor Paul describes are not unique to him, but references of their use can be found in other parts of Scripture. What is interesting about the list is what is missing. Some commentators have pointed out that the protective shields worn on the legs are not mentioned, but just as noticeable is the lack of protection for the soldier's back. The armor is designed for the person of war. Battles are not designed with the intent to retreat. Soldiers who are confronting their enemy need not protect their backs, as the battle is before them. In God's army, one never hears the call for retreat.

Having informed his readers of the reality of their enemy, and the necessity for preparation to stand against it, Paul gives one more command—**Stand firm . . .** (Eph. 6:14). This seems almost ridiculous in light of the topic, but Paul is too much of an expert in human nature to overlook the importance of this statement. His warning is against the human tendency to get all dressed up and then go nowhere. The Christian is not to become arrayed for battle and then sit at home cowering, away from the conflict. If we are to find the power of God by which we wage our war, and suit up with the armor necessary to stand against the Enemy, we need to follow through and strike a blow for the Lord. Yet, how often are we guilty of just the opposite?

We spend our time in preparation for the battle. We pray and worship, study God's Word, and strategize programs for the church, but then become mysteriously absent when the call to arms is sounded. We always seem to have a more pressing responsibility, a too restrictive schedule to actually go to war. We become muscle-bound, because our strength is never exerted in war. Our armor, shield, and sword are like new, having never been tested in the heat of battle. They sit in our homes, gleaming brightly, attesting to our preparedness, while indicting us of our sloth. If only they had a few dents from conflict. If only there were scorch marks on the shield from Satan's darts. If only the sword were nicked or bent, revealing its use, it would speak a proper testimony. The pride of a warrior is not the shine of his armor, but the telltale marks of his conflict. Paul's command to stand is a military charge to be about the work of a soldier.

No doubt, Paul's allegory was influenced by the Roman army, the strongest fighting force known in his day. Supposedly, the strength of this army depended upon the individual soldier's doing his task. Each soldier was trained to protect a certain space around himself, with the understanding that, in battle, any enemy entering that space did so at the loss of his life. Their space was to be defended to the death. With each man trained in this way, the soldiers were grouped in rows forming a square. These squares were then arranged in a staggered form resembling a checkerboard. At the command, the groups began moving forward en masse. As they encountered the enemy, each soldier did exactly what he was trained to do—defend his space by standing his ground to the death. This, no doubt, is Paul's picture of the Christian army going into conflict with the Enemy—Christians empowered by God, encased with His armor, equipped with His weaponry, dedicated to stand their ground against the opposition. No wonder, when He spoke of the church, Jesus said that the gates of hell would not be able to stand against it (see Matthew 16:18). Paul's conviction of the Christian's invincibility in battle is expressed in Romans 8:28-39, where he declares that we are already "more than conquerors." He was convinced that no principality or power on earth or beyond could take us away from the love of God in Christ. What a blessed promise of victory to carry into battle! However, this is only possible if we do the work we have been empowered and equipped to perform.

As Paul lists the different pieces of armor, he describes their figurative natures: truth, righteousness, gospel, faith, salvation, and spirit. Reason tells us that warriors go to war armed in defense against the enemy's weapons. Those items deemed unnecessary are soon shed to lighten the load. In World War II, our soldiers were outfitted with gas masks to protect them from the dreaded mustard gas used in World War I. However, realizing that this was not a threat in battle, the mask was one of the items quickly disposed of by the G.I.'s. A soldier's enemy can be defined by the weapons the soldier uses against them. By realizing this, we can develop an understanding of what this spiritual enemy intends to use against us.

We are told to buckle the **belt of truth** around our waists (Eph. 6:14). Why would we need belts of truth? Is it not because we battle against an enemy who is a liar? Jesus describes our enemy in John 8:44 as a liar and the father of lies. In his deception, he can even pass himself off as an angel of light (see 2 Corinthians 11:14). He is so deceptive in his messages that "even the elect" can be misled (Matt. 24:24). How important it is for God's warriors to wear about themselves the truth of God so that it can reveal each message and statement for what it truly is. If it is truth, the statement will shine as the belt itself. If it is a lie, it will be revealed by its dullness. Isaiah 11:5 speaks of an allegorical belt. This is in a passage describing the promised Messiah as a stem coming from the root of Jesse. This one who was to come would be girded with a belt of righteousness, a sash of faithfulness.

We are told to have **the breastplate of righteousness in place** (Eph. 6:14). The breastplate covered the greatest area on the warrior, protecting his most vital organs from harm. Its appearance helped to suggest the strength of the soldier and his army. Enveloped in this protection the soldier was enabled to stand against the weapons that would otherwise mortally wound him. Isaiah 59:16 speaks of God's "arm," which is an allusion to Christ, as the one who came in righteousness to fill the void in the world our sin had created. In His coming, he put on "righteousness as His breastplate." Since our armor reflects our Enemy's nature, the presence of a breastplate of righteousness reveals the Enemy's propensity to use unrighteousness to destroy God's people. Paul adds to this armor's purpose in 1 Thessalonians 5:8, by encouraging his readers to put on "faith and love as a breastplate." His obvious concern at this point is for the weapons of doubt and hatred that the Enemy uses against us.

Our **feet** are to be **fitted with the readiness that comes from the gospel of peace** (Eph. 6:15). Paul is referencing Isaiah's message: "How beautiful on the mountains are the feet of those who bring good news"

(Isa. 52:7). The good news Isaiah is talking about is the salvation of Israel back from Exile. Our modern word *gospel* literally means "good news" and refers to the salvation message of Jesus Christ. Paul makes specific mention of Isaiah's message in Romans 10:15, where he points out the logical understanding that the people of this world will never be changed from their sinful lives unless they have the opportunity to hear the message. This message will never be heard unless someone is sent to proclaim it. The good news of Jesus Christ gives us motive and message. It shods our feet to go and proclaim to those who know no good news. This, then, is the Enemy's weapon against us. In his deception, he convinces humankind that there is no hope, no reason for rejoicing, no future to live for. But we do battle armed with the gospel. We share good news in the face of the world's despair.

We are told to **take up the shield of faith** because we can use it against the **flaming arrows of the evil one** (Eph. 6:16). One of the strategic weapons of ancient warfare was the spear, and later the arrow. These were weapons able to inflict harm on the opponent while he was still at a distance. If used effectively, they would serve to reduce the force of an army before actual hand-to-hand conflict ensued. Unless there was something to protect the encroaching army against these airborne attacks, their numbers would be decimated easily. The shield was used for this very purpose. As the distance of battle closed, and the airborne weaponry was used, the soldier could defend himself by allowing the missile to strike the shield instead of the body.

Faith becomes that means which enables us to continue forward, even in the face of Satan's onslaught. His "flaming arrows" are the arrows of doubt that, once finding their mark in the believer, burn with an all-consuming fire, incinerating us. Doubt comes as a result of our experiences in life, especially those that challenge our safety and comfort. Doubt is a by-product of faith, as faith moves us into realms beyond our own ability. Yet, faith is the contradiction of doubt. It is that which enables us to stand opposed to even the most impossible of situations and proclaim, "Never-the-less God!" John wrote that it is the very means by which we overcome the world, the exercise of our faith (see 1 John 5:4).

Our heads are to be protected by **the helmet of salvation** (Eph. 6:17). We know that the brain maintains total control of the body. Without it, we are in trouble. Encasing this vital area with salvation assures the protection and direction of our life. Isaiah includes this piece of armor in his description of God's "arm" previously discussed above (Isa. 59:16), as does Paul in 1 Thessalonians 5:8. To wear the helmet of salvation is to fend against its opposite—damnation. This is the weapon that takes away our life immediately. It removes the hope of living and returns us to being dead in our sins. This was the condition the Ephesian readers were once in because of their sins and trespasses, but because of Christ they are made alive, having been saved by grace (see Ephesians 2:1, 5).

The last part of the warrior's preparation is not so much a part of armor as it is a weapon of war. The **sword of the Spirit** (6:17), like the soldier's sword, can be used as an offensive or defensive tool. The soldier could use it aggressively by inflicting wounds upon his opponent, or it could become the means by which he repelled the attack from his opponent. As Paul is quick to point out, this sword is actually the Word of God. In John's vision on Patmos, he describes Christ's tongue as a sharp two-edged sword (see Revelation 1:16), illustrating His Word (what comes out of His mouth) as a weapon of God.

Jesus gives us an excellent example of its use as a means of defense during His wilderness struggle with Satan (see Matthew 4:1-10). Each time Satan tempted Jesus, Jesus struck it away by quoting the truth of God. Three times He countered Satan by quoting Scripture. "It is written" (Matt. 4:4, 7, 10) becomes the preface to our greatest defense against any aggressive attack the Evil One wishes to make.

The Word of God as an attacking weapon is described in Hebrews 4:12, where the writer relates that it is sharper than a two-edged sword and penetrates and divides the soul and the spirit. It judges the thoughts and attitudes of humankind. It reveals every hidden thing within creation. Surely we have little idea of how powerful a weapon God has bestowed upon His people. But, like any weapon, it must be used with care, for improperly applied, it can wreak havoc on the innocent in our surroundings.

2. PRAYING CONTINUALLY 6:18-20

Having instructed them to be strengthened by the Lord and protected by His spiritual armor, Paul encourages his readers to one last action of warfare—prayer. In a much more abbreviated way, he shares the same exhortations with the church at Colossae (see Colossians 4:2-3). In his elaboration here, Paul makes a number of distinctions that this exercise is to take.

First, they are to **pray in the Spirit** (Eph. 6:18). What a wonderful encouragement to be led by the Holy Spirit! John, while on the island of

Patmos, refers to his experience on that splendid Lord's Day as being "in the Spirit" (Rev. 1:10). Paul instructed the Romans to pray utilizing the influence and power of the Holy Spirit (see Romans 8:26-27) who benefits the believer in several ways: (1) He helps us in our weaknesses; (2) He intercedes for us while we pray, praying for those issues that we are ignorant of—His groaning within expresses messages that words cannot convey; and (3) the line of communication is perfect since God knows the mind of the Spirit as He intercedes and the Spirit knows the will of God. Thus, to pray in the Spirit is to rely upon His helpful control and intercession as we speak to God. Some have come to understand the practice of being in the Spirit as a totally ecstatic experience often expressed though unintelligible words and expressions. Paul cautions against such complete abandonment to ecstasy in our prayer life as he reminds the people that prayer in the spirit is also an exercise of the mind (see 1 Corinthians 14:14-15).

Second, we are to pray **on all occasions** (Eph. 6:18). Luke explains that this is the reason why Jesus shared His parable concerning the persistent widow who continued to come before the local judge with her petition for justice. We should always pray and not give up (see Luke 18:1-8). To the Thessalonian church, Paul gives the exhortation, "Pray continually" (1 Thess. 5:17). Prayer is to be an ongoing, habitual experience in the Christian's life. However, some may err in placing certain confines on prayer. Some may see prayer as an action to be observed in the worship service on Sunday, or in the immediate fellowship of other Christians. Others may reserve prayer for their times of trial or need. Understanding the benevolence of God, and His power to do the impossible in our lives, we often turn to Him in desperate times. It just seems natural. However, there are those who choose just the opposite, especially in very intense times of trial. Depression can so weigh a person down that the thought of doing anything is too great a burden, so prayer is forfeited. The old adage instructs well in this situation: "Whenever you find it the hardest to pray, pray your hardest!" Others find their prayer lives slipping in the face of prosperity. When everything is going well with no clouds on the horizon, it is easy to become complacent in our communication with God. Paul's command stands in contrast to these attitudes. We are to pray on all occasions, among those who are unspiritual as well as spiritual, in our times of need and in our times of plenty, in the heights of our joys and in the lows of our despairs. The soldier of Christ battles on through prayer. **Be alert,** Paul says, **and always keep on praying for all the saints** (Eph. 6:18).

Third, we are to pray **with all kinds of prayers and requests** (6:18). What a joy to hear from God that He is a God of variety. There is a danger among some who desire to limit the meaning and expression of prayer to a particular style or approach. Some feel it can only be done on the knees. Others require the eyes to be closed. Still others feel prayers must be spontaneous, not quoted or read. Every action bears with it the potential for abuse. But in the same way, it carries the power of its own function. Prayer can be done in a number of ways that befit different occasions and needs.

Sometimes our prayer lives suffer from want of variety, leaving us wallowing in a rut of sameness. Invigoration can be found through an infusion of different prayer expressions that bring on new experiences of worship. Written prayers sometimes help us to express more accurately thoughts and feelings that we could not otherwise express. They also help to stretch our understanding of God to a broader perspective, and to praise God in ways we have never done before. Hymns, poetry, and even prose can be read before God as prayers. A trip through the Psalms becomes helpful as we encounter David's experiences, shadowing our own. His words to God can help us express our thoughts as well. Prayers can be short or long, verbal or mental, sentences or paragraphs, on our knees or on our feet, with eyes open or closed, with heads bowed or faces raised toward heaven, with hands folded or open toward the Master, expressing praise or petition. It is important that we recognize the different approaches to prayer, but more important to utilize them before God in petition and praise. Paul exhorts the people to not only keep on praying, but to do so on behalf of the saints. We need to be in prayer for one another, realizing not only our dependence on prayer, but our need of it.

Paul adds to this request a personal desire for their prayers: **Pray also for me** (Eph. 6:19a). He wants them to pray that, by God's grace, he will have the words necessary to speak fearlessly, to **make known the mystery of the gospel** which has been entrusted to him (6:19; see also 1:9; 3:2-3). Paul realized his dependence upon prayer for the furtherance and ability of ministry. His call to prayer becomes the means by which his readers are able to put on the spiritual armor of God. It is the means by which we are strengthened. It is the stability by which we stand. Prayer for God's people is the means by which God's good provisions are made real to us. Without it, we are left naked and vulnerable.

Paul's request gives us an excellent insight into the human frailty of this man. He realizes his weakness and potential for failure without this intercession. If this is true for Paul, how much more so for us. Paul's earlier command to pray on all occasions is, no doubt, more an expression from his own experience than merely good information.

A secondary note can be heard in Paul's request for prayer, as we are reminded that he is an **ambassador in chains** (6:20). Paul writes this letter while under house arrest in Rome, awaiting his opportunity to make an appeal to Caesar himself (see Acts 25:11). The seriousness of the occasion is likely weighing upon him. In his attempt to flee any semblance of a kangaroo court, he has succeeded in bringing himself before the most powerful political authority of his day, an authority that was not too sympathetic to causes outside the interests of Rome, an authority that believed in a pantheon of pagan deities. The outcome of this encounter would be either his release or death. This reality he expresses to the church at Philippi (see Philippians 1:19-26). He is thankful for their prayers on his behalf, and desires that whatever the outcome—life or death—he would have sufficient strength to glorify God in his body. The question that this request raises is apparently answered in 2 Timothy 4:16-18, where Paul relates how he was alone during the experience, and yet the Lord stood by him, giving him strength so that through him the message was proclaimed.

What a powerful privilege it is to read Paul's letters in this light! They illustrate for us the experiential truth of what he claims. The command to arms and armor does not come from one far removed from the battlefield, but from one who shouts above his own encounter to those who stand behind him. His command is by example. His encouragement is fulfilled by his experience. Let us heed his call and, by prayer, put on and take up that which is necessary for doing spiritual battle, strengthened by God himself.

13

CLOSING

Ephesians 6:21-24

A s the saying goes, "All good things must come to an end." Paul abruptly ends his instructions and brings the letter to a close. The conclusion serves to introduce Tychicus, Paul's postman and fellow servant of Christ. He ends the letter with a final benediction bestowing peace, love, and grace upon his readers.

1. TYCHICUS: PAUL'S MESSENGER 6:21-22

As with every letter, the Ephesian epistle required some means of delivery for the information to pass to its recipients. The means of delivery for this letter is found in one named **Tychicus** (Eph. 6:21). The first mention of him is found in Acts 20:4, where Luke records Paul's exit from Ephesus. This followed the riot precipitated by Demetrius, the silversmith. Luke lists Tychicus as among those who accompanied Paul. He was originally from Asia. In Colossians 4:7-8, Paul repeats almost word for word his statement in our present verses. In reality, Tychicus is delivering three letters: Ephesians, and the letters to the Colossians and to Philemon.

To Paul, Tychicus is a **dear brother and faithful servant in the Lord** (Eph. 6:21). This is evident from the different ways Paul used him in ministry. In his second letter to Timothy, Paul mentioned that he was quite alone except for the company of Luke; one man had fallen away from the faith, and Paul had sent others away on journeys of responsibility (see 2 Timothy 4:12). This included Tychicus, whom he had sent to Ephesus, quite possibly to deliver these letters. To Titus, Paul's man in Crete, Paul says that he plans to send either one named Artemas or Tychicus as an apparent replacement, so as to free Titus from his responsibilities and make it possible for him to meet Paul in Nicopolis, where he planned to winter (see Titus 1:5; 3:12).

The purpose of Tychicus's coming to Ephesus is threefold. He is, first, to deliver the letters entrusted to him by Paul and, second, to pass on additional information regarding Paul and his companion's present situation. Since so much was hanging in the balance for Paul regarding his imprisonment, there was, no doubt, much that could be shared with those interested. It was more reasonable to have this information shared by mouth rather than in writing, because of the amount of information that could be shared, along with the explanations. Though at times Paul shares some insight into his personal experiences in some of his letters, it was not his custom to elaborate. He has told the readers on several occasions about his imprisonment (see Ephesians 3:1; 4:1; 6:20). The fine details of his experience, condition, and activities would be shared by this faithful brother. Tychicus's purpose was, third, to encourage the recipients of the letter, presumably in the faith. In Paul's sister letter to the Colossians, Paul shared how he was struggling against strong opposition as he served the Lord for the people of Colossae and Laodicea (see Colossians 2:1-5). It was his desire that, as a result of his struggle, they would be "encouraged in heart and united in love." Paul's purpose for sending Tychicus is the same—for the encouragement of the people.

Encouraging the churches was of vital importance to Paul. His stated purpose for going to Rome was that he might impart a spiritual gift among them and that he and the church at Rome might be mutually encouraged (see Romans 1:11-12). His second missionary journey was begun with the intent to go back among the churches he had established to see how they were doing (see Acts 15:36). Implied in this is his desire to encourage those he found serving the Lord.

2. PAUL'S FINAL BLESSING 6:23-24

As was Paul's custom, he concludes his letter with a blessing extended toward his readers (see the discussion regarding his greeting in Ephesians 1:2). His blessing is extended toward two groups, though probably they are meant to be the same people described in different ways: (1) **Peace . . . and love** are extended to **the brothers . . . with faith from God the Father and the Lord Jesus Christ** (Eph. 6:23); and (2) **To all who love our Lord Jesus Christ with an undying love,** grace is bestowed (6:24).

The purpose of a benediction is to bring a blessing from God. Here Paul is exercising upon the church his authority as an apostle, by proclaiming the blessing of God upon the people and their efforts. The blessing is made possible by two influences: (1) because of the nature of God and His attitude toward humankind; and (2) because of the nature of the brethren and their love for God ("with an undying love").

Each Christian should guard against making light of the reality of God's blessing in the life of the believer. To say "God bless you" is a statement of faith in the benevolence and mercy of God. It assumes that the Father is a God of blessing and not wrath. We are assured of this by Paul's elaboration of His salvation plan found in 1:3-10. Paul's **faith** is expressed in this blessing, trusting **God the Father and our Lord Jesus Christ** to bestow **peace** upon these people (6:23). It is a faith that believes God is a God of love, and that this love can be both known and experienced by His people. It is an expression that humankind can and does find unmerited favor at the hand of God—better known as grace—and that all this is determined and experienced by one's faith in God and the very nature of His being.

The words **the brothers** and **all who love our Lord Jesus Christ** (6:23-24) describe people with a special relationship toward God. They are brothers with Paul because of their mutual claim to the Heavenly Father. They hold faith in common by their mutual love for God.

Paul began this letter by bestowing a blessing of grace and peace. He concludes by repeating this and adding love for good measure. These are words resulting from the truth contained between these two entries. They are not merely platitudes of pious jargon, but anticipated and resultant testimonies of the nature of God, verified by the fulfillment of everything Paul has shared to his Gentile readers of this wonderful letter written by the prisoner of God.

APPENDIX

WHAT DO YOU MEAN IT IS NOT IN THE BIBLE?

In recent years, a number of new versions of our Bible have come into existence representing the result of many years of study and translation. Many things have been discovered within the past several hundred years that have helped scholars working on these projects. Much of this has come from archeology in the form of early manuscripts of parts or all of the Bible. These finds have revealed that some of the wording of the Bible has undergone changes and variations over the centuries, which has resulted in some differences in translation in today's versions of the Bible.

In an attempt to present a version closely aligning to the earliest writings, some portions have had to be omitted or written differently. When this happens, there is usually a notation made which states that the earliest or most accurate manuscripts do not contain the word, phrase, or section in question. This has caused confusion, if not mistrust among some in relation to our modern versions. People often ask, "Why is this necessary, and how is it determined?" To give an exhaustive explanation of this science would take a book in itself, but it may be helpful to consider the topic in general.

To begin, we need to remove ourselves from our modern technological culture with its copying machines, faxes, and computers. Even printing presses did not exist at the time these manuscripts were created. Anything printed or copied in the first century A.D. was done so by hand, by people known as scribes. Scribes were either people who were well educated in language skills, or simply illiterate slaves trained to copy the letters from one paper over to another. Because this was a human process, it was susceptible to human error.

We all have had experiences of making errors while copying something by hand. Whether it was a homework paper, report, or recipe, our best efforts sometimes resulted in an error which made the copied paper different than the original. The same is true with the scribes of old. Although they took painstaking care in their task, inevitable mistakes slipped by them which became variations in the document.

Some of the more prominent errors have been given names. Haplography is the omission of a word or portion of phrase from a line or document. This most likely resulted when the scribe remembered the last word looked at in the original before attention was turned to writing the copied page. Upon completing the transfer of the present phrase, the scribe looked again to the original document to relocate the place where they had left off. Finding the word they *remembered* leaving, they read the next portion to copy, without realizing they had returned to the same word, but later in the document, leaving out of the copied document everything in between.

A dittography is much like a haplography, except that when the word was found the second time, the scribe had returned to a point earlier in the original document and was actually repeating what was already copied. Scribal notes were notations written in the margins of the manuscript as an explanation for certain passages to help readers better understand a text. The problem with these notations was that they were sometimes read as corrections that were also noted in the margins. Later scribes copying the document might mistake a scribal note for a correction, and include it as part of the text. An example of this can be found in John 5:3, where it is explained why the crippled were brought to the pool of water for healing.

Another major area of change to the manuscripts was the result of actual editing done by scribes in an attempt to correct what they felt to be incorrect grammar or to make a difficult passage fit into its context more smoothly. In later times, the use of scriptoriums became popular—a room full of scribes would sit making copies of a manuscript being read to them. This process depended heavily upon accurate reading and precise hearing. Words which sounded alike, yet held different meanings, were sometimes exchanged for those of the original.

Given these numerous means of error, the modern scholar is faced with the task of comparing the different manuscripts to determine what is error and what is not. It is much like solving a two-thousand-year-old mystery. A number of accepted guidelines help in the process to assure the highest degree of probability in determining the original. Some of these guidelines include the following: (1) the shortest variation is to be accepted first; it is likely the least adulterated since changes for clarity tend to make portions longer, and not shorter; (2) obvious errors such as haplographies and dittographies are to be weeded out; and (3) the roughest translation is to be preferred over the smoothest, since in many cases the smoother the grammar, the higher the potential of editing.

In addition to these and other guidelines, the scholar traces the history of the manuscript, attempting to determine from which document it was copied and which documents were copied from it. Some feel that if a high number of manuscripts contain the same word or phrase, that number alone would argue its accuracy. However, a high number of copies could merely mean that an errant manuscript was copied by a large number of people who did not recognize the error.

There are actually a number of manuscripts that have been studied and are believed to reflect the most accurate expression of the original documents. These are the ones most often referred to in the phrase, "The oldest and most accurate manuscripts do not contain. . . ." Since we have no existing original manuscripts of the Scriptures, this determination is merely an assumption. However, it is probably an accurate assumption.

Once a variation in the text is recognized and explained, the translators of the Scriptures endeavor to reflect the more accurate wording. Sometimes this is done by adding a note of explanation. Other times this is done by omitting the section altogether with an explanation of why it has been omitted. It is not always possible to make an exact determination, which leaves the scholars faced with a question of probability. They are able to recognize the cause, but unable to argue convincingly for any one particular translation.

To talk of these difficulties in the process of translating Scripture makes us uncomfortable, because it implies that our Scriptures are inaccurate and untrustworthy. Nothing could be farther from the truth. While there may be questions regarding certain words or phrases, these variations do not jeopardize the message of God in any way. The way to God through Jesus Christ is just as accurately explained in our Bibles today as it was from the pens of its writers. Our Master's love is just as endearing as ever before. God's desires for humankind are just as clear. The variations in question are minimal in impact, but nonetheless noticeable when we read that they were not a part of the original work.

SELECT BIBLIOGRAPHY

Albright, William Foxwell and David Noel Freedman, eds. *Ephesians 1–3,* vol. 34. The Anchor Bible. Garden City, New York: Doubleday and Company, Inc., 1982.

Albright, William Foxwell and David Noel Freedman, eds. *Ephesians 4–6,* vol. 34. The Anchor Bible. Garden City, New York: Doubleday and Company, Inc., 1982.

Arndt, William F. and F. Wilbur Gingrich, trans. *A Greek-English Lexicon of the New Testament and other Early Christian Literature.* Chicago: The University of Chicago Press, 1957.

Barclay, William. *The Letters to the Galatians and Ephesians.* The Daily Bible Study Series. Philadelphia: The Westminster Press, 1976.

Brown, Colin. *Dictionary of New Testament Theology,* vol. 2. Grand Rapids, Michigan: Zondervan Publishing House, 1976.

Bruce, F. F. *The Epistle to the Colossians, to Philemon, and to the Ephesians.* The New International Commentary on the New Testament. Grand Rapids, Michigan: Wm. B. Eerdmans Publishing Co., 1984.

Driver, Samuel Rolles, Alfred Plummer, and Charles Augustus Briggs, eds. *Ephesians, Colossians.* The International Critical Commentary. Edinburgh: T. and T. Clark, 1991.

Hope Publishing Company. *The Singing Church.* Carol Stream, Illinois: Hope Publishing Company, 1985.

Metzger, Bruce M. *A Textual Commentary on the New Testament.* New York: United Bible Societies, 1975.

Morris, Leon. *Expository Reflections on the Letter to the Ephesians.* Grand Rapids, Michigan: Baker Books, 1994.

Pfeiffer, Charles F. *The Dead Sea Scrolls and the Bible.* New York: Weathervane Books, 1969.

Purkiser, W. T., Richard S. Taylor, and Willard H. Taylor. *God, Man, and Salvation: A Biblical Theology.* Kansas City, Missouri: Beacon Hill Press of Kansas City, 1977.

Ridderbos, Herman. *Paul: An Outline of His Theology.* John Richard DeWitt, trans. Grand Rapids, Michigan: Wm. B. Eerdmans Publishing Co., 1975.

Stoeckhardt, George. *Ephesians.* Concordia Classic Commentary Series. Martin S. Sommer, trans. St. Louis: Concordia Publishing House, 1952.

Von Rad, Gerhard. *Wisdom in Israel.* James D. Martin, trans. Nashville, Tennessee: Abingdon Press, 1972.

Wesley, John. *Explanatory Notes,* vol. IV. Salem, Massachusetts: Schmul Publishers, 1975.

Wesley, John. *The Works of John Wesley*, 3rd. ed. Grand Rapids, Michigan: Baker Book House, 1986.